CANDIDLY CAINE

Michael Caine's life and career have been colourful, chequered, poverty stricken and well rewarded. A Cockney who has never forgotten his roots, he has become an international film star. Packed with anecdotes and revealing stories from Caine himself and from such close friends as Roger Moore and Sean Connery, reviews and opinions, *Candidly Caine* gives an unmatched insight into this outspoken and charismatic star.

CANDIDLY CAINE

Written by Elaine Gallagher,
Edited by Ian Macdonald
and incorporating original conversations
with Michael Caine and comments from
his friends and co-stars

CHIVERS PRESS
BATH

First published in Great Britain 1990
by
Robson Books Ltd
This Large Print edition published by
Chivers Press
by arrangement with
Robson Books Ltd
1991

ISBN 0 86220 461 5

British Library Cataloguing in Publication Data

Gallagher, E. J.
  Candidly Caine.
  1. Cinema films. Acting   2. Caine, Michael, 1933–
  I. Title
  791.43028092

  ISBN 0–86220–461–5

CONTENTS

CONTENTS

'I'd Just Like To Thank My Agent'

ACKNOWLEDGEMENTS

So many people helped, willingly and graciously, in the making of this book that we must apologize in advance to those not thanked by name below. We just don't have room to thank each and every actor and actress, director, producer and writer who shared with us their memories of Michael Caine. But we're no less grateful for all that; and to everyone who's credited in the main body of the book, and to everyone else we pestered over the last 18 months, our heartfelt gratitude and our eternal respect for, above all else, their patience.

Of the people who helped pull the book together, our greatest thanks must go to Lorna Dickinson, producer of *The Trouble With Michael Caine*, and Mark Tinkler, a researcher on the programme; both of whom were in on the book from the start. It's no exaggeration to say that it wouldn't have been written without them.

At LWT, many thanks are due to Bea Adams, Sandra Thompson, Dave Headdon, Claire Nye, Trevor Popple, Claudia Rosencrantz, Graham Stuart, Librarian Sarah Adair and the Library staff. Nicholas Barrett, as always, gave his unfailing support and encouragement. Outside LWT we'd like to thank Mrs A Butterworth, Theo Cowan, David G Croft, Beverley Cross, Cy Endfield, John Gilbert, Lewis Gilbert, Denys Graham, Kenneth Griffith, Mrs Joyce Hawkins, Robert Mill, Dennis Selinger, Alexander Walker and Sam Wanamaker; Barrie

MacDonald, Sue Fewell, and the IBA Library staff; the staff of the BFI, particularly Janice Headland, Virginia Hennessey, Joan Ingram, Tony Mechele, Janet Moat, Pat Perelli, Markku Salmi, Peter Todd and Tise Vahimagi; Granada TV's Archives department; the Theatre Museum's Enquiries staff; and the BBC, particularly the Written Archives Centre and Jacqui Kavanagh.

Finally, we'd like to thank Mr Maurice Micklewhite for being a decent geezer about it all.

INTRODUCTION

Bob Hoskins:
'What do you think about this show?'

Michael Caine:
'I'll do it.'

Bob Hoskins:
'Do what?'

Michael Caine:
'Whatever the show is, I'll do it. Who am I?'

Bob Hoskins:
'Michael Caine.'

Michael Caine:
'No, who am I in the show?'

Bob Hoskins:
'Michael Caine! It's a show about you!'

Michael Caine:
'Right, I'll do it.'

Bob Hoskins:
'You're doing it already! You're doing it right now.'

Michael Caine:
'Good. Well, I should be able to fit another couple of films in at the same time then, won't I . . .'

The show in question was London Weekend Television's *The Trouble With Michael Caine*. The above conversation actually took place in the programme, but it was impressionists Enn Reitel and

Jon Glover who spoke the lines. They were the voices for two Spitting Image puppets of Bob Hoskins and Michael Caine, in a sketch written by Geoffrey Perkins and performed in front of the real Hoskins and Caine. Afterwards, host Michael Aspel asked the real Michael Caine, 'Did any of it strike home?'

'Yes, a lot struck home,' replied Caine. 'That's why it's funny! Only the truth is funny.'

The truth, or at least an original insight into the character of the star guest was of course what the programme was intended to reveal. And to reveal it as entertainingly as possible.

The completed programme was the first hour-long TV portrait of Michael Caine since LWT had made the documentary *Candid Caine* twenty years before. Transmitted on 1 January 1989 it delighted everyone by reaching 10.9 million viewers in the UK, and later by winning a gold medal at the 1990 New York Film and TV Festival.

Michael Aspel kicked off by saying, 'Tonight his friends are going to tell us what makes him tick, and possibly explode. Michael Caine has worked with 25,421 people so far in his career, at least until tonight. Many of those people are all around us. Some of those love him, but for those who don't, Michael, watch your back . . . !'

Michael Caine had warmed to the idea of the show some months before, but he knew nothing of the structure of the programme until the moment he walked on. Everything from then on was a complete surprise.

Every member of the 250-strong audience had some connection with Michael Caine, and they rose to the occasion magnificently. Frederick Forsyth, Nigel Havers, John Hurt, Saeed Jaffrey, Millicent Martin,

Roger Moore, Peter Ustinov and film critic Alexander Walker were just some of the names who contributed; along with faces from Caine's early career, like the director of *Zulu*, Cy Endfield, and the director who gave Caine his big break into films as well as television, Julian Amyes.

The power of that audience was not lost on Caine. As he said just after he had described his technique for acting drunk, 'I'll need an aspirin after this show, I can tell you! . . . Do you know what's intimidating about this audience? It's very difficult to sit up here as a celebrity in front of an audience of people who should be up here instead of you. It's very hard to sit with your peers and put across the fact that you're somebody that somebody else isn't—because they all are!

'It's very difficult to make you understand, Michael. [Turning to audience] A glaze came over his eyes in the middle of that!'

Aspel: 'I was just trying to act drunk.'

Caine: 'Well, you've mastered it. Now try to act like an aspirin!'

Michael Caine's career spans nearly forty years and encompasses dozens of plays and television programmes as well as nearly eighty films. It's been colourful, chequered, poverty-stricken and well-rewarded; he's been both criticized and awarded some of the highest honours in show business. Whatever else, Michael Caine has certainly packed a lot in. So it was inevitable that even two hours of concentrated TV discussion from the unedited tapes of *The Trouble With Michael Caine* could only be the starting point for a book like this—a portrait of the man who once claimed 'I'm not really star material . . .'

Candidly Caine comprises hundreds of hours of research and interviews. It features much original comment—many stars and other key people, whether or not they appeared in the show, gave their recollections individually. And of course Michael Caine himself, in discussions before and after the programme, provided more information and more stories—often capping what had already been said with yet more anecdotes.

So, in the following pages you'll find everything you ever wanted to know about Michael Caine's career; from his early life and loves to what he thinks about retirement. There are stories from his Army days, his stage days, and the rave reviews for his one and only West End play. There's one of many rejection letters he received from the BBC, and stories about Caine the TV actor—most of whose appearances were limited to the part of 'Second Police Constable'! There are the bit parts he played in films in the 50s, and the real story of how he landed the part which launched him to stardom—in *Zulu*.

Actors, actresses, directors, writers and critics have all contributed; from the actor who remembers him as an office boy, to the director who nearly killed him. There's Caine's very first leading lady, the footballer who Caine taught to act, and Bob Hoskins on the time Caine got him a 'diabolical bollocking' for being drunk, even though he wasn't!

Woody Allen, Sir Richard Attenborough, Bryan Forbes and Ken Russell give their opinion of Michael Caine the actor, and Caine tells us what he thinks of directors! There are original quotes and stories from Sean Connery, Nigel Davenport, Nigel Havers, Glenda Jackson, Saeed Jaffrey, Roger Moore, Tim Pigott-Smith, Peter Ustinov, Shelley Winters and over fifty others.

Everybody knows, of course, that the minute Michael Caine is told about something he becomes an expert on it, whatever the subject. Peter Sellers knew it so well he originated the now famous catchprase—'And Not Many People Know That!'—while doing an impersonation of Caine for his own answerphone. Naturally it stuck. What not many people actually know is that even experts come unstuck sometimes, even when the expert is Michael Caine and the subject is himself. Overheard at the pie-and-mash party after the recording of *The Trouble With Michael Caine* was Caine confiding in Bob Hoskins: ''Ere, Bob—these people know more about me than I do!'

CHAPTER ONE

'WE USED TO CALL HIM MICK IN THOSE DAYS' 1933–1952

'Being a cockney isn't just a matter of geography. It's an attitude of mind.'

Michael Caine

In 1986, as a favour to his old friend Bob Hoskins, Michael Caine agreed to play a cameo role as a gangster in the film *Mona Lisa*. The film's production offices were located in a disused hospital in the old London docklands area of Rotherhithe, fast becoming more fashionable as a residential district for City businessmen. At his first production meeting on the film, the surroundings seemed more than a little familiar to Caine; but not until he was told that he was sitting in what used to be St Olave's Hospital did he realize what was causing those feelings of déjà-vu. As Maurice Joseph Micklewhite, he'd been born there fifty-three years earlier, on 14 March 1933. Michael Caine is convinced this is some kind of record—he must be the only actor ever to have made a film from the hospital where he was born!

Michael Caine is proud of being a cockney, although Micklewhite is an unusual name in London. Originally it may have been an Irish gypsy family name, where the tradition was always to name the first-born son 'Maurice'—Michael Caine's real first name, and that of his father before him. But the Micklewhites have lived in London for

1

generations; and Michael Caine's birthplace in Rotherhithe is, as required by convention, well within the sound of Bow bells. Geographically, Michael Caine is as cockney as bangers and mash.

Traditionally, your average cockney was supposed to be a cheery 'cock-sparrow' who doffed his cap and called you 'Guv'nor'. He liked his eel and pie for tea, he had the occasional 'bull and cow' (row) with his 'trouble and strife' (wife), and he always knew his place. In reality, the working-class cockney of the 1930s had a great deal in common with the urban blacks of the USA—he was poor, he lived in a virtual ghetto and he stuck to his own traditions.

As cockneys go, however, Maurice Micklewhite was never typical. He might have been brought up as such, but he never 'knew his place'. For years he refused to accept that he couldn't make it as a professional actor just because he was working-class. And, at a time when social barriers in England were rarely crossed, if a working-class lad was even 'half-way bright' (as Caine once described himself) life could be hard.

Life was hard enough anyway, right from the start. A between-the-wars baby, Maurice Micklewhite was born at a time of high poverty and low optimism. His father, Maurice Snr, was one of the 'irreducible million', searching ever hopefully for work but rarely finding any. His mother, Ellen, was normally expected by her husband to stay at home to look after the family, but when the going got hard financially she found herself taking occasional jobs, such as sewing on buttons at a local clothing factory.

Ellen Micklewhite was skilled at making ends

meet, and throughout those difficult early years of Maurice's life she made sure her family never suffered. Her determination won her son's enduring respect. Even into her old age she played an important role in his life, and strongly influenced his views on what a wife and mother should be.

Their living accommodation was cramped. For six months the family lived in a slum in the Old Kent Road, until it was demolished. Then the three of them moved to a two-roomed flat in Urlwin Street, Camberwell. Despite these conditions and the endless money problems, it was, as Caine has often repeated, a secure and happy home life. Many years later Caine would decide against sending his second daughter Natasha to boarding school, because he wanted her to know the same strong sense of family which he remembered so well.

Maurice Micklewhite's was a traditional working-class childhood. His father was a man's man who showed his family great love and support, but was definitely in charge, spending his evenings in the local pub and regarding tasks like washing up as strictly women's work. Caine acknowledges that a lot of his own attitudes came from his father and indeed he has often been accused of having a highly conventional attitude to the roles of men and women in society.

In 1936 Maurice Snr got a regular job in Billingsgate fish market, keeping up a family tradition that could be traced back several hundred years. That year the Micklewhites' second son, Stanley, was born, joining the rest of the family in the now severely over-crowded flat off Camberwell Road.

The family spent the six years from 1933 to 1939

3

in Urlwin Street, a row of Victorian houses, which is still standing and now shows signs of gentrification. When the Micklewhites lived there the house was occupied by three families. The one toilet was in the basement and shared by all twelve occupants.

The Micklewhite parents were determined that their sons should have a better start in life than their own and so at the age of four Maurice started at the John Ruskin Infant School, just around the corner in John Ruskin Street.

Eighteen months younger than the other children, and with long fair curls and blue eyes, he was soon labelled 'teacher's pet', and often came home with battle scars from defending himself.

No Time to Wave Goodbye

In 1939 the by now stabilized fortunes of the Micklewhites were thrown asunder by the outbreak of war. Clutching his Mickey Mouse gas mask, Maurice was initially evacuated to Wargrave in Berkshire. However, what started out as an adventure soon turned into a nightmare for the six-year-old boy. He and another boy lodger were mistreated by the policeman's wife who had taken them in. She locked them in a cupboard when she went out and refused to feed them properly. Caine can still remember vividly his first few minutes in this house. As he said to Ben Wicks, author of *No Time to Wave Goodbye*, 'At first everyone was very nice and then the woman who had taken us there left us and we sat down to eat. The woman said, "Here's your meal", and gave us a tin of pilchards between the two of us and some bread and water. Now, we'd been in this rich woman's house so we

4

said, "Where's the butter?" and we suddenly got this wallop round the head. From then it started.'

Eventually a teacher observed sores on Maurice's legs and, recognizing the signs of malnutrition, contacted the National Society for the Prevention of Cruelty to Children. The woman, it turned out, hated children and was only taking in evacuees for the money, hence feeding them the cheapest diet possible, canned fish and bread. Caine did not talk about these occurrences until many years later when he agreed to make a film on child abuse for Dr Barnardo's. He is still passionate about children's welfare, and is a strong supporter of children's charities.

However, as for all actors, no experience is ever wasted and it is those memories of the abuse he suffered that Caine summons up to trigger anger for a scene. 'When I need to get angry I go straight back to that. And I hate all adults at that moment and then I can go *bang*! That gets me extremely angry, it still does. Not about myself obviously but about other people who do it. But you know the extraordinary thing is I've done a lot of work in that area and when you see a child victim you think, if I could get hold of the person who did this I'd strangle him with my bare hands. And then you see the person and they are just so pitiful you couldn't think of touching them ... it's quite strange actually. They're usually quite pitiful people.'

By contrast, his second experience of evacuation couldn't have been happier. Reunited with his mother and brother, he was sent to the Norfolk village of North Runcton. It was the first real experience of the countryside for the boy from the inner city, and he was immediately captivated. The

5

next six years he counts as the happiest of his life, spent in an oasis of green rolling fields. This love of rural England would eventually prompt his return from America in 1987 after eight years of self-imposed exile. It is even now culminating in his new garden at his home in Oxfordshire, with its special plants to attract wildfowl; and in his increasing interest in conservation.

Ellen Micklewhite took a job as cook to a local timber merchant, and Maurice would wait avidly to sample the leftovers that came back to the kitchen from the table. It was his first glimpse of the good life and he determined that one day he would have some of this for himself: 'I used to watch the food when it came back and I would taste half a glass of wine that was left, or a pheasant leg or a cigar butt. I used to steal those things and go out in the garden and smoke, eat and drink them . . . and then throw up! Now I do it without throwing up, and that's what you call the good life. The good life consists entirely of being able to do all these things without throwing up.'

It was at North Runcton that, in Christmas 1943, he made his stage début, with the villagers unwittingly making up the first audience of a famous-actor-to-be. His starring role was as Baron Fitznoodle, father of the Ugly Sisters in *Cinderella*—'I went on and got a load of laughs and the local MP gave me five shillings as the best act of the evening. When I came off I found my flies were undone. Ever since then, just before I make my entrance I check that my flies aren't undone.'

'A Skinny Schoolboy with a Mop of Fair Hair'
On 8 May 1945 the idyll ended. The war was over

6

and the family came back to London, only to discover that the old house and the rest of the street had been damaged by the Luftwaffe and needed extensive repairs.

They were rehoused in a 'prefab', one of the instant prefabricated homes made of cheap materials which became so common after the ravages of the London blitz. It stood in nearby Marshall Gardens, and was to remain their home for the next ten years. A block of flats now stands on the site, although even today there are other 'prefabs' still standing nearby.

Maurice took up his scholarship place at Hackney Downs Grocers' School having passed the scholarship exam while an evacuee. Before long he went on to Wilsons Grammar School, near Camberwell Green, where he found himself disadvantaged by class and out of place among the more privileged boys. It was tough, and he rebelled. He became known as 'The Professor', by now having acquired his first pair of glasses to aid his short sight. Although he hated school he had a desire to learn, and he spent endless hours reading in Southwark Public Library.

Like most of his generation, Maurice's main recreation was going to the pictures. The cinema bug had bitten him in a big way and he passed most of his free hours under cover of darkness in the cinemas near his home. 'I went to the cinema six, sometimes seven times a week. And that's where not being satisfied with my lot as a working-class kid stemmed from. I wanted to be a star from the very first B movie I saw as a kid of seven or eight. I thought it must be great to be up there on the screen.'

He would often jump off the bus on the way to the school's playing fields and spend the afternoon playing truant in the Tower Cinema in Peckham, watching his heroes, Humphrey Bogart, Errol Flynn and John Wayne.

It must have seemed an unattainable dream. It wasn't just lack of money that stopped working-class kids going into acting and the creative arts, it was years of social conditioning. Declaring an ambition to become an actor was seen as renouncing your own kind; a combination of thinking you were better than the other kids on the street and being a cissy. It would need to be a very determined child who could shake off all this, endure the ridicule and stick to his objective.

As Caine himself has put it, this was the 'french windows and Bunty's having a party' era of acting. It seemed that every actor had a Home Counties, plummy accent and had been to drama school. Where would a working-class kid from the wrong end of town find the opportunity to gain any experience at all in the actor's craft? Watching actors on the screen might have been as far as Caine's career would have gone if it hadn't been for Clubland.

Clubland was a youth club set up by the Reverend James Butterworth in memory of his pals who didn't come back from the First World War. It was run along democratic lines with its own parliament and various committees, and the only condition for membership was attendance on Sunday evenings at the church next door. Located on Camberwell Road, round the corner from the Micklewhites' former home in Urlwin Street, Clubland aimed to involve children from the age of

8

fourteen in all kinds of activities, and to give them the challenges and opportunities that they would never otherwise encounter. One of those activities was a drama group.

The Reverend Butterworth was a man who had been at the front of the queue when they were handing out powers of persuasion and charm. Not only did he persuade many celebrities to become patrons of the club, from the footballer Tommy Walker (Chelsea and Hearts) to the young actors Richard Attenborough and John Mills, but he actually managed to encourage the then Queen, Queen Mary, to take an interest, and she visited the club on several occasions.

One of the Reverend Butterworth's major coups came when he made a fund-raising trip to America and visited Hollywood. He so impressed another London boy, Bob Hope, that Hope gave a fortnight of benefit shows for Clubland at the Prince of Wales Theatre, London, raising the extraordinary sum (for 1951) of £20,000! Bob Hope even visited Clubland, bringing with him Marilyn Maxwell, his blonde American co-star in *Lemon Drop Kid*. Many years later Bob Hope would make sure Caine paid his dues to Clubland. 'I was in the Acapulco Film Festival, and Bob did *The Bob Hope Show* from there,' says Michael Caine, 'and I did the show with him. My fee was $10,000 but I never got it, and my agent rang the Bob Hope company to check. He got a message from Bob saying "Check with Clubland". He'd sent it straight to the Club. He said he'd been supporting them all these years and it was about time Michael Caine started supporting them!'

Caine has always said he came to acting by accident. He was really after a girl called Amy

9

Hood, the object of a teenage crush he was experiencing at the time. Going up to the gym class he went past the activity rooms in which some classes were going on. Looking through the glass doors, he saw Amy Hood and told his friends to go on upstairs while he waited to catch a better glimpse of the object of his affections. When he asked what the class was, he was told 'drama'. He thought quickly and realized he could have the field to himself. 'None of the boys would join in because they thought it was cissy. But all the prettiest girls were in there . . .' It might have been the first time, but certainly not the last, that he followed his own instincts and swam against the tide, even though he knew his mates wouldn't understand. 'All the guys were up in the showers together and they're calling *me* a woofter.'

And so Maurice Micklewhite, known as 'Mick' to his friends, joined the Clubland drama group. The Reverend Butterworth, now deceased, also clearly remembered young Maurice hanging about outside the drama class. 'He used to hang around the theatre door breaking the rule that no one went in unless they were rehearsing. This boy was always trying to get in there to watch, and the times I had to clear him out were innumerable. One day he said, "Do you think I could have a part in there?" We were doing *Rossum's Universal Robots* at the time, I think. And as soon as he got up on the stage I thought, there's something special.'

Caine too can recall that production. 'The first play I ever did was a Czechoslovakian play, very esoteric, called *Rossum's Universal Robots, RUR*. I played a robot. The critic in the *South London Press* wrote 'Mr Caine was very convincing as a robot.'

10

It must have been a memorable production, and earned a special mention in the Clubland annual review of 1948.

What courage in producing a four-act play. Yet not for many a year has anything been done so brilliantly as the most difficult *Rossum's Universal Robots*. Mr Stuart Ready deserved the great ovation he received for his masterly production of *RUR* and for giving comparatively new members their first chance of staging real drama . . .
    . . . With not one weak link in the Robots we were thrilled with clear forthright acting. Most varied personalities were magnificently portrayed by John Bradwin, Maurice Micklewhite, Henry Law, Eileen Thompson, Ivy Warner. All the cast should be happy in having staged a great play which held an appreciative audience spellbound for two hours.

But in fact it *wasn't* his first Clubland appearance—both the Reverend Butterworth and Michael Caine had forgotten an even earlier performance. Maurice Micklewhite first took to the Clubland stage in November 1947 when he appeared in a play called *And This Our Life*. All the cast had to make spoofs of their own names so Mick became Maurice Ficklewhite, one of the prisoners in Stalag 8X. A perceptive talent spotter, the chairman of the drama club at the time, Derek Coles, recorded in his log the performance of 'an up-and-coming star, Maurice Micklewhite'.
    In 1949 Maurice Micklewhite appeared in a one-act play called *Low Bridge*. When he was cast, the then chairman of the drama club, Alan

11

Thompson, wrote in his log book, 'I will say no more than a certain fair-haired actor has the male lead. He's the best actor in the club.'

From those schoolboy parts, Maurice's interest in the techniques of acting began to develop. His visits to Southwark Public Library took on a new purpose as he avidly read up everything they had on the subject. He began to think about each movement and each expression. He took out a book on acting technique by the Russian actor Pudovkin and carefully studied it. He was especially impressed by two particular pieces of advice: to remember that film acting is not acting but *re*-acting, and never to blink before the camera. Caine can remember putting the second into practice: 'Not blinking was the first thing I learnt. It makes your eyes water after a while, and my mother used to say, "What's the matter with you, why are you staring at everybody?" At school they used to call me "snake eyes" because I had very heavy-lidded eyes and I never blinked. I never used to get a kick or anything because everybody was frightened to hit old snake eyes!'

Maurice had also scored a hit with Amy Hood, now Amy Power, who can still remember the young Mick. 'He was a skinny schoolboy with a mop of fair hair, and a very good talker which was unusual for a young lad. We used to sit on the wall outside my house talking until 2am and then he'd give me a hasty kiss and rush off home. It was all very innocent ... a long time before *Alfie*.'

For his part, Caine remembers that Amy was the first girl he ever danced with. 'Clubland was the first place I ever held a girl very close to dance with. If you see the photographs of me when I was

12

fourteen you'll realize just how few dances I got. The first dance I ever had was with the most beautiful girl in the club, Amy Hood.'

The teenage sweethearts shared a love of films and would sometimes skip school to go to the movies, Amy bringing jam sandwiches to sustain them. Another of Mick's teenage friends, Sylvia Stowe, recalls that his particular favourite actor of the time was Danny Kaye and that he went to see *Up In Arms* seventeen times. Caine too recalls those teenage trips to the cinema and the variety of emotions which they stirred up within him. 'I can remember being very angry, sitting there watching the way working-class people were portrayed in British movies. They were always lovable idiots, always servile and always condescended to. I thought then in becoming an actor I would have a chance to play some of those minor characters with dignity. And I remember we used to laugh a lot at English theatre-trained actors who tried to play gangsters. They seemed so effeminate to us, and they always got the fights all wrong.'

After their play-readings at Clubland Mick would confide his hopes for the future to Amy. 'He would walk me home and talk about acting and say that he'd like to direct too. In those days acting was thought to be "cissy" around where we lived.'

Sylvia Stowe also remembers that young Mick was becoming increasingly expert on the subject of acting, as a certain famous actress was about to find out. 'One Sunday Fay Compton came to talk to the drama club after the service. Mick began to tell her about the Royal Academy of Dramatic Art, which he was particularly keen on at the time. "Yes, I *do* know about it, dear," she said to him.'

Mick joined the Clubland summer camp in Guernsey in the summer of 1948, his first trip away from the English mainland, and a welcome reminder of the open spaces and countryside that he had come to love when he was an evacuee in North Runcton.

Amy and Sylvia were there too and while Amy remembers that Mick chivalrously carried her bag across the cliffs for her—and got sunburn as a result—Sylvia recalls that when the time came to do the chores they had each been assigned Mick often conveniently happened to be missing!

'You Grow Up Tough In The Queen's Royal Regiment'

Although he was generally quite shy, when it came to acting young Maurice was as confident as he could be. After leaving school he knew, like all the young men at the time, that he'd have to 'do his bit' in the Forces, as his National Service. But he wasn't going to hang around waiting for his call-up papers to arrive. He jumped straight into the film business—as filing clerk and messenger boy for Peak Films, Victoria Street, London, SW1.

After that he was hired as an office boy by Wardour Street film producer Jay Lewis. Sitting in Lewis's office he saw a whole host of British actors troop past; John Mills, Michael Medwin, and Richard Attenborough among them. One of them, Victor Maddern, clearly remembers the by now cocky sixteen-year-old sitting behind the switchboard when he arrived for his appointment: 'I told him I had come to see Jay Lewis, and the lad called up to the office. After a pause he said to me, "How do you get into this fucking business, then?"

14

I was a bit taken aback, but told him to join an amateur company and try for a RADA scholarship.'

In 1950 Jay Lewis gave Maurice the chance to be teaboy/messenger on the film *Morning Departure*, a story of heroism at sea, starring John Mills and Richard Attenborough as the commander and the stoker of an imperilled submarine. Casting his mind back forty years, Sir Richard Attenborough, who would later direct Caine in *A Bridge Too Far*, can just about recall the teenage version. 'In retrospect I do remember him, though I'm not sure that if I hadn't been told I would have connected that cheeky little bugger running everywhere with Michael Caine.'

In May 1951 Maurice finally got his call-up papers as a private in the Queen's Royal Regiment—of which he jokes: 'You grow up tough in the Queen's Royal Regiment. You have to walk along with "Queen's" written on your shoulder. You're frightened to go out at first'—and was sent to join the British Army on the Rhine in Germany (where, coincidentally, the lieutenant who vetted him at BAOR headquarters in Iserlohn was Patrick Newell, later to play 'Mother' in *The New Avengers* TV series).

But Mick was not designed for army life. He hated the discipline and the hierarchy. The Army being organized and run according to British 'class' divisions probably had something to do with it too. Private Micklewhite became so deliberately inconspicuous that the sergeant began to mistrust him and put him in the middle of the front row to be under his eye. However, his time in Germany, if boring, was at least peaceful, and even afforded the occasional opportunity to escape into the more

15

desirable world of the movies, as one of his commanding officers of the time, Lieutenant-Colonel W G Pettifar of the Royal Fusiliers can recall: 'In Berlin we were not allowed to wear civilian clothes at any time. One night I saw Caine coming out of the cinema resplendent in full riding outfit, jodhpurs, silk shirt, everything. I said to him, "Micklewhite, what are you doing out of uniform?" He said, "I've just been riding, sir," and I said, "Oh no, you haven't! I've just seen you coming out of the cinema." I sent him back to barracks to change.'

But the safe, if dull, sojourn in Germany was not to continue. Half-way through the first year of their service Micklewhite and his fellow privates were asked if they wanted to sign on for an extra year, an offer which they were about to refuse wholeheartedly when the officer announced, 'Wait a bit, we haven't told you it all yet. Those who don't sign on are going to Korea.' Caine was so out of touch with what being a real soldier meant that he thought he would rather go to Korea and die than stay in the army for any longer, and promptly put his name down. But irony was to play its part as he found out; 'The funny thing is, as we were coming home from Korea the blokes who had signed on for longer were being sent out there.'

The Korean war had begun in June 1950 between the Democratic People's Republic of Korea (North Korea) and the Republic of Korea (South Korea). North Korea got military aid from China, and the United Nations intervened on the side of the South Koreans. It was as part of these UN forces that the British Army got involved. The war finally ended inconclusively in July 1953, with a total loss of life

16

estimated at five million.

Private Micklewhite was transferred to 9 platoon of the 1st Battalion, Royal Fusiliers, and in early April 1952 began training for Korea at Warley Barracks, near Brentwood, Essex. The date of the battalion's departure for Korea kept changing, and soon the members of the platoon were passing the time by setting up a sweepstake on when they would eventually leave. The lads in the platoon were much of the same age, and Mick soon became firm friends with several who were also from South London, like Fusilier Jack Hawkins, a bricklayer from Blackheath. Mick, Jack and the others naturally made the most of the odd spots of leave they got, but Jack even then realized that Maurice was interested in more than just birds and booze. Years later Jack recalled of him, 'He always had his nose stuck in a book.'

Micklewhite's platoon commander was 2nd Lieutenant Robert Mill. Later Caine would base his portrayal of Lieutenant Gonville Bromhead in *Zulu* on Mill (with several of Prince Philip's mannerisms thrown in). Lt Mill kept a record of the build-up to their departure for Korea in his personal platoon book.

'I joined the battalion on 28th April 1952. At that time Sgt Walters was commanding the platoon which had just finished the first week of training at Stanford battle area in Norfolk. Training was done on a company basis. We returned to Warley Barracks in Essex on May 9th. Embarkation leave began on May 15th after a few practice parades and ended on June 5th.

On June 9th the battalion marched through the

17

city of London with colours flying, drums beating and bayonets fixed, and after had lunch at the Guildhall as guests of the Lord Mayor and the Corporation.

On June 26th we sailed from Liverpool in TSS Empire Halladay for Korea—ports of call Port Said, Aden, Colombo, Singapore, Hong Kong and we are due at Pusan on August 4th.

Five days in transit camp during which time five joined us from the Royal Norfolks, then two weeks in a training area and on August 26th we took over the slackest part of the Commonwealth division line from the Kings Shropshire Light Infantry. A couple of days later Sgt Davies was at length replaced by Sgt Smith, a habitué of C company and at one time of 9 platoon.

Robert Mill also kept an entry in his book for each of the thirty-five men in his platoon, including Fusilier 22486547 Micklewhite, M. An actor himself in Civvy Street, Mill recalls it was odd to meet a lad of Micklewhite's social class who candidly expressed such ambitions. 'At the time an actor seemed an unlikely thing for him to want to be!' Interestingly, Micklewhite told Mill he was a 'camera mechanic' at Denham Studios, something he probably worked at for a few days at the most. Mill's book also records Mick's interest in emigrating to the USA—a desire Caine always denied until he finally went to Hollywood over twenty-five years later, in 1978.

The weeks of training went on, and as the youngest platoon commander in the Battalion, Robert Mill had his work cut out—especially as his batman was the *oldest* in the battalion, a fact which

18

sometimes led the Company Commander to wonder who was actually doing the commanding! Apparently the men of 9 platoon also had a particular penchant for rabbit pie.

But despite the light-hearted moments they were preparing to fight a war, and underneath the bravado everyone, including nineteen-year-old Fusilier Micklewhite, knew it. 'I remember the boredom and the bull. I also remember the sheer naked terror of finding that I, a kid from the Elephant and Castle, actually had to go out into a paddy field at night while Chinese soldiers were trying to kill me. And I think that those who don't want us to remember these things probably never knew them in the first place.'

On arrival in Korea the Battalion took up their position on high ground overlooking the Sami Chon river. Two thousand yards away across the flat river floor were the enemy, the Chinese. It was trench warfare, with the attendant boredom, long periods of inactivity followed by bouts of gunfire. It was also extremely uncomfortable; as the report of the conflict in the Chronicle of the Royal Fusiliers for that year put it, 'After living for six weeks in the same hole in the ground one feels like a rabbit whose hutch wants moving.'

Caine vividly remembers his feelings in the trenches of the Sami Chon valley. 'There were Chinese troops opposite us. The amazing thing about them was their numbers; there were thousands of them. After an attack you would find their bodies in groups of four. They only had one rifle between them. When one fell, the next one picked it up.'

There were more comic moments too, like

19

Caine's first night on watch: 'I was sent to guard a train. I was beside this enormous pile of rubbish, twenty or thirty feet high. And it started to move. I had had a beer or two, but not that much. I looked closer and it was rats. All of it was rats. I ran to the other end of the train. A couple of Americans guarding a freight train offered me a Coca-Cola. They didn't just have a wagonload. Their whole train was Coca-Cola! And that train got priority over us when we moved out. I thought, "We're going to be all right in this war, lads."'

As the Royal Fusiliers' Chronicle records, much of the everyday life of the battalion was monotonous routine, apart from the ever present threat of the Chinese burp guns. Each day would start with 'stand-to' in the early hours. After this the routine varied according to the particular problems of each company, but during the day, every man had to put in four hours' work improving the defences in addition to any other work or periodical inspections.

At some point during the day there would be an organized rest. By sunset, patrols were on their way out. Usually patrols had thirty-six hours' warning, so that they could be briefed and, maybe, rehearsed. Patrolling was always a hazardous and nerve-racking job, and there seemed to be no way of keeping warm when lying down in a freezing paddy field, and yet not be overdressed for climbing hills. One patrol sticks out in Caine's memory. 'One night, the only time in my entire life, I *knew* I was about to die. Four of us were out on what was laughingly called Observation Patrol. The first inkling we had was when we smelt the Chinese. They ate garlic like apples. For years after I

20

couldn't eat garlic.

'Then we heard them talking and we knew they had sussed us; it was very eerie, in the moonlight in a paddy field, knowing that we were about to die.

'None of us had the least idea why we were fighting in Korea; but the odd thing was, we all thought, "We're going to die expensive. We'll take as many of them with us as we can." Our officer shouted "Run!" and by chance we ran towards the Chinese. Which is what saved us; in the dark we all lost each other. I grew up that night.'

Lt Mill offered Fusilier Micklewhite the chance of promotion to Lance-Corporal, but he turned it down. He had come into the army a private and that was how he was going to leave it, preferably alive.

Fusilier Micklewhite was actually very lucky. Not all the members of Nine platoon survived the war unscathed. Some were wounded, like Jack Hawkins, who received a bad head wound from which he never recovered. Hawkins returned, disabled, to England, where he spent the next thirty-two years until his death in 1984 suffering frequent bouts of withdrawal, depression and confusion.

And although The Royal Fusiliers did not suffer the huge casualties of regiments like the Gloucesters and the Argyll and Sutherlands, Caine had to endure the experience of seeing his friends die: 'It wasn't the brutality of the death that got you—it was the suddenness. You were talking to somebody and a minute later he wasn't there. We never knew we were becoming experienced; but it was always the replacement recruits, the new boys, that died.'

A few months later Fusilier Micklewhite was on

his way home. He would later admit that the Army influenced him more than he knew at the time, and in 1987 he launched the annual Poppy Day appeal. Mick may not have been a total innocent when he went to Korea, but he came home an adult. And one with a future to plan.

'At the Tower of London on our last day we were slouching home, civilians. The band was practising. The Parade sergeant never said a word. He just signalled to the band, and they started the regimental march.

'We had always been a bolshie lot. But with our baggage and our trilby hats and whatever demob clothes we were wearing, free at last, we straightened up and formed into threes with the band playing. That's how I left the Army.'

CHAPTER TWO

'IT'S THE THEATRE, DEAR, AND THEY CAN'T SEE YOU FROM THE BACK': THE THEATRE CAREER 1952–1955

'To me, movies are like being in love with a woman who cooks, washes your socks and is great in bed. The stage was like being in love with a tarty broad who couldn't care less if I lived or died.'

Michael Caine

After his stint in the Korean War, Maurice Micklewhite came home to join his parents in the prefab behind the Elephant and Castle in London. The future was hardly brimming over with possibilities. He was twenty years old, fresh out of the Army and determined to become an actor, but with no clear idea of how to go about it.

After a couple of weeks he took a job at Smithfield meat market, just down the road from his father's workplace at Billingsgate. Working for the company of Lovell & Christmas, and attired in a white apron and clogs, Maurice's job was to mix different qualities of butter in large vats. The butter then came out of the packing machines with cheap or fancy labels according to whether it would end up in the corner shop or at Harrods. It was hardly stimulating work, but at least it gave him time to think about the future and his next step.

One of Maurice's colleagues was an elderly man suffering from foot rot who shuffled around stacking empty cartons. He was a gentle, sad man

23

who had once known theatre people like James Agate, the drama critic. Hearing of Maurice's interest in acting, he brought in a copy of *The Stage*, the trade paper for actors, which Maurice had never heard of before. Scanning the pages, he spotted an advertisement for an 'Assistant Stage Manager, Horsham Repertory Company. Occasional walk-on parts', at a salary of two pounds ten shillings a week.

So Maurice Micklewhite made the first phone call of his life—to the general manager of the company, a man called Alwyn D Fox. Fox was one of the old school, an actor-manager who also chipped in with the occasional script. His company, The Westminster Repertory Company had only recently taken over at the Theatre Royal in Horsham, Sussex, in March 1953, after the previous company had moved out saying that it was impossible to make the rep work commercially. The director of the last company had seen only two alternatives, as quoted in the *West Sussex County Times* of 13 March 1953: 'One, to limit the size of casts and the type of setting so severely that some of the company's appeal would inevitably be lost in a series of bedroom farces. The other—and it might not work in Horsham—would be to go in for leg shows, pure and simple.'

While the citizens of Horsham were still reeling at the prospect, they were saved by the arrival of Alwyn D Fox and his company. The new tenancy at the Theatre Royal was heralded by the *West Sussex County Times*:

Next week Play Fare Productions will present The Westminster Repertory Company under the direction of their resident London producer Alwyn D Fox. Mr Fox played in and produced *Cold Turkey* at the Comedy Theatre, London, last year and also appeared in *Vintage Wine*. He has also written six radio plays...

If Horsham had been saved from leg shows, it was not deprived of its fair share of farces and mystery thrillers. Among the productions in those first few months were *Jane Eyre*, *The Witch*, *Art and Mrs Bottle*, *Third Time Lucky*, *Treasure Island* and *Lace on Her Petticoat*.

Into this mix stepped Maurice Micklewhite, Assistant Stage Manager and aspiring young actor. One of his fellow actresses at the rep, June Wyndham Davies, now a drama producer at Granada Television, can clearly remember him arriving for his audition: 'Mike Caine came for his interview wearing crepe-soled shoes and a leather jacket that really stank of fish. He had an extremely broad cockney accent, but he really worked at it.'

Caine recalls that his first ever line was 'Come along with me, sir', with which he became more than familiar as the arresting officer in several dozen mystery thrillers. As he progressed, Alwyn D Fox entrusted him with a few bigger parts but decided that something would have to be done about the young actor's name. Eye-catching it might be, but snappy it was not.

The cast, like everyone else from schooldays through to the Army, had already abbreviated his surname to 'Mick', so Michael became his first name. As for a new surname, they chose 'Scott'; joining him with Randolph and Janette in a name that hopefully bestowed star status. Oddly, his

25

stage surname would be one of the very few things that didn't survive his transition to stardom. As Mike Scott he never got an Oscar, but he did get his first taste of public acclaim.

His first review as a professional actor came out on 10 July 1953. The front page of the *West Sussex County Times* for that week was devoted to the question of whether ewe mutton was being used to make up part of the local meat ration. Barbara Stanwyck and Clark Gable were on at the pictures and at the Theatre Royal the Westminster Repertory Company had just presented a play called *The Case of Lady Camber* by Horace Annesley Vachell. A certain young actor received the following notice in the *West Sussex County Times*: 'Michael Scott never convincingly dons the years as a fashionable physician.'

The following week Alwyn Fox gave him the opportunity to play Hindley Earnshaw in *Wuthering Heights*. It gave Michael Scott his first chance at playing a drunk, a technique he was to perfect over the years in roles like Charley Fortnum in *The Honorary Consul* and Frank Bryant in *Educating Rita*. But as the drunken Hindley he was initially less than convincing: 'The producer said, "What the hell do you think you're doing?" and I said, "I'm playing a drunk, sir." And he said, "No, you're not, you're an actor who's trying to walk crooked and trying to speak in a slurred voice. Don't you realize that a drunk is a man who's trying to walk straight and speak properly?" He told me to go back and do it again, so then I had to try to walk straight and speak properly. And there is something you can do to make yourself go sort of giddy, and then you really have to try hard to walk straight and speak properly. It's quite difficult, but that was the way I learnt to act drunk.'

It must have worked for it earned him a far more enthusiastic review in the *West Sussex County Times* of 17 July 1953. 'Michael Scott has his best opportunity to date as the drunkard Hindley.'

But by the end of the week's run of *Wuthering Heights* things were not going so well. June Wyndham Davies recalls that Michael struggled, shivering and very pale, to get through the matinée performance. On leaving the stage he collapsed in his dressing-room and was taken off to hospital on a stretcher.

It was the first sign of the malaria that would, a few months later, force the young actor to leave the Horsham rep and reunite him in hospital with some of his old comrades from Korea, suffering the same fate. Meanwhile his indisposition made it into the paper although his ailment had changed somewhat. 'Michael Scott, member of the Westminster Repertory Company', said the *West Sussex County Times*, 'went down suddenly with tonsillitis on Saturday afternoon and was unable to play the part of Hindley Earnshaw in the two final performances of *Wuthering Heights . . .*'

By early August Michael Scott was back with the company to take on the role of the cockney butler in Gordon Harker's *The Sport of Kings*, 'an ultra English comedy with occasional excursions into farce.'

'Michael Scott's hypocritically sanctimonious butler is the best thing he has done locally,' said the *West Sussex County Times*. 'His transformation on learning of his master's misdemeanours is a grand piece of comic contrast.'

27

Michael Scott was learning fast. Six months previously he had been just another soldier doing his National Service and now he was fulfilling his dream to become an actor. He was learning a great deal from Alwyn D Fox and from the more experienced members of the company, but other things he would just have to pick up for himself: 'I asked if someone could help me with my make-up. All the guys in the rep were gay and they all said, "Yes, we'll help you!" And I came on at the end as the detective-inspector to arrest the suspect looking like a tart!

'There was a still photo taken of the play and when I next went home I was proudly telling my mother all the parts I'd done, and my father who was a very tough old Billingsgate porter came over and picked up this still, and looked at it and said, "I thought so." He was convinced I was gay. If you can imagine, I was wearing a trilby hat and a mackintosh and I had on false eyelashes, blue eyeshadow and pink lipstick. I'd kept saying to the guys, "Isn't this a bit over the top?" And they said, "No, it's the theatre, dear, and they can't see you from the back!"'

Word had got round town that there was a new and extremely good-looking young actor working at the rep and the girls of the local High School suddenly began to find an evening at the theatre a very attractive proposition. June Wyndham Davies remembers how Alwyn D Fox decided to capitalize on his new star attraction: 'In *Love from a Stranger* they dyed Mike's eyelashes for the first time. They'd realized that the schoolgirls kept coming because they were nuts about Mike and with the dyed eyelashes and the tan, Mike looked a dish.'

The *West Sussex County Times* of 14 August was enthusiastic about his performance as well as his looks.

In *Love From A Stranger* the handsome stranger dominates the scene throughout. Blessed with the looks for the part, Michael Scott nevertheless turns in a performance that is astonishingly good to those who have only seen him in limited minor roles.

The part is one which could easily drift into melodramatic interpretation, more funny than chilling, but Mr Scott switches alarmingly from quiet charm to maniacal frenzy in a manner which certainly promoted a succession of spinal shivers in the idolizing bevy of High School beauty which surrounded your critic on Monday.

June Wyndham Davies became his first leading lady when he was called upon to play a seducer, plying a girl with alcohol to try and weaken her resistance. Thanks to Michael Scott's opening night nerves though, the scene did not go according to plan. 'I'd forgotten to take the cork out of the bottle and the audience began to laugh at that straight away. 'June very dutifully got drunk, but the audience was in hysterics. She had to succumb to my advances because she was supposed to be inebriated—she was rolling around the stage dead drunk but she hadn't had one drop.

'June was hissing at me, trying to tell me to take the cork out of the bottle, but when you're really nervous your heart beats so loud that it's the only thing you can hear. I was actually deaf with nerves. I could see her lips moving and every time she

29

stopped talking I just said my lines. I was trying desperately to remember them anyway.'

Michael's inexperience frequently led to similar situations for the rest of the company. One of their August 1953 offerings, *The Case of Mrs Barry*, was one such example. 'We told Mike he should always have a spare line of dialogue ready in case anything went wrong. Mike played a sexton for which he had to wear a very tall hat. When he came on he forgot to take it off and it knocked the top off the door. We all waited to see what was going to happen and Mike said beautifully, "Ma'am, your house falls about our ears", which corpsed me. Then I knew he'd be a star.'

The drama critic of the *West Sussex County Times* wrote, 'As the village sexton who investigates his friend's suspicious sudden death and devises a horrific way of disclosing the merry widow's guilt, Michael Scott is all quiet, implacable determination.'

Gradually Michael Scott grew in experience and capability and his reviews in the *West Sussex County Times* became more and more favourable over the months he spent at Horsham. September brought him: 'Michael Scott's playing of the arrogant ignorant local squire gains effect from resisting the temptation to overdraw the part,' for *The Corn is Green*; 'I liked especially the performances of Michael Scott as the gauche miner whose interests, as Sally (June Wyndham Davies) points out, were dogs, darts and Sally in that order,' for *The Gay Dog*; and 'Michael Scott as Clarence, the Cockney thief, keeps us amused in his too-rare appearances on the stage,' for *The Strange Affair at St Hilda's*.

In those days repertory companies performed a

different play every few days, and the young Michael Scott acquired a maturity in his portrayals of characters that could easily have taken him several years if the runs had been longer. It was difficult for him not to go over the top sometimes, though, as the local reviewer picked up when Scott played Robert Crosbie in Somerset Maugham's *The Letter*.

'There was always a hint of over-acting about Michael Scott's portrayal of Robert Crosbie,' he wrote in the 25 September issue of the *West Sussex County Times*, 'and it was only when the first faint wisps of uncertainty drifted into his mind, and later, when his belief in his wife was finally shattered that he exhibited the requisite emotional stress.'

But there were times when over-acting stood him in good stead. On 9 October the same paper carried a review of *Sweeney Todd*:

Apprentice June Wyndham Davies (if only her mother could see her now, ginger wig and all) and seafaring hero Michael Scott, an upstanding example of masculine rectitude if ever there was one, successfully overplay their parts in matching the machinations of the trio of villains.

By the end of October 1953 though, Mike Scott had exchanged Horsham for Queen Mary's hospital in Roehampton, where he spent seven weeks being treated for malaria. It was goodbye to acting for the present. But there is a postscript to his time at the Horsham rep—twenty-five years on, when he was finally an international superstar living in Los Angeles: 'I was sitting at home on my Beverly Hill

31

with all the toys—the swimming pool, the tennis court, the jacuzzi, the Rolls-Royce—when I got a letter from the DHSS in Hammersmith. I thought, "Christ, what have they got me for now?" I opened it and it said, "We have here, very sick in hospital, a man called Alwyn D Fox who is completely impoverished and keeps telling everyone he discovered Michael Caine. Could you write a letter and perhaps include a little money for us to get him some extras because he is completely penniless." So I wrote a letter saying it was Alwyn D Fox who gave me my start in show business and I sent a cheque for $5,000 or something. About six weeks later I got my cheque back uncashed and they said, "Unfortunately Mr Fox passed away before he could spend your money but not until he had received your letter to tell everyone that he had discovered you."'

'We're Finishing Early Today So Romeo Here Can Get Married'
By the time Michael Scott had recovered from the malaria it was 1954, and time to look for another season's work. Luckily he landed another post in rep, this time at Lowestoft, on the Suffolk coast. His fortunes changed, though not in the way he anticipated.

He fell in love and got married.

Mixing business with pleasure, he married his leading lady, Patricia Haines, a few months after he joined the company in Lowestoft. Patricia Haines was the leading lady of the company, a little older than him and an experienced actress. Sadly, the marriage didn't stand the test of time. The pressure of rival careers and ambitions fighting each other

32

was hard enough, but the arrival a year later of daughter Dominique, plus the never-ending money problems, proved just too much for their fragile relationship; and their marriage foundered.

But back in 1954 the only inkling of trouble was their slightly 'artistic', occasionally tempestuous, relationship. Professionally they spent the summer entertaining the holidaymakers with the usual round of rep offerings. Michael Scott became the male juvenile lead, on four pounds ten shillings a week. His opposite number, the female juvenile lead, was an actress called Jean Marlow who spotted a potential problem as soon as Michael Scott arrived in Lowestoft. He'd come with only the clothes he stood up in—and the actors were each supposed to supply their own wardrobe!

But for now it was his first night and Jean gave him his choice of the miniature bottles of liqueurs which the theatre manager brought back from abroad for the theatre bar, and which were used for the actors' treats.

The stipulation about the actors' clothing soon caused problems for the new recruit: 'The first week I was there I only had a small part so I came on in a suit, did my bit and went off,' Michael Caine remembers. 'The second week I had about four changes, so I went off and came on again, still in the same suit from the week before; and I came on twice more, still in the same suit. And Jackson Stanley, the manager, came round and he said, "Why didn't you change in the last act?" And I said, "Into what?" He went on, "A different suit! It's three weeks later, and you're in the town instead of the country—you're supposed to change!" I said, "But I've only *got* one suit."'

33

Michael soon settled in, but the months he had been ill had caused his burgeoning talent to turn slightly rusty, a relief to Jean Marlow: 'I was about the worst in the company and I was jolly glad when Michael turned up because he was even worse than me.'

Their first production together was less than slick. 'Michael was awful—he didn't know the script as he was brand new. I had an awful squeaky voice, and the whole show was carried by Patricia Haines. Mike and I were on stage together all the time—he'd whisper to me "What do I do now?" and I'd say, "Sit down", and then say all his lines as well as my own.

'We did a play called *But Once A Year* in which Michael and I played man and wife. I had a lot of costume changes and some embraces with Michael. I made the embraces last as long as possible so I could think about my next costume change.'

Jackson Stanley, the actor-manager of the company at Lowestoft was a formidable man in his seventies with a strong North Country accent and a short temper. He had a tendency to sack staff if they disagreed with him and then to hire them straight back again. Jean Marlow remembers being sacked for complaining that Stanley didn't pay their National Insurance stamps, and Mike Scott was sacked for marrying the leading lady. However, as with Alwyn D Fox at Horsham, Caine can still remember the advice that he was given by the older man. This time it was on the subject of what to do whilst waiting for your next line of dialogue.

'He said to me, "What are you doing Michael?"

'"Nothing, sir."

'"What do you mean, nothing?"

'"I haven't got anything to say."

'So he said, "What do you mean, you haven't got anything to say? Of course you've got things to say, you've got wonderful things to say. But you sit there and listen, think of these extraordinary things to say and then decide not to say them!"

'That is the greatest piece of advice I can give to someone who wants to act in movies—to listen and react.'

But little could dampen Michael Scott's enthusiasm for life. He was young and in love. When they weren't working, the company went to the cinema where Mike taught everyone how to blow smoke rings and gave his criticisms of the films as he had always done on his visits to the cinema with his Clubland pals. One week *Quo Vadis* came under his scrutiny, as Jean Marlow remembers—'We all fell about after the first line "You can see Rome from the top of the hill". During the film Mike said to me, "One day I'm going to be a film star."'

Eventually the day of the company wedding between Michael Scott and Patricia Haines dawned. 'We're finishing early today so Romeo here can get married,' announced Jackson Stanley before they all went off to celebrate.

Shortly afterwards, Jackson Stanley had another talk with Michael Scott. 'He said to me, "You've got a hell of a long way to go, my boy, but there's something different about you. There are about three actors who can listen on a stage, who can act as if they're really hearing the other actors' words instead of just waiting to speak their lines. You know how to do this."

'After a few months he said, "I can't teach you

any more. You should go to London." So I went and fell flat on my face.'

'I Could Have Been Michael 101 Dalmatians...'
After he and Patricia left Lowestoft, towards the end of the 1954 summer season, Michael Scott decided he had had enough of rep and the endless grind of appearing in a different show every single week, learning a fresh set of lines and running around to find props. The newly-weds returned to London where they lived first with the Micklewhite parents, and then in a two-roomed flat in Brixton.

The young actor's big break was still nine years away, and over the next few years he was frequently 'resting' for long and often depressing periods. But in London there was TV, and occasionally even film, work to be sought; though the parts were probably only one-liners, if he was lucky.

Television work under union agreements meant he should now register with the actors' union, Equity. Only he couldn't. There was already an actor on their books called Michael Scott and of course no two actors can have the same name. He needed to find another name, and fast, if he was to keep the new part he'd just got ... 'I was in a phone box on Leicester Square and my agent had got me a job. She said, "You're now a full member of Equity but you've got to change your name because there is another Michael Scott."

'I said, "I'll keep Michael", and she said, "Yes, you can keep Michael but you've got to change the Scott." So I looked round and *The Caine Mutiny* was on so I thought "Michael Caine"; and as I looked round I thought, "Well, I could be Michael Mutiny." But under the Leicester Square Theatre

36

there was *101 Dalmatians*. I could have been Michael 101 Dalmatians if the trees had been in a different place!'

The demise of 'Michael Scott' in favour of TV work didn't mean that he was about to abandon the theatre entirely. At the end of 1954, the brand-new 'Michael Caine' spent a few months with Joan Littlewood's Theatre Workshop in Stratford East. He was a member of the 'alternative' company brought together to hold the fort at Stratford while the 'A' team was on tour. It wasn't a great success. He appeared in a play called *The Chimes*, which was roundly condemned by the critics, the *Daily Herald* referring to its 'artless crudity of adaptation and acting.'

Caine and Joan Littlewood had different approaches to their craft and after the run of *The Chimes* Caine was not offered any more work, or as he succinctly puts it, 'I went to Theatre Workshop for an inglorious three months before I was thrown out.'

However, his time at Stratford East had not been wasted. Again he had picked up a piece of advice which would stay with him all his career: 'I learned a very valuable lesson from Joan Littlewood. One day she said to me, "Rehearsal is the work—performance is relaxation." That is fabulous advice for movies. All the hell Joan put me through was worth it for that one sentence.'

Years later, in 1983, Caine bumped into Joan Littlewood in London. 'I've just seen *Educating Rita*,' she told him. 'It's the first fucking performance you've given in twenty years.' 'Thanks a lot, Joan,' said Caine. 'Don't worry,' she said. 'I suppose you've made millions not acting.' 'I have,

37

Joan, I have!' Caine replied.

Over the next few years, Caine's time was almost totally taken up with trying to get into TV and films, but he did make the occasional foray into the theatre with companies like Sam Wanamaker's New Shakespeare Theatre in Liverpool in 1958. Robert Shaw was appearing as the lead in a play called *One More River*, and Michael Caine had a small part as a sailor. They used to drive back to London whenever they could in Robert's beaten-up Humber Saloon. There was no M1, so they would cut across country to the accident-prone A1. At that time there was a road safety campaign with posters at accident blackspots, and Robert Shaw's reaction to these always terrified Caine—'As Robert spotted one of these hoardings showing a picture of a widow and the message "Keep death off the road", he'd press his foot down hard on the accelerator and shout, "Let's get the fuck out of here!"'

While they were in Liverpool Charles Laughton came through to direct a play called *The Party*. But the talk was not of Laughton but of the new kid who was apparently, unbelievably, acting Laughton off the stage. Caine went to see for himself. The 'kid' was Albert Finney.

Albert Finney was also the actor for whom the role of Private Bamforth in Willis Hall's *The Long, The Short and The Tall* was conceived. But it was Peter O'Toole who shot to stardom in the role in January 1959, first at the Royal Court and then at the New Theatre; Michael Caine was O'Toole's understudy in that production.

Peter O'Toole once said he'd never missed a performance in his life, but for Michael Caine there was always that possibility. They were three

38

terrifying, frustrating months; every night O'Toole left it until the very last minute before he turned up, by which time Caine would be dressed and quaking, preparing to face an audience who hadn't come to see him at all. Then O'Toole would leap in, shout a greeting and bound off stagewards, leaving Caine totally drained. But, as Caine recalled later, the atmosphere backstage was so free and easy there seemed no point in saying anything about it. Caine gritted his teeth and got on with it. He was also given two other important tasks by O'Toole: to go out and buy the brandy and to find the girls. As he says, 'I'd have made a wonderful pimp.'

After O'Toole left to take up his role as *Lawrence of Arabia*, Caine took over as Private Bamforth in a six-month provincial tour of the play. It was on that tour that he first met Terence Stamp, with whom he would share a flat in swinging London for the next four and a half years. Stamp has said that for him Caine was the definitive Bamforth. 'He understudied O'Toole, literally waiting in the wings while the star was being hauled, legless and roaring, out of the Salisbury and on to the stage. I never heard Michael Caine say a word against O'Toole, but in private he could do a wicked imitation of Peter's nasal, Leeds-Irish-cockney rendition of Bamforth.'

The tour of *The Long, The Short and The Tall* took them to Nottingham, Edinburgh, Hanley, Dublin, Bradford, Bournemouth and Sheffield, to name just some of the venues. Along the way Stamp was picking up tips from the streetwise Caine. When they arrived in a new town on a Sunday evening they would make their way straight to the stage door for a sighting of the digs list. In his

39

autobiography, *Coming Attractions*, Stamp remembers what would happen next.

Caine explained to the newcomers: 'It's essential to be quick off the mark before the good digs get snapped up.' He had change at the ready for the stage door pay-phone and was armed with a few loaded questions for prospective landladies: How big were the rooms? What were the other boarders like? Was the grub any cop? Last, but certainly not least, was the house averse to outside talent—female company? From town to town the digs varied enormously ranging from great to duff; a common factor being landladies who generally liked 'theatricals' and had a field knowledge of their needs.

When the tour arrived in Cambridge Michael Caine appeared with a black patch over one eye. The hospital had told him that the eye had probably become infected from stage make-up. Terence Stamp recalls that the director was less than happy when he heard that Caine planned to go on stage wearing the patch.

Jerry [the director] objected, and a heated discussion followed, with Mike holding his ground.
Finally Jerry said, 'Well, wear your usual make-up but don't put anything near the bad eye.' Mike couldn't believe it. 'Wot, and come on looking like a bloody Bonzo?'
He wore the black patch.
That was my first inkling of Mike's phobia about his lashes. He would take great care to

40

mascara them whenever he performed but it would never have crossed his mind to wear make-up in the street. Later, when Mike and I were living in Ebury Street in Belgravia, he came up the stairs one day holding two small glass bottles and announcing triumphantly, 'This is it! Someone's finally cracked it.'

'Cracked what, Mike?'

'The eyelashes. Look, a dye! You put it on yourself.'

'Does it work?'

'I dunno. I thought it'd be worth a try.'

He rushed up to his bathroom on the top floor. Ten minutes later he came down. The stuff had worked all right, but in his haste to transform his lashes, Mike had omitted to protect his eyelids. He really did look like a Bonzo for a couple of days.

In 1960 Caine was offered a part in a work by a new young playwright at The Royal Court Theatre. The playwright was called Harold Pinter and the new play was *The Room*.

The paths of actor and playwright had already crossed on more than one occasion. Pinter had also been a pupil at Hackney Downs Grocers' School, although several years before Caine. Later, while he was still acting under his stage name of David Baron, Pinter had appeared in the West End production of *The Long, The Short and The Tall*, but not at the same time as Caine was understudying O'Toole.

Caine can recall meeting Pinter at the point where he was about to make the transition from the stage to behind the pen: 'I met an actor called

David Baron and he said, "Sod this, I'm giving up acting. I'm going to write but I'll use my real name." And so I said "What's your real name, David?" He said, "Harold Pinter". And I met another actor who'd just been fired from Maudie Edwards' rep in Swansea and he said, "Fuck this acting lark, I'm going to try writing." And he told me that in fact he'd already written a play. I asked him what it was called, and he said *Look Back in Anger*. It was John Osborne.'

By the early sixties Caine was making some kind of headway, however tortuous, in television. The theatre no longer really occupied his thoughts, but a one-week run playing Terry Stamp's older brother was certainly OK. So he appeared in the world première of *Why the Chicken*, a play based on a musical theme by Lionel Bart.

'An Extremely Promising West End Début'
There was just one more production in Michael Caine's theatre career and it was simultaneously his West End début and his farewell performance.

Next Time I'll Sing To You by James Saunders was a strong avant-garde piece based on the true story of a man called Jimmy Mason who died in 1942 at the age of eighty-four, having lived alone for forty-four years in a barricaded hovel in Great Canfield, Essex. The only person he spoke to in all those years was his brother who brought him food.

The production was really an anti-play. The actors would move in and out of their characters, borrow matches from the audience—whom they would often taunt—and lounge around on a lilo. No wonder the play came as a great shock to those who had expected *Next Time I'll Sing To You* to be a musical!

It opened at the New Arts Theatre on 23 January 1963, and a month later transferred to the Criterion in the West End. *Next Time I'll Sing To You* was an immediate success and became the hottest ticket in town. Famed critic Harold Hobson was so impressed that he managed to find a reason to review the play almost every week in the *Sunday Times*. '*Next Time I'll Sing to You*,' he said, 'is the best directed play in London. It is the best acted play in London. It is the best play in London.'

This prompted the following response from Bernard Levin in the *Daily Mail*:

When Mr Harold Hobson says that a non-French play is the best to be seen in London and goes on saying so for weeks on end, it clearly behoves me, as the final arbiter in these matters, to go and see it myself, and pronounce ... Mr Hobson is not quite right, but he is nearer right than wrong. *Next Time I'll Sing to You* is, in fact, the best non-play in London.

Michael Caine came in for his share of praise, too. The *Daily Express*'s Herbert Kretzmer wrote, 'The jaunty performance of Michael Caine came as a most pleasurable revelation'; while *The Stage* added, 'Michael Caine makes an extremely promising West End début'; and J W Lambert, writing in the *Sunday Times*, had this to say:

I cannot resist commending the astounding range of half-hinted feeling which Michael Caine draws from his knockabout role by the flick of an eye, a grin, the twist of a hip: granted that he has been

43

given a flying start by his author, his communication across the footlights works on the audience like an electric charge.

The play continued to attract a growing following, and it was standing room only for most of the performances. Michael Caine had finally, triumphantly, made it to the West End.

His part involved a very long monologue at the start of the second act which included asking the audience questions that were for the most part unanswerable. Once, though, Caine was caught out as Denys Graham, another member of the cast, remembers—'One night someone *did* actually react to one of the questions, and said, Yes, he *was* a Lithuanian clock-maker or some such. Michael ad-libbed and got the man up on stage. Afterwards the man whispered to Caine that he was a resting actor, and wanted to be able to say he'd appeared on the West End stage.'

Michael Caine was certainly enjoying himself in the West End. Denys Graham recalls that Caine's friends from home often came up to see him and Michael would usually take them out for pie and mash after the show. And as well as his pals there was female company to think about. Between them, Caine and his new friend Terry Stamp made a formidable team as another member of the production, Michael Bryant, clearly remembers: 'On the first night we heard the click of stiletto heels. First Terry Stamp, and then six mini-skirted dolly birds went past on their way down to Mike's dressing room. "The birds love me 'ooded eyes," Mike always said.'

Barry Foster and Michael Bryant shared a

44

dressing room at the Criterion and both enjoyed working with Caine whom they thought of as 'a smashing bloke and a great cockney character actor.' When Michael told them that he hated 'the fucking theatre' and intended to be a film star they were highly amused. According to Michael Bryant, 'At that time all film stars looked like Richard Todd. "How's a hideous-looking chap like you going to be a film star?" we used to ask him.'

The cast were paid around £9 each per week, plus, of course the glory. But while appearing on the West End stage and receiving enthusiastic reviews might have led other young actors to think their stage career was assured, Caine had other ideas.

In February 1963 Michael Caine was poised to break through as a successful actor. But he had a choice to make between the theatre and the movies. He was just starting a run in a West End play, when suddenly he was offered a part in a film. Should he risk a virtual certain West End hit for the one-off movie that might be a flop?

For Michael Caine there was no contest—he'd do the film. That film was called *Zulu*.

In twenty-seven years he has chosen never to go back to the theatre. Many offers have been made, but all have been politely but firmly refused.

'I remember early on a very famous theatre company offering me an international tour of, I think it was *Henry V*, which was very artistic and I was very flattered. I went to see the man and he said, "Of course you know the theatre doesn't pay anywhere near as much as films," and I said, "Of course not, I don't expect that, but how much does it pay?" And he said, "Twenty-five pounds a

45

week." So I said, "Forget it. It may be Art, but I can make a film and buy a Van Gogh. That's Art, and it'll last!" I wasn't really sure that what *I* was going to do with *Henry V* was going to be Art, either.'

CHAPTER THREE

'TELEVISION IS A ONE-NIGHT STAND': THE TELEVISION CAREER 1955–1962

'I went up and said to him, "I thought you were bloody marvellous ... and I think you're going to be a very big star."
And the first words that this articulate, intelligent and sensitive young cockney said to me were "Cor, fuck me—really?"'

Roger Moore

'Michael Scott' might have been raring to take London by storm after his return from Lowestoft, but it seemed London was less than ready for him. While his new wife Patricia Haines was getting parts here and there, his most regular spot was as a washer-upper at the Ecu de France restaurant in Jermyn Street or at the Dorchester Hotel.

Visits to agents were less frequent than visits to the labour exchange in Smith Street. There he was allocated an odd mix of short-term jobs, and during the mid-fifties, Michael Scott found himself tackling a variety of supporting roles, from plumber's mate to loading Lyons individual fruit pies, and working in the Brixton laundry—where his ability to withstand the heat earned him the nickname of 'Sanders of the Steam Room' from his black colleagues.

Occasionally his agent, Josephine Burton, succeeded in getting him the odd walk-on part on TV, but nothing he could crow about. He was

47

never going to make it with *The Adventures of Sir Lancelot*, for example. For a start, the series didn't get transmitted for ages, until ITV had got off the ground. And the parts were virtually invisible anyway; as 'Third Knight' in one episode, he rode slowly and gingerly up to the camera, delivered his one line, and plodded off again. He wasn't even recognizable, his helmet and visor conspiring to obscure his face completely.

Changing his name didn't bring instant success either. 1955 was a difficult time for the newly-minted Michael Caine. He'd leapt from the crucible of repertory theatre into the fire of a new young marriage—made more stressful by lack of money and by what he saw as his failure to make it as an actor in the place which really counted, London. Two years later, in 1957, an article in the *Observer* in the form of an imaginary interview with a 'bit-part' actor, graphically illustrated the exact problems facing Caine.

'I used to work in twice-nightly rep. Came the TV. The local audiences were apparently tired of seeing the likes of me playing different parts week after week, and the rep had to close. Most of us came to London to play "bits" in TV shorts. So the local rep audiences still see me and the likes of me night after night. It's not for nothing that they call television "rep in an iron lung."' ...

... 'Who then—all things being equal—will get the part?'

'The nicest guy in the bunch. The one that badgers [the producers and casting directors] least; the one who makes no fuss about money, costume, studio dates; the one who doesn't fluff his lines, or hog the camera or try to act the star off the screen. In short, the pleasant, conscientious, modest, honest plodder.'

'Are you one of them?'

'Yes. My job-hunting therefore consists of nothing more forceful than showing my face at regular intervals. I just look in, usually when I am about to start another job and can't be suspected of cadging, just to say "Hello" and "How about a quick cup of coffee?"'

'Not a drink?'

'They don't drink nowadays, except on the BBC where their jobs are safe.'

To add to his uncertain professional existence came domestic upheaval. In 1955 he and Patricia became parents with the birth of their daughter Dominique. All was not well with the marriage, however. Six months after Dominique was born they split up; and not long afterwards, in early 1956, Caine's father died aged only fifty-seven. It all hit Maurice Micklewhite very hard. His father had always been a bit suspicious of his choice of career, and Maurice had tried very hard to prove to him that it was OK, and that he could succeed at it. Now it was too late.

Teetering on the brink of a really damaging depression, he was rescued by his mother. Ellen Micklewhite packed him off abroad with a small sum that came through on a life insurance policy, and the future millionaire Michael Caine spent several months of Orwellian existence in Paris, seeing life from pavement level. He spent most of his time on his own just watching everything, unconsciously saving it up for the day when it

49

might come in handy.

This was Cardboard City, 1950s style. Sometimes he would find a bed for the night and at other times the air terminal at Les Invalides provided his place of rest. He was even befriended by the gendarmes at the Place de la Concorde who took pity on the young wanderer when it rained and allowed him to sleep in their huts. It was rough but it was formative, and he learned from it. There was another side-effect too. During those months in Paris Caine became a fluent French speaker, a skill he would later put to good use when he became a connoisseur of good food and wine.

When he returned to England a few months later, Caine went back to the endless round of trying for parts in television and films. In the years before *Zulu*, he estimates, he made over a hundred TV appearances. He kept a written record, counting them up as they came and went. At the end, or rather at the beginning of his film career, he threw the file away. Much of the television of the time was live, and many of Michael Caine's unbilled performances are now virtually untraceable.

Even this humble TV career had to start somewhere; and it began, strangely enough, in films. Films were, of course, where Michael Caine wanted to be and mid-1956 brought him his first speaking part in a movie. Called *A Hill In Korea*, it was shot in Portugal and portrayed the Korean War which Fusilier Micklewhite had so vividly experienced. Of course, this was only a movie and Portugal wasn't much like Korea—Caine later remarked, 'Wales would have been more appropriate'—but that didn't stop him claiming expert knowledge in order to get the part. It

50

worked; his National Service had come in useful after all, and director Julian Amyes took him on to play one of the soldiers. He first met Amyes at 144 Piccadilly and was rather quieter than usual as Amyes recalls, 'He was very shy, until someone said he'd worked at Stratford East and then he got animated. He said that it had been far too left-wing and full of communists!'

A few months later, after the shoot of *A Hill in Korea* was over, Amyes began work on a production for television, an abstract-looking version of a modern classic about Joan of Arc, called *The Lark*. Thinking about his cast he remembered the young actor whom he had taken on for *A Hill in Korea* and decided to offer him a part. Michael Caine is eternally grateful: 'The hardest thing to get in your life is your very first speaking part in a film. Julian Amyes gave me both mine, he gave me a part in *The Lark* on television and he gave me a part in a film called *A Hill in Korea*. Those were my first two parts.'

In those days of live TV, audiences had to accept the occasional fluff or forgotten line. But it must have been hard to accept Michael Caine's first real TV outing. As a prison guard, and wearing a helmet that looked like the nose cone of a cannon-shell, he found himself so nervous that he forgot his words—all three of them—tried to exit with Joan of Arc through the wrong door and, finding his way blocked by a large and ungainly TV camera, walked right up to the lens and said, in close-up, 'Oh, bugger it!' To cap it all, he then made his exit, still with Joan, but straight out of the window of what was supposed to be a Norman castle, eighty foot high.

51

But the surest sign that his luck had turned, however humbly, was the letter his agent got two weeks later. In the days before videotape, plays were sometimes 'tele-recorded' or filmed as they went out, so they could be repeated later. If mistakes were made during the performance, they could do the odd re-take afterwards and then insert it into the final tele-recording. On 26 November 1956, a member of the BBC's TV Bookings Department wrote to Michael Caine:

Re: The Lark 11/11/56
I understand that you kindly agreed to stay on after the transmission of the above play to appear in some re-takes for the tele-recording.

In view of the additional time involved, I am asking our Accounts Department to enclose a cheque for 11 guineas.

So not only had Caine made a hash of his best chance on TV yet, he'd got paid extra for it!

Live television put a great strain on any TV drama. Actors would have their suits joined together with velcro so they could be ripped off in a second. At least Michael Caine had one advantage: 'I was very thin so I could wear two suits.' However, having to worry about an instant costume change did make it difficult to devote himself fully to the role, as Caine remembers—'You'd be standing in front of the camera, playing someone who was about to go to prison and the actress playing your girl would be crying and saying "It's all right, darling." And then they'd say "cut" and someone would literally rip the whole suit off, and you've got another suit on underneath and you're coming out of prison five years later and it's really the same shot.'

On the day Caine received his contract for *The Lark*, he also got one for an episode of a drama serial called *Crime of the Century*. It was the kind of part he often got in the next couple of years, well down the credits in the 'Other parts played by' section. He found himself supporting such actors as Sid James and Ballard Berkeley (who was playing a major—the kind of character he was still playing twenty-five years later, when he was 'The Major' in *Fawlty Towers*)

'I Didn't Even Know He Was In It!'

Caine's agent Josephine Burton lost no time in striking while the iron was hot. By mid-January 1957 she was again putting his name forward to the BBC, this time suggesting him for the part of a young Australian. The career résumé which she attached to the letter shows her determination, at least, to do her best for him. Michael Caine, the BBC was told, could speak with an Australian accent, had served with the Australian army in Korea (*alongside* would have been more accurate) and had even lived in Australia! Moreover, he was, they were told, a boxer.

What happened about the Australian part isn't clear, but Caine certainly got a boxing role in March 1957. It was in Rod Serling's classic boxing story *Requiem for a Heavyweight*. The star character in the story was boxer 'Mountain McClintock', who is used by his manager and then thrown aside when he is past his best. When McClintock is penniless on the streets his manager comes along with his latest boxing 'discovery'—played by Michael Caine. 'The

53

director was Alvin Rakoff, who gave me quite a lot of little parts,' says Caine. In fact, the part was so 'little' that viewers probably only saw the back of Caine's head; in any case, they were far more interested in the face that was being catapulted to fame in the lead role of Mountain McClintock—Sean Connery.

Warren Mitchell was also in the cast of *Requiem*, but like many of Caine's early co-stars can't remember him at that time: 'Was he?' he says. 'I didn't even know he was in it.'

It wasn't the first time that Michael and Sean Connery had met. Michael Caine claims to have first met the ex-coffin polisher from Edinburgh, variously, in an agent's waiting room, auditioning for the same part in *How To Murder a Rich Uncle* (which Caine got), and when Connery was appearing in the chorus of *South Pacific*. In the years ahead the two actors were to become close friends, and co-star in one of Caine's own favourite movies, *The Man Who Would Be King*.

Anonymous Michael Caine might still be, but by spring 1957 work was definitely coming his way. ITV, the commercial TV channel, had now been around since 1955, giving struggling actors another potential employer apart from the BBC. Most of the drama for ITV was, though, rather different from that of the Corporation. And although *The Adventures of William Tell* provided employment, unfortunately the *Sir Lancelot* problem reared its head again: the viewing public didn't actually *see* Michael Caine's performance until well over a year after he'd done the part.

'The Prisoner' is probably an episode of *The Adventures of William Tell* Michael Caine would rather forget, especially as it meant concealing his blond locks under a dark wig. Caine played a prisoner on a chain gang, as Conrad Phillips, who played William Tell, recalls: 'He was being sprung out of prison and I took his place. He was supposed to be doubling up for me and we were both wearing convict gear and looking rather dirty. I thought at the time "that's a likely lad!" He was a very positive young actor.'

Despite the advent of ITV the BBC still remained the largest producer of television drama, and there were many more unbilled appearances for Caine still to come. *Joyous Errand* was one such, in which Caine appeared in the last episode as an airline pilot. There was nothing notable about it at all, except that the star, Peter Arne, had already quit by Episode 3, claiming complete loss of patience with the poor quality of the scripts.

Ronald Eyre remembers directing Michael Caine in a series about great wartime escapes, taken from stories by Aidan Crawley and called appropriately enough *Escape*. Caine appeared in an episode set in 'Prison Camp Stalag Luft III, NCO's compound, Spring 1942' and Ronald Eyre noticed a particular quality in the young actor. 'He was a powerful, startling actor. I couldn't make head or tail of him. He seemed dozy, but underneath there was a power, a coiled spring. It was very mysterious—*he* was very mysterious. His technique was slightly special, but it wasn't a veneer, as with some actors. He's a *real* actor.'

Gradually, as the fifties wore on, Caine's fortunes began to improve. From not being in the credits at all he had made it into the 'other parts played by' section and sometimes even got a credit of his own.

55

His ascent from then on was so slow that it sometimes appeared not to be moving at all, but he was gaining in experience and contacts all the time. A couple of months after his appearance in *Escape*, he had a part in *Mister Charlesworth*, a series of six crime stories set in Soho in which Nigel Davenport—later to co-star with Caine in *Play Dirty* and in *Without A Clue* and *Jack the Ripper*—played a trusty sergeant to Wensley Pithey's Detective Chief Inspector.

But the series that regularly gave Michael Caine the odd chance was the one which was to become the most popular crime series of its day—*Dixon of Dock Green*. When it first started, though, no one could have foreseen the popularity that lay ahead. Even the star Jack Warner only saw it as a short-term bet. 'This series in six episodes—if I'm lucky it'll be extended to thirteen!' he told a friend, Harry Landis, who had been in Portugal with Caine on *A Hill in Korea*. *Dixon*, or rather its producer, Douglas Moodie, gave many struggling actors their first taste of TV in rather more comfortable surroundings than some other TV dramas. The format was familiar to everyone, and the regular actors were old hands. And it was usually well received by critics as well as the TV audience.

The series was based by its originator, Ted Willis, on personal stories sent in to him regularly by some two hundred policemen and women, and for that reason the series was generally regarded as 'authentic'. But there were limits to the 'authenticity'—as casting blond, blue-eyed Michael Caine in the unlikely guise of an Indian pedlar suggests!

Crime drama was very much the order of the TV

day in the 1950s. Raymond Francis is still remembered as Chief Superintendent Lockhart in ITV's *No Hiding Place*, which started life as *Murder Bag*. Michael Caine popped up in one episode of *Murder Bag*, which strangely enough, never appeared in *TV Times* though it was shown in four ITV regions.

A less well known series, that was sold to America, and which has occasionally surfaced in TV archive re-runs in the USA, is *Mark Saber*; about a one-armed former Scotland Yard chief inspector turned private eye, played by Donald Gray. Caine was definitely in one episode—about the theft of a collection of art treasures, directed by Dick Lester (of *Help* and *Superman II* fame)—and possibly others.

'I'm Afraid The Part Has Now Been Cast...'
In 1958 Michael Caine's agent was still hammering away at BBC producers to give Caine a chance. He got the occasional interview, like the one on 25 February, where the un-named interviewing producer noted, 'Profile still too long, but liked.' He read the part of a 'copper', and the pencilled note reads 'Must use. V. good type.' Nobody knows if he got the part, but more often than not letters would arrive at his agent's office (or even at his mother's address in Marshall Gardens) thanking him for coming and saying more or less the same as the one sent him on 23 April 1958. 'I am afraid that the part for which you read has now been cast, but there will, of course, be many other characters in the series when it starts, one of which may be right for you.'

By a strange quirk of fate, however, Michael

57

Caine did get to play in a BBC version of the production that gave him his name—*The Caine Mutiny Court Martial*—made, according to the *Radio Times*, with the generous assistance of the Royal Navy. He played one of the court orderlies. Sometimes it must have seemed there was no escape from the actor's graveyard of bit parts. Sunday night plays on the BBC like an adaptation of Edgar Wallace's *The Frog* (in which he played third police constable) might pay the rent, but Caine was hardly the star. On other occasions, producer Douglas Moodie varied Caine's employment on *Dixon of Dock Green* by making him a gunman instead of an Indian pedlar.

The New Year, 1959, dawned and found Michael Caine in almost the same state as 1956, '57 and '58 had done, still waiting for his big break. Life was an endless round of auditions—a process that every actor knows so well. First Caine would need to psych himself up, to convince himself he would get the part and then, if he was successful, the perpetual question would arise—would this be the part which would finally get him noticed? By now he was working more regularly, but still in minor parts; for instance in *The Dark Side of the Earth*, a big BBC production about the Hungarian Revolution, in which Caine found a small niche as a Russian guard.

March 1959 saw him back in *Dixon of Dock Green* again, as a character called 'Tufty'. In one of his many appearances in *Dixon* he worked with Angela Douglas, and made an immediately favourable impression: 'One day I caught a bus with Michael. "'Ere, 'ow much are you gettin' paid?" he asked me. I told him I was getting twelve guineas. "Well,

58

put your purse away, dear," he said, "I'm doing better than that—I'm on fifteen.'''

Next, Michael Caine discovered Manchester and Granada TV, landing a small part in a series, starring Gerald Harper and Lisa Gastoni, called *Skyport*, about crime and dramatic happenings around an airport. One of the producers was Michael Scott (not the actor who had forced Maurice Micklewhite to change his stage name to Michael Caine, but the man who later became Granada TV's Programme Controller, and presenter of many different television series) who went on from *Skyport* to direct *Knight Errant '60*. This was a popular Granada TV series starring John Turner as Adam Knight, a modern-day Sir Lancelot who sets himself up to help anybody, in any situation. The flexibility of the format meant the series could run and run, at least in theory, as long as the ideas for each episode kept on coming. Reviewers liked it because it gave them a rest from the usual crime fare—'The absence of crime and violence in the usual sense is a welcome departure for any regular drama series on ITV,' said the long-suffering Philip Purser of the *News Chronicle*. His relief was premature, though; crime provided several situations that required the services of Adam Knight. Michael Scott gave Caine a small part in the episode *Man on the Pier*, about a man who pleaded guilty to an offence his wife is certain he did not commit.

Call for Action, a BBC series which mixed actors in fictitious situations with real-life emergency services and their 'anonymous heroes', was a little different from what had gone before. One aspect of it, however, was more than a little familiar to

Michael Caine: it called for location filming—at Lowestoft. Caine played Chief Engineer on a North Sea trawler which runs into trouble. He spent a week on location and a day at Ealing Film Studios, and was paid 42 guineas, plus his board and lodging and two pounds twelve shillings rail fare.

Then it was back to, yes, more detectives and the like in drama serials, such as *Golden Girl*. Based on an idea like 'The Perils of Pauline', *Golden Girl* featured Katie Boyle (or Lady Boyle as she was then known) as an heiress in danger of her life and mixed up with a journalist who sends her poisoned fruit.

Golden Girl didn't benefit from the full attention of the cast and crew. It was made at the time of the 1960s Olympics and, according to another of its stars, Michael Aldridge, they had the television on in the studio during transmission, much to the annoyance of the producer.

One scene was filmed at night on Wimbledon Common and involved Katie Boyle being gagged, blindfolded and locked inside a case. She couldn't stop giggling, and neither could Michael. Throughout his career Caine had been plagued by fits of the giggles at inopportune moments. 'I always was a giggler. I still am—I still laugh when I can't take it all seriously. When it gets too pompous I get giggly. Robert Bolt took me to see *The Oresteia* or *Clytemnestra* or something, and as the heroine came on she was screeching "Woe is me!", and tore her eyes out, and I pissed myself with laughter. Robert never forgave me.'

Michael Aldridge, who played the detective-inspector, can't remember meeting Michael Caine at all—he had too many other things on his mind: 'I think I was too busy chatting up, unsuccessfully

60

I'm afraid, Miss Boyle who was very beautiful and very sexy.'

Julian Amyes then called on Caine once again, to play what seemed to be becoming a standby part—'Second Constable'—this time in a six-episode adventure serial called *No Wreath for the General*. Episode Three must be a bonus-point answer in all the 'Early performances by Famous Faces' competitions—it featured Patrick Cargill (later better known as *Father Dear Father*); upper-class type James Villiers; future 'Schhh ... you know who' spy William Franklyn; and Stratford Johns, famous in later years as the nasty Inspector Barlow in *Z Cars* and *Softly Softly*. Even the music was composed by someone who went on to better things, the man who later composed the music for *Doctor Who*—Ron Grainer.

Caine's next role was a rather more intellectual venture; a part in a dramatization of a book extract for a newish series called *Bookstand*. The 'Script Associate' was a young man called Dennis Potter, and it was obviously a challenging kind of programme; not until towards the end of the first series was it commended by one reviewer for resolving 'the various contradictions involved in viewing what is read' (*Time and Tide*, 13 Jan 1961). Caine played a character called O'Toole in an extract from Murray Sayle's novel *A Crooked Sixpence*.

Granada TV still had Caine on their books, though he only ever seemed to get the ubiquitous 'policeman' role. In *Ring of Truth*—a comedy about the loss of an engagement ring, directed by the man who had given him a small film role a few months before in *A Foxhole in Cairo*, John Moxey—Michael

61

Caine played one PC Wimbush. The play got good reviews: '. . . an amusing fireside comedy, especially the police part' said the *Observer*, and, added the *Daily Mirror*, 'It moved from the faintly funny to the uproarious . . . played delightfully by as nice a collection of characters as I've seen for a long time.' Caine had *nearly* been noticed. It was a small thing but it was encouraging, and maybe even a portent of things to come.

'I Think You're Going To Be A Very Big Star'

By 1961 Michael Caine was known in the business as a reliable actor who could possibly have some promise, although he obviously wasn't a newcomer. But the climate was gradually altering to benefit Caine. In the fifties, working-class actors had stood less chance than their 'betters' at making it in serious drama, but now it was the sixties and things were changing fast. The era of kitchen sink drama was just over the horizon and to be working class was about to become fashionable. And Caine's experience had reached the point where producers felt *able* to offer him better parts. One play that had a particular impact on Caine's fortunes was *The Compartment*, written by Johnny Speight. It focused on two men travelling alone in a railway carriage. Caine played a young lout, a drummer in a jazz band, who unnerves a middle-aged, middle-class businessman, played by Frank Finlay.

Peter Sellers originally wanted the part played by Caine, but because of filming commitments he was unavailable. John McGrath, the director, told writer Johnny Speight that they had another actor in mind, but that they wouldn't book him until Speight had seen him. It didn't take Johnny

Speight long to make up his mind. 'Caine only read four pages for me before I said "OK"; and off we went to the bar. It turned out afterwards that Caine had been rehearsing it with Terence Stamp.'

If there was a turning point for Michael Caine this was probably it. *A Hill in Korea* may have been his break into movies, but *The Compartment*, in August 1961, marked the first time he got noticed by the national newspapers' critics, though their praise was tempered by some fairly pompous fault-finding, as in *The Times*:

... In his effort to hold our attention throughout he became monotonous, not giving us the opportunity of deciding which moments of the monologue were the most significant and so of giving an insight into the character...

The actor was quite successful in suggesting that the young man had altogether lost control of himself when threatening his victim with what was in fact a dummy pistol, but it is doubtful whether this was the sense of that incident as the author had intended it.

More importantly, *The Compartment* got him noticed by the agents. As it happened, Caine was temporarily with The Bill Watts Agency, the estimable Josephine Burton having died suddenly in New York a few months previously. After *The Compartment*, one agent in particular, Dennis Selinger, departed from his usual practice and wrote to Caine offering his services. Caine accepted, knowing Selinger's reputation as one of the best in the business. By February 1962 he was exclusive to Selinger's agency. Later he reminded Dennis of a letter he'd received from him before *The Compartment* went out, giving Caine the stock answer young actors always got from agents who were less than keen—he 'wasn't taking on any clients at the moment'! Selinger is still Michael Caine's agent nearly thirty years later.

After years of bit parts going out in dribs and drabs, Michael Caine suddenly found he had three major parts going out in three successive weeks. After *The Compartment* came *Tickets to Trieste*, in the BBC series *Storyboard*, about three beatniks who upset an international spy network when they go to Trieste to rescue a beautiful girl in distress. Caine played one of the beatniks, in a script written by Troy Kennedy Martin, who later created *Z Cars* and would go on to write the screenplay for one of Caine's later movies, the ever popular *The Italian Job*.

A week later Caine was on TV again, this time as an ageing, frequently drunk 'raver', in an ITV drama he had made at Granada TV entitled *Goodbye Charlie*. One of a series called *The Younger Generation* it starred John Thaw. Manchester-born Thaw came from a similar background to Michael Caine, but unlike Caine he had won a scholarship to the Royal Academy of Dramatic Art, where he was taught to speak 'properly'. Ironically though, Thaw's international success came years later from playing the cockney policeman, Inspector Regan, in *The Sweeney*. In a neat twist, when *The Sweeney* started to play on the American TV networks Michael Caine, as the newest Englishman to arrive in Beverly Hills, began to host *Sweeney* parties for his new American friends—and provided a running translation service to explain John Thaw's 'cockneyisms'!

Also in the cast was Johnny Briggs, whom Caine had met briefly in 1959 while working on the film *The Bulldog Breed*, and who was later to become famous as Mike Baldwin in *Coronation Street*. On one occasion, according to Johnny Briggs, rehearsals weren't going too well. 'Michael only had about four lines but he kept gabbling them. The director said to Ronnie Lacey and me, "Take him over to the pub and see what you can do with him."

'We were in the pub going through his lines and I kept saying to him, "Pause between the lines, Michael; pause."

'In the end I got fed up and left the pub. Ronnie Lacey stayed, and years later Michael helped him out when he got to Hollywood. If only I'd stayed!'

Television was still frequently 'live', and on the night of transmission director Gordon Flemyng found himself impressed with Caine's professionalism: 'There was one scene where Michael had to come crashing into a cellar drunk and holding a bottle and guitar, and fall over. We were using real bottles and the bottle broke. Because it was live we couldn't stop. Michael had put his hand in the glass but he just carried on without stopping.'

The BBC wasn't about to lose out to Granada TV if it could help it. In the planning stages at TV Centre was a drama series which, in the event, became the hottest TV property of 1962—*Z Cars*. At the casting stage, though not for any role in particular, Caine was brought in. It was less than a month after *The Younger Generation* had gone out. The interview was a success, but Caine wasn't interested. *Z Cars* was a good bet, and he was mindful of what it meant to his career, but he was gambling. Movies was what he wanted, and he was still trying.

By the end of 1961 Michael Caine was commanding good parts; such as in *Somewhere for the Night*, a play written by Bill Naughton. This was a comedy about an Irish girl, newly arrived in London and searching for her sister. Caine's character, Tosh, decides to help her, although his motives are somewhat dubious.

Even as *Somewhere for the Night* went out on TV, Bill Naughton was preparing to hear, in just over a month's time, the radio première of his newest play, featuring a character not unlike Tosh, which later had far more effect on Caine's career than any TV part—*Alfie*.

As a bit of light relief, Caine next turned up in a comedy sketch written by Johnny Speight. He played a trainee burglar being taught the ropes by Arthur 'Up to me neck in muck and bullets' Haynes, who finished up playing the piano in the upper-class house they were robbing, while Caine did the twist!

According to Johnny Speight, the night of the recording was cold and foggy, 'the last of the great London pea soupers', and only half the audience turned up. The fog had worsened by the end of the show, and after leaving the Wood Green Empire, he and Caine were soon lost. 'We kept seeing muffled figures looming up out of the gloom, and Mike and I started shouting, "Oi, do you know the way to Wood Green tube station?" "Wood Green?" came the reply, "I can't even find fucking London!"'

The next year, 1962, brought in some good solid parts, such as that of Paul Latimer in *So Many*

Children, a BBC play starring Thora Hird as a landlady who boards ex-prisoners and the like. Paul Latimer is one of her lodgers who firmly believes that tomorrow will see him in the perfect job. 'Excellent performances all round,' said the *Daily Mirror*'s critic, who thought rather less of the play itself.

The *Playmates*, a two-hander by Johnny Speight, was an even better chance; a second crack at the same character he had played in Speight's *The Compartment* the year before, this time with the loutish youth calling at an isolated cottage in the country. The part gave Caine plenty of scope to develop his technique of dealing with both comedy and tragedy within the same character; and it helped him keep up his by now fairly high public profile. 'Michael Caine repeated his brilliant earlier performance . . . a piece of hypnotic television,' said the *Daily Mail*, while the *Daily Telegraph* praised the 'good work from Michael Caine'.

The Playmates, together with *The Compartment*, had caught the attention of someone else, a young actor called Roger Moore, who was busy making his name as The Saint. One day, seeing Michael Caine and Terence Stamp strolling along outside the London Pavilion in Piccadilly, he decided to go up to Caine and tell him what he thought. 'I went up and said to him, "I thought you were absolutely bloody marvellous . . . and I think you're going to be a very big star." And the first words that this articulate, intelligent and sensitive cockney said to me were "Cor, fuck me, really?"'

In his next play, *Luck of the Draw*, Caine was cast as a lonely young man in search of a mate. The meek character of his co-star, Ann Lynn, contrasted nicely with Caine's rougher, but still sensitive, cockney one, in a rather overlong drama set in London's bed-sit land. High spots were few, although when Caine's character describes in authentic London dialect what French delicacy he has in mind for a 'diner à deux', the result is a wonderfully mis-pronounced 'ooves a la provonsale'!

Perhaps Michael Caine, as a cockney actor and labelled as such, was lucky to ride the tide of working-class drama into the 'kitchen-sink' era. Luck or not, there was certainly the danger that it might typecast him for years to come, even after his success as an officer-and-a-gentleman in *Zulu*.

Occasionally Caine got the chance to do something which wasn't a cockney part, but he wasn't well served by his repertoire of regional accents, other than the 'sarf London' one he was brought up with. With a northern accent for example, he was heading for 'Trooble at t'mill'. Seeing him in *Hobson's Choice*, a fellow actor thought, 'He was the strangest choice for Willie Mossop I can remember. I didn't think he'd go very far.'

The critic of the *Daily Mail* seemed to agree with him. '... Caine who, of course, originally came to notice as the half-crazed cockney interloper in Johnny Speight's two experiments in television drama, could not cope with the change of accent.'

Others were kinder: 'Michael Caine's Willie Mossop ignored tradition and was all the better for it,' said the *Evening News*; while the *Daily Mirror*'s reviewer thought that 'Michael Caine, despite his youthful looks, got his teeth firmly into the part of Willie,' and the *Birmingham Mail* praised the actors

68

for giving *Hobson's Choice* 'its full North Country flavour', adding that 'Michael Caine is collecting a record of several impressive TV appearances.'

Less than six months after *Hobson's Choice* went out, director Cy Endfield sent word to Caine's agent, Dennis Selinger, that he'd like Michael to try out for a new war film he was casting. It was called *Zulu*. Caine's television career, like his theatre career, was about to give way to bigger things.

'That Exceptional Young Actor, Michael Caine'

It always seems as if Michael Caine's success was instant, the minute *Zulu* hit the cinemas. But it wasn't. It took three years for him to make it to international star status, which is, in fact, quite quick. But while people noticed him after *Zulu*, the dwindling British film industry of the sixties still didn't have a lot to offer him straight away, and he continued working in TV as well. This time, though, his parts were starring ones, with decent previews attached as well. Before *Zulu* came out, Caine starred alongside Ian McShane, Madge Ryan and Caroline Mortimer in *Funny Noises with their Mouths*; he was billed in the *Radio Times* as 'that exceptional young actor, Michael Caine'. The producer, John Elliot, immediately snapped Caine up again for the lead in another play, *The Way with Reggie*, a part which echoed some of the dilemmas Caine had faced in his own career. Reggie, an intelligent London docker, begins to be aware of his own imaginative potential and goes through some of the alienation from family and friends that self-education can bring. 'Just because I can read and think about things outside of myself, it don't mean I'm that far removed from my own kind, that

69

I'm a stranger,' says Caine's character, Reggie Downes. The play was also notable for a strange dream sequence featuring Caine with hooks instead of hands, being taunted by his workmates. The cast included the girl whose bus fare he had paid a few years earlier, Angela Douglas, but as she recalls, there was little time available for reminiscing. 'It was a very cold winter's afternoon and I remember we just about had time to say, "Hello, do you remember me?" before we had to get straight into bed together for a scene.'

The cast also included the woman who later became almost as famous as Michael Caine, Jean Alexander—better known as *Coronation Street*'s Hilda Ogden.

The Way with Reggie got appreciative reviews, mainly for raising in drama a real-life social problem. The *Daily Worker* didn't like the dream sequence much, but felt that the actors' 'working-class accents were pitched at a reasonably accurate level of realism'—which must have raised a laugh from all who knew Maurice Micklewhite's background!

Caine's parts might have been good, but he was still fighting his way to the stardom he thought he should have. As late as April 1964 he took on an uncharacteristically theatrical role in the BBC TV co-production of *Hamlet at Elsinore*, filmed on location in Denmark. He's reported to have told the lighting director, Robert Wright, 'I don't understand a word of what I'm saying, [but] I have a feeling you get seen on this kind of thing. The right people will watch it.'

Whatever the story, he went on to give a rendering of Horatio that impressed a young actress with whom he would later work on *X, Y and Zee*, Susannah York: 'The very first time I saw Michael act was when he played Horatio in *Hamlet* on TV. I vividly remember thinking at the end of the play, "My God, he's a bloody good actor that guy." He was a very moving Horatio, especially watching him weeping. I remember asking him how he managed to weep, and he said it was a technical trick, something he could do with the back of his throat. I've never been able to get to the bottom of it, I would rather like to have learnt how to do it.'

Unfortunately the critics didn't seem to agree, *Television Mail*'s among them:

Michael Caine's Horatio was a very dry stick indeed—hardly the chosen friend of a prince at Wittenberg. Even in the last holocaust he seemed strangely matter-of-fact, as though the deaths of his friend, his king, his queen, and the son of the late Prime Minister, were somewhat annoying interruptions to a morning's fun with the foils.

If 1964 was Caine's last year as a 'real' television actor, he went out on a high note in what was at the time the longest (at 2 hours 15 minutes) and possibly the largest single play ever mounted by ITV, *The Other Man*. With a script which ran to over 240 pages, there were over two hundred actors (sixty with speaking parts) taking part in a serious attempt by director Gordon Flemyng to show that TV was, like the cinema, capable of presenting good drama on a large scale. Caine led the cast.

The part was a prestigious one and important to Caine. The deal had been negotiated with Dennis Selinger, and had finally got to the point where the

71

huge part was Caine's.

About half an hour after the deal had been agreed, Gordon Flemyng was surprised to find Michael turn up at his offices to collect the script. 'You needn't have done that,' he told him. 'We would have sent it.' 'That's OK,' replied Caine, 'I wanted it now.'

'He didn't really believe he had the part until he had got the script,' says Flemyng. 'He really wanted to give it a good cuddle.'

In the play England has become a German satellite and Caine plays a hero of the Anglo-Germany army. In a battle he is blown up but doctors completely reconstruct him, using transplants, as a complete man—an early version of the *Six Million Dollar Man*. Siân Phillips plays his wife who, when she meets him again, starts to scream and go mad, the reason being that his eyes are different. Everyone then realizes he's been reconstructed.

During one scene Caine had to wear a straitjacket, an experience he found deeply unnerving because of a phobia dating back to his childhood when his mother put him in a tie and shirt for a special occasion. Caine hated the tight, restricted feeling and as a result developed a liking for the polo neck jumpers and open-necked shirts that have become his trademark.

For Flemyng Caine was now a director's dream, a professional in every way: 'During that film I realized that Michael could cry on cue. You could just say to him, "This is it, this is where you go", and that would be it.'

Caine found the experience of over two hours of live television invaluable. 'In movies someone will say, "We're going to do a long take now"—and a long take in a movie is somewhere between two and five minutes. I always look at them and smile because I did a take that was three and a half hours.'

Since 1964 Michael Caine has been too busy being a film star to take much notice of television. There have been umpteen TV interviews, profiles and charity appeals, but until 1987 there was only one more real TV performance. In 1969 he made a charity appearance in *Cornelius*, one of a trilogy called *The Male of the Species* featuring Anna Calder-Marshall and introduced by Laurence Olivier (with whom Caine was to co-star in *Sleuth* three years later). His role was as a modern-day Lothario, romancing the suspicious daughter of the character played by Sean Connery, who had appeared in the previous week's play. In a twist on *Alfie*, Caine gets his come-uppance, but for the wrong reasons; and the girl ends up feeling somewhat fed up. It was good enough to win Anna Calder-Marshall, but not Michael Caine, an Emmy.

The press, of course, had been fed the *Alfie* storyline, anyway.

Taking over another man's girlfriend [announced the press release] is not something of which bachelor Michael Caine approves.

'I wouldn't do anything like that in private life,' he avers. 'If there is one thing that can be said to my credit, it's that I have a strong proprietary sense. I've been around with a lot of birds in my time, but I've never stolen one from a pal.'

On the other hand, the Cornelius he portrays

73

in the show doesn't really steal the girl. He acquires the girl at the request of his friend, who wants to get her off his hands, and makes a habit of persuading Cornelius to do this when his girls become too serious.

Michael Caine agrees that he would do this for a friend.

'In fact,' he confides, 'me old pal Terence Stamp and I have often done this for each other!'

In 1987 Caine returned to television to reveal another side to himself. This was in BBC TV's *Acting—Acting in Film*, the first of a series of masterclasses held in camera by acknowledged masters of the craft. And in 1988 he revealed his talent as wit and raconteur in LWT's *The Trouble with Michael Caine*.

But as a professional actor, Michael Caine has not genuinely returned to television acting, except for *Cornelius*, since 1964. His recent TV appearances, *Jack the Ripper* and *Dr Jekyll and Mr Hyde*, have been in blockbuster productions designed to look just as good as the movies, and made in exactly the same way. It's completely different from the old days of TV studio plays, when virtually everything was done in the studio almost as if it was live theatre, with several cameras at once.

Given the differences between television in the early sixties and the big screen, it's a tribute to Michael Caine that he trained so long and so hard in television solely to achieve success in the cinema. But it's simply not credible that he didn't enjoy it; more that he knew the end result on the big screen was so much more satisfying.

As he says:

'To me the theatre was a woman who I loved dearly, and who treated me like dirt.

The movies is a woman who I adore, and she just showered me with gifts.

But television is a one-night stand.'

CHAPTER FOUR

'NOT WANTED ON LOCATION': THE FILMS TO 1962

'The girls I used to go out with would say, "You're very charming." But I used to say, "I can't be. I can't get into the Charm School".'

Michael Caine

It would be fair to say that Michael Caine pulled himself up by his own bootstraps. He didn't *win* his acting spurs, he *earned* them. He never won a place at the Royal Academy of Dramatic Art or any other acting school, and he didn't get into the Rank Films' Charm School, attended by such stars as Diana Dors, Joan Collins, and other big names, in the fifties. He never enjoyed the patronage of important producers or directors; and he wasn't approached by a top-notch agent until he'd already got himself a starring role on television.

For someone who badly wanted to be a film star, film experience was not easy to come by; there was even less work in the movies than there was in TV. Even so, between 1956 and 1964 Michael Caine appeared in about thirty films. As with his TV work, the details are very hazy and no record exists of the exact number of his appearances.

It was his Army experience which got Michael Caine his first movie role, as a private in *A Hill in Korea*. As he told his colleague from the Lowestoft rep, Jean Marlow, he'd given the producers a logical reason for casting him: 'Well, I've been there, ain't I!'

Shot in Portugal, the thirteen weeks of location work was to be more important for Caine than he originally imagined. Stanley Baker, who was starring in the film, later remembered the young actor, and backed Cy Endfield when casting Caine in *Zulu*.

But first Caine renewed old acquaintances. Victor Maddern—the actor whose advice Caine asked in such a direct manner in Jay Lewis's office seven years earlier—was also in the cast. As they waited at Northolt airport for the plane to fly them out to Portugal, Maddern was confronted by Caine for a second time: 'A chap came up to me and said, "You don't remember me, do you?" He reminded me of how we'd met and then announced, "Well, I'm on my way up!"'

In contrast to the plush suites and sumptuous villas that were to become his location residences in his later career, Caine spent his first stint on location sharing a hotel bedroom. 'One night we were talking late into the night,' recalls his room mate, Harry Landis, 'and Michael said that he thought the theatre was fucking boring, and that he'd much rather do films. I told him rather pompously that the theatre was the mother of our craft, and if he felt like that then he might as well pack it all in!'

In their free time the actors went down to the Texas bar in Lisbon, a potentially dangerous place, as Victor Maddern remembers. 'It was full of pretty girls, but we didn't realize they were whores at first. Once we found out, Mike would have nothing to do with them,' he says.

'Unfortunately, three of them fell for *him*, and

77

wouldn't take no for an answer. So all through the rest of that night all we could hear were these three, outside the front of the hotel, yelling, "Mike! Michael, Michael!"'

When the film opened, in the autumn of 1956, Lindsay Anderson, writing in the *New Statesman*, was not overly impressed: 'Presented with a certain ineffective good taste, it is a pointless reworking of stale conventions: the isolated patrol, the inexperienced lieutenant, the fatherly sergeant, the coward—and of course the inevitable chorus of indomitable cockney wit.'

In the years that followed Michael Caine thought more than once about packing it all in. In fact, it sometimes seemed as if the decision was being made for him—as often as not he would end up on the cutting room floor rather than in the final screen version. But the experience was good; bit by bit Caine was learning his craft—watching others and waiting for the time when he could put the knowledge he'd gained into practice.

Being a bit player, turning up for just one or two days' shooting was, in some ways, even more stressful than being the star of the film. By the time Caine rolled up to do his piece the rest of the cast would already know each other; everyone would be shouting, 'Good morning, Joe. Hi, Bob,' and he would feel an outsider. Suddenly it would be time to deliver his few lines and he knew that no one was going to make allowances for someone who wasn't a full member of the team. He remembers the feelings well: 'A lot of people, especially in Hollywood, started as stars. They don't know what it's like to be on the receiving end of that; what it's like to be a stranger on the set and not know anyone—you're standing there, terrified you're going to blow your lines and the star or director is going to scream at you. When I used to do small parts, one-liners, some of the stars were pretty shitty to small-part players like me, which is why I don't behave like that myself.'

Not long afterwards, Caine got a part in another film, *Sailor Beware!*, adapted from a stage play. It starred Ronald Lewis as a bridegroom facing pre-marital strife from his mother-in-law, played by Peggy Mount. Michael Caine played a small part as a sailor in the background on board ship.

August 1956 saw Caine in another military role, this time on the other side as a German soldier in *The Steel Bayonet*. Set in Tunis in 1943, it was the story of a British observation post fighting off a German tank attack. Nobody noticed the actors playing the German soldiers except when they spoke, and then only because of the over-enthusiastic sub-titles. 'It piques me to have to be told that the English for "Allo! Allo!" is "Hello! Hello!"', remarked the *News Chronicle*'s critic.

In neither *Sailor Beware!* nor *The Steel Bayonet* did Caine get a credit, but he fared slightly better in his next film, *How to Murder a Rich Uncle*, although his part wasn't particularly big. It *had* been larger, but director and star Nigel Patrick cut it from several lines to just two words, both the same. In this rather strange, pedestrian black comedy Caine played, of all things, an Irishman, who rescues a rich old man from drowning. His accent is hilarious. All he says is 'Aye' twice, and even that comes out as 'Oy'—which might suggest why his other lines were cut! But at least he was in the credits at the end.

Caine's next movie, *Carve Her Name with Pride*, was even more important for making contacts; which was just as well, as his part was so small as to be virtually non-existent. Star Jack Warner was to work with Caine a few months later in *Dixon of Dock Green*, but more importantly the film was being directed by Lewis Gilbert, the man who later made Caine famous as *Alfie*, and who also directed him in what many people regard as his finest performance, as Frank Bryant in *Educating Rita*.

Michael Caine once said that Lewis Gilbert fired him from *Carve Her Name with Pride*, but Gilbert remembers nothing of that. Instead, it's more than possible that nobody actually noticed him; it's almost impossible to *see* him physically on screen, and his name does not appear among the credits.

Carve Her Name with Pride is the classic British war movie about the activities of spy heroine Violette Szabo, played by Virginia McKenna. It's the film trivia buffs are always trying to remember, as it ends with the poem 'The Life That I Have', by Leo Marks, a genuine piece of wartime code which still remains very moving. However, only with the help of a good video-recorder is it possible to find another piece of astounding trivia. Freeze the picture at the scene in the railway cattle-truck, and try to identify the prisoners-of-war clutching at Miss McKenna through the bars and calling out 'Water!' One of these voices is distinctly Michael Caine's, but the scene is so dark his face could belong to anyone from Richard Todd to Shirley Temple.

Caine made good use of most of the B-movie producers still active in the 1950s, such as the Danzigers, for whom he also worked at around the

80

same time on the *Mark Saber* TV series. *A Woman of Mystery* was a crime story about a newspaper reporter investigating the suicide of a young woman, and getting involved with a gang of forgers instead.

From being virtually invisible in *Carve Her Name with Pride*, Michael Caine found himself totally absent in *The Key*. His one and only scene was cut from the final version. It was just bad luck in what should have been a terrific film, given a screenplay by Carl Foreman and direction by Sir Carol Reed. As it turned out, it looked more professional than brilliant.

As a sailor who gets hysterical during shelling from a U-boat, Caine had to fall from his ship and drown. His big moment took place in the tank at Shepperton, with special effects explosions and water pouring from a great height. Caine gave it his all, but he got a bit more than he bargained for as fifty tons of water shot over him. 'I went right through the bleedin' scenery! I went through the side of a battleship, which was made of hardboard ... I just didn't know where I was. They had said, "There'll be some water", and I thought a bloke was going to be there with a hose. They didn't tell me it was going to be a big explosion!'

Everyone applauded, and Carol Reed congratulated him. His scene was fine, and Caine was elated. But when the film came to be edited it was the preceding bit of special effects that scuppered him. 'The first special effect went wrong ... I had to run along the deck shouting that there was a submarine, or the enemy; and with that they fired fifty tons of water over me. [But] then it looked ridiculous because the "shell" [that came over] just went *plop!* into the water, and then you cut to me with this mountain of water coming over me. They had to cut it out because it looked silly!'

Disappointing though it was to be totally cut out, Caine filed it away mentally under 'useful experience.'

He never actually met the star of *The Key*, Sophia Loren, but he later met up with some of his friends from those days on other productions, and occasionally they became his employers. Bryan Forbes was one—he was an actor in *The Key*, he co-wrote *Danger Within*, which Caine worked on a year later; and he later directed Caine in *The Wrong Box*. They are firm friends, theirs the kind of friendship which comes from sharing the bad times as well as the good. 'I've known Michael since we were both impoverished,' says Forbes. 'We used to eat at a place called the Under Thirties Club, which was behind the stage door at the Theatre Royal in the Haymarket, run by actors for actors. You used to be able to eat very well there for under one pound.'

Blind Spot was an altogether better proposition for bit-part actors. The eagle-eyed viewer might even spot a youngish-looking, uncredited, Arthur Lowe; and for Michael Caine it meant a stronger part than he'd seen for some time. That doesn't mean it was a large part; for most of the film he only appears in a photograph anyway. But, as a baddie involved in a smuggling racket, he's generally rather nasty for a few minutes at the end until he's pursued by the police and crashes his car. He doesn't get a mention in the credits, though.

In his few lines he appears rather more aristocratic than you would expect from a working-class actor, with just a *hint* of his later performance as Lt Bromhead in *Zulu*. There's no warmth in the character though, which he played with some menace; quite an achievement in a few short lines.

If 1958 had started reasonably well with *Blind Spot*, Caine's luck didn't last. He slid out of the credit list in his next movie, and the next, and the next. The first of these, *The Two-Headed Spy* was directed by the legendary André de Toth, with whom Caine was later to work on *Billion Dollar Brain* (with De Toth as Executive Producer) and *Play Dirty*. For now though, Caine was just one of a pair of jackbooted German soldiers who manages to execute a rather smart salute and turn without falling over.

Following *The Two-Headed Spy*, and again unbilled, was a part in an unlikely story entitled *Passport to Shame*, about a French girl being tricked into prostitution in London. This time Caine's contacts hadn't led to much—the director was Alvin Rakoff, for whom he'd already worked, as a 'court orderly' in the TV production, *The Caine Mutiny Court Martial* that year, and this part was probably even smaller. He appears handsomely, but fleetingly and silently in Reel 2 as a bridegroom coming out of the church where the luckless French girl is about to marry an Englishman for the sake of his passport.

Caine's next uncredited performance was in *Danger Within*, a prisoner-of-war film of slightly higher calibre than usual. If you check the list of his total number of appearances in this picture, it presents a snapshot of a typical part for Michael Caine in 1958; just one more film in the frustrating and cheerless life of a bit-part player:

Reel 1
1 4 seconds of Michael Caine sitting on a box at the edge of the shot.
2 Another 4-second shot of the same.
3 MC is dismissed. 2 seconds.

Reel 2
1 MC in the middle of a crowd shot.

Reel 3
1 MC standing around when Dennis Price marks out an imaginary stage on the ground. Then MC helps to stop fight.
2 Back on the box again. 2 seconds.

Reel 4
1 MC at the side of the stage as Dennis Price does *Hamlet*.
2 MC in crowd.
3 MC speaks(!): (referring to pin-up) 'Think I can take her with me?'
His mate: 'What are her measurements?'
MC: 'Forty-one, twenty-three, thirty-eight.'
Mate: 'You'd never get her through the tunnel!'

Reel 5
1 MC as prompt in performance of *Hamlet*.
2 End credits. MC not listed.

And this was one of his more active films!

Frustration in his career wasn't the only problem

Caine had to contend with at the time. His marriage had broken up and he was in severe financial difficulties, often having to go hungry. He was constantly on the lookout for cheap accommodation, almost as hard to come by as acting roles: 'I remember going to newsagents' shops in Earls Court to look for rooms, and on the cards in the windows where they were advertised, the landladies used to say, "No Irish, dogs, blacks or actors". We couldn't even get good billing on the postcard.'

That year, 1959, was a particularly lean one for Michael Caine as far as movies were concerned. The theatre took up some of his time with the touring version of *The Long, The Short and The Tall,* and he spent a good deal of his spare time with Terry Stamp, Robert Shaw, Edward Judd and the others who hung out at various actors' retreats, like the Salisbury pub in St Martin's Lane. Conrad Phillips, who had thought Caine 'a likely lad' on *William Tell* also used to drink there: 'I used to see Michael in the Salisbury, together with Peter O'Toole, Ronnie Fraser, Robert Shaw and so on. We used to chat and I would say, "How are things? Got any work?" I think he hated being an understudy, but he was very positive. He was already being seen around and getting his face known.'

Caine and Stamp hoofed around London in their Clark's desert boots from one haunt to another—the National Film Theatre, Foyle's Bookshop, with coffee bars by day and 'Arry's' (The Arethusa Nightclub) by night. As Terence Stamp wrote in his autobiography, *Coming Attractions:*

Our plan for the day always incorporated several

showbiz haunts where Mike could pick up information about possible productions currently in the pipeline. Mid-afternoon we would hit the best tea room in London. Housed in Gerrard Buildings, it was called Le Grain; everybody knew it as 'Not Wanted on Location' because it was always filled with out of work 'crowd' (film extras). If our finances hadn't stretched to a proper lunch, we'd have a lamb sandwich, then linger over milky tea in a glass, changing tables until we wound up at Mike's favourite. Being at the back of the room, against the wood-panelled wall, it gave the best view of the action.

In 1960 it was back to war pictures, and attempts at a German accent in *A Foxhole in Cairo*. Though Caine himself would vigorously deny it, foreign accents, for him, have never been the easiest technique to master. In this case, playing a German soldier caught behind the British lines, the script gave him no chance anyway; with lines like 'It is only necessary to give our name and number'. On the credit side, there was more than just one line for him to deliver, he appeared in three scenes, and he had a billing.

And then ... Caine to the rescue of Norman Wisdom! An unlikely scenario, but true nonetheless. In *The Bulldog Breed*, also released in 1960, Wisdom played a variation of his usual character; this time he was a small grocer who is unlucky in love. The object of Norman's affections is a cinema cashier who witnesses (in a rather uninterested fashion) Norman being pushed around by a gang of rowdies led by Oliver Reed—an early small-time role for him, too. Enter sailor Caine and his friends who see Reed off, and inspire Norman to join the Navy. But, once again, Caine did not get a credit.

The swings and roundabouts of the outrageous cinema business then put Michael Caine back into a smaller and (yet again) uncredited role as a policeman during a state of emergency in *The Day the Earth Caught Fire*. An ecological disaster occurs after US and Russian nuclear test explosions have shifted the Earth's orbit, causing climatic changes. Caine is reduced to redirecting traffic—'Keep moving, please. Down to the Embankment, this district's out of bounds.' Even Bernard Braden, as a news editor, got a bigger part.

In 1962, the balance was back in Caine's favour. He landed a part as an Irish gangster in a short supporting feature based on the Edgar Wallace story *The Gunner*, and re-titled *Solo for Sparrow*. Caine had more lines to say, and several scenes including the final shootout. However, director Gordon Flemyng was perplexed by Caine's attitude: 'Every time we came to one of his lines Michael would say, "I don't need to say that line, do I, Gordon? I could do this instead, couldn't I?" By the eighth day I realized that Michael actually hadn't spoken at all; he'd found a reason for not saying any of the lines until in the end he didn't have any. Then we came to a scene where a woman is kidnapped and Michael had to say, "Just be quiet, missus." He said it in an Irish accent and I could immediately see why he had got out of the rest of the lines. He played a mute in that film.'

Flemyng exaggerates slightly, and Caine does still have a few lines left intact. The film itself is now hugely enjoyable as a period piece. Glyn Houston played the policeman who finally got Caine by throwing a chicken round the corner of the barn where Caine was hiding, in order to surprise him. Even death by battery hen in a B-movie doesn't detract from the value to Caine of decent movie experience.

Everything went quiet again on the film front, although television work was by now coming his way regularly. Domestically things had improved and Caine was now sharing a flat with Terry Stamp, at a Harley Street address that was a considerable improvement on Earls Court. Stamp was doing rather well, but there was no sign of anything decent for Caine just yet, at least not in the movies.

Terry Stamp felt the time was right to invest in some decent clobber and asked tailor Doug Hayward to assist. 'My first customer was Terry Stamp,' recalls Hayward, whose Mount Street premises are still visited frequently by Caine and other star clients. 'He wanted four suits and a tailcoat. I'd never cut a tailcoat before, and it's a very skilled job. Anyway, I did the coat; and then I got a desperate call one night. It was Michael Caine. "For Crissake get round here! How do you put this bleedin' thing on?" Apparently, Terry was due to go to some première or other. After that I got into the habit of doing the fittings at home. Michael was always there; it was the best non-homosexual relationship I've ever seen between two men living in a flat.'

Michael Caine's last unbilled film role was in a comic romp called *The Wrong Arm of the Law*. Described as 'by Ealing out of TV comedy', it featured several of Britain's best-known comic actors ranging from Peter Sellers to Arthur

Mullard. Caine had no lines and played a policeman; but in the finished version he's nowhere to be seen. All his hard-won success on TV counted for naught when it came to getting his big break in films. If anything, for Michael Caine, *The Wrong Arm of the Law* underlined once again the precarious nature of his actor's existence; and the irrelevance of previous movie experience to the job in hand when you're an unknown.

There must have been times, especially as Caine approached his thirtieth birthday in March 1963, when he doubted if the break he was so patiently waiting for would ever come at all. Everyone else he knew seemed by then to be on their way—Terry Stamp had scored with *Billy Budd* and Albert Finney with *Saturday Night and Sunday Morning*; and Richard Harris was, by January 1963, about to hit the big time with *This Sporting Life*. Was Michael Caine going to be the one left behind, the nearly man of his generation?

'I could have been the one to discover Michael Caine,' reflects Barry Norman. 'I was friendly with Terence Stamp who kept telling me to meet his flatmate, an actor called Maurice Micklewhite who would soon be very big. I laughed and said it was impossible for anyone with the name of Micklewhite to make it anywhere. Terry said he'd changed his name to Michael Caine, and I said that name was equally improbable!

'And then came *Zulu* and soon after that *Alfie*, by which time it was too late because everyone had discovered Michael Caine.'

CHAPTER FIVE

'WHO IS THIS BUM WITH THE GLASSES?':
1963–1966

'One night I was in the Crazy Elephant Club and I saw Caine come in. Later in the gloom I said to him, "I saw you in *Zulu*. I thought you were very good." The voice replied, "I wasn't in *Zulu*, but if I had been I would have been very good." It was Peter O'Toole.'

Johnny Speight

The Battle of Rorke's Drift was the less-than-catchy title of a filmscript which, by 1962, had been doing the rounds of the major film companies for a year or two. Co-written by director Cy Endfield and John Prebble (later historical adviser on the memorable BBC TV play *Culloden*), it had been through several 'almost' situations, but the film moguls were still wary. There were no big name stars involved, they argued; and they thought the budget was too large for a film that was unlikely to take off anywhere except Britain. Only one studio, Columbia, had shown any definite interest, but they said they would only make the picture if Endfield could get Burt Lancaster to do it!

Most of these refusals seemed like stock answers to the experienced Endfield, who was convinced there was a much simpler solution to the problem of getting his script accepted. He'd suspected the cumbersome title might be putting people off, and he clearly remembers the day when, while crossing

Grosvenor Square in London, the flash of inspiration came. He'd call it simply *Zulu*.

It worked. Not long afterwards, lead actor and co-producer Stanley Baker phoned Endfield to say that Joe Levine of Paramount Pictures had already started imagining 60-foot-high Zulus on the publicity hoardings, and the money was there! Casting began.

Someone suggested to Endfield that he see a play at the Arts Theatre called *Next Time I'll Sing to You* whose cast included an actor called Michael Bryant who might be suitable for *Zulu*. Endfield went, but the actor playing the narrator also caught his eye—Michael Caine. 'It was a sort of "Alfie" role,' says Endfield, 'and he had to keep speaking to the audience. I thought he was marvellous and the next day I said to the casting director, "See if you can get that kid over." I was thinking of him for one of the cockney private roles.'

Early in 1963 Caine was summoned to the bar on the first floor of the Prince of Wales Theatre, which Bernard Delfont had lent to Endfield for the auditions. 'It was a very long bar and if it hadn't been for the length of that bar, Michael would never have got the part,' says Endfield. 'He came in to read and as I watched him there was something about him. He had tremendous good looks with that shock of blond hair, and he had power.'

However, when Caine read the part of the cockney private, Endfield felt he somehow looked wrong for it. He thought about some of the other roles and made Caine read those as well. Caine was getting a little restless and other actors were arriving for their readings, Endfield recalls. 'But I didn't want to let him go. I thought he'd be good to

91

have in the picture. Finally he said to me, "Is there anything else?" and when I said no, he said, "Well, OK, thanks", and started to walk away down this great long bar, and the next two guys came forward. He was at the end of the bar, about ninety feet away, when I said, "Hold on ... come back!" If that had been a normal room he would have been long gone.

'I said, "Listen. I want to ask you a question. You've read the script—do you think you could handle the accent of the gentleman officer, Bromhead?"

'Mike said, in his thick Elephant and Castle accent, "I think I could, but I wouldn't have the nerve to say it to anyone except you." So I asked him to wait for Stanley Baker to arrive and to read the part of Lt Gonville Bromhead for both of us. As a result we gave him a screen test.'

In fact, the part Caine had originally been called for, that of Private Hook, had in any case already been promised by Stanley Baker to another actor, James Booth. Booth had initially been offered the part of Sergeant Bourne (eventually played by Nigel Green), but had to turn it down as he was working at the RSC at the time and couldn't go to South Africa. Baker thought again and then came up with a solution.

'Stanley said, "Right, you can play Private Hook. You can film during the day and go to the Aldwych at night,"' says Booth. 'So all my scenes were done in England. Each evening I rushed back from the film studio to play Edmund to Paul Scofield's King Lear. I never met Michael at all, except once briefly, at Stanley's house.'

Caine was deeply nervous about the screen test

92

and had borrowed a mascot from his co-star in *Next Time I'll Sing to You*, Liz Fraser. She loaned him her lucky mouse—a real, but very dead mouse. He had of course already met and admired Stanley Baker during *A Hill in Korea*, and when he arrived for the screen test Caine was delighted to see Baker waiting to do the scene with him. 'I'll never forget the way Stanley put everything into my screen test, and he did it for me. He even wore his uniform. I mean, they could have got anybody to stand in on the test. Not Stanley. He stood there in his uniform with his back to the camera and played the scene with me. He knew how important it was for me—and to him of course. But I'll never forget him for that. This was a professional attitude by a professional man. That was Stanley, always the professional.'

When they had begun casting *Zulu*, Endfield and Baker had gone to see actor Kenneth Griffith who had knowledge of both South Africa and military history and was interested in the Battle of Rorke's Drift. Griffith offers a slightly different version of how Caine got the part in *Zulu*: 'They brought with them the very first draft of the script,' recalls Griffith, 'and offered me a part, but I couldn't do it. Afterwards I passed the script on to my agent, Dennis Selinger, and he nominated Michael for it. It was an astonishing choice, but full marks to Dennis.

'Around the time of *Zulu* Dennis asked me if I knew of Michael Caine and I replied that I had met him in the bar of the Arts Theatre. "I think he could be a big star," said Dennis, "bigger than O'Toole." I replied, "Oh, Dennis, for God's sake don't talk such bloody rubbish."'

A few days after his screen test, while he was eagerly awaiting the outcome, Caine went to a party with Terence Stamp—a party Cy Endfield was coincidentally also attending. From across the room Endfield spotted Caine with a certain apprehension: 'I was conscious of the fact that I didn't have anything to say to Michael. And I became increasingly aware that wherever I moved there were a pair of eyes staring at me. Finally I said, "I know you want to know about this. Look, the test was no good." And his face fell. I went on, "Don't worry about it. I think you should play the part but there are diplomatic problems." (I had to convince the executives at Paramount.) "I'm going to make this picture and you're going to be in it, but you'll have to be patient."'

Later that evening, at about 10 pm, Endfield saw Caine again. 'I could see he had tears in his eyes,' he remembers, 'and I reassured him, "You're going to have the part." And he said, "You know why I'm acting like this—it's because I've resolved that if I haven't reached a significant position by the time I'm thirty, then I'm going to forget it forever."'

Terence Stamp wrote of that evening in the third volume of his memoirs, *Double Feature:*

In between the chat I looked across at Mike. He and Cy appeared to be hitting it off. Both were laughing. Someone asked Martine to dance. I glanced again in Mike's direction. He came towards me through the crowd, towering above them like a schooner under sail. Tears were streaming down his face—I didn't move. His lips curled back; he was speaking but I could hardly hear the words, only a tense, high-pitched whisper. He came closer. 'I've got the part. He liked my test. I've got the part. I'm going to play Bromhead!' His face was wet. I hadn't a handkerchief and he wasn't aware he was crying anyway. I looked at my Rolex; eleven-thirty. Mike is thirty tomorrow. He's made it, with half an hour to spare.

As history shows, Endfield did manage to convince the Paramount executives, and back at the Criterion theatre Caine's fellow actors in *Next Time I'll Sing to You* were delighted, and wryly amused, when they heard about Caine's big triumph. 'When Barry Foster and I heard that Michael had landed a part in *Zulu*,' says Michael Bryant, 'we assumed it would be as a cockney private. When we heard that it was as an officer we cried with laughter. "Who's going to dub you?" we said.'

Denys Graham, who was playing the hermit, had also tested for *Zulu* but decided to stay for the whole run of *Next Time I'll Sing to You* at the Criterion. Like James Booth, he had been offered a role that would only involve filming in England. 'Our producer threatened, half jokingly, that the play would have to close if anyone else went,' he remembers.

Now that Caine's role was finally confirmed there was little time to get everything ready before he had to leave for South Africa. Caine's costumiers on *Zulu* were, as they would be for many of his subsequent films, the old established firm of Bermans and Nathans. In Monty Berman's office there hangs a colour picture of the *Zulu* cast in all their finery, inscribed: 'Dear Monty, thanks to you

Zulu looks magnificent. Yours, Stanley [Baker].'

Bermans and Nathans had carried out their usual meticulous research and discovered that, in fact, as an engineer officer Stanley Baker would have worn a *blue* uniform. But in order to get the dramatic effect for the film Monty Berman and Stanley Baker decided to have *all* the major characters (including Baker) in the red uniforms that made the picture so memorable.

Caine was having a great time, rushing around for costume fittings and getting his injections for the trip. He even took the precaution of asking Liz Fraser if he could take her lucky mouse to South Africa for the filming as it had worked so well so far. In between Caine still visited his favourite haunts, and one day Gerald Campion, actor and the owner of the famous sixties hang-out, Gerry's Bar, was surprised to see some customers come in for lunch carrying a very strange cargo. 'Stanley Baker and Michael Caine came in carrying yards and yards of leopardskin cloth. I said, "What the hell's all that for?" Michael replied, "We've had this leopardskin made up in Shoreditch, and we've got to take it out to Africa to dress all the Zulus up in it."'

Caine was also intent on preparing for his role as Lt Gonville Bromhead as thoroughly as possible. Bromhead had been, in real life, a rather short, dark and somewhat deaf man who was left behind with the garrison at Rorke's Drift because (it was rumoured) his superiors couldn't trust him to hear their orders in the thick of battle. The tall, fair Michael Caine decided it would be useless to attempt an accurate reconstruction of Bromhead; so his best bet would be to portray him more generally as a product of the officer class, and show up the distinctions between the man and his men.

Thinking back to his time as an ordinary soldier in Korea, Caine had some of his own memories of the officer class to draw on, particularly of his platoon commander, Lt Robert Mill. But he needed more information, so for two weeks he went off daily to have lunch with Guards officers in London, telling them he was researching the background to the film, and all the while watching their every word and movement. Then, realizing things would have been different in Victorian times—an era when, if anything, class divisions were even more pronounced and privilege far more apparent—Caine decided to copy the most privileged man he could think of, Prince Philip, the Duke of Edinburgh. 'He always walks with his hands behind his back,' says Caine, 'and in *Zulu* I walked the whole time like that. No one found it out, but they knew unconsciously who I was, because Prince Philip is so familiar. I also realized that privileged people like him speak very slowly, because they don't have to get your attention. You're already hanging on their words.'

Soon Caine and the rest of the cast and crew left for South Africa and shooting began. Four thousand Zulus had been brought in from their kraals a few miles away to act as extras for the film. Led by Chief Mangosuthu Buthelezi, now a significant black leader in the political struggle for South Africa, they were the descendants of the original Zulus who had fought the real Battle of Rorke's Drift in 1879. They nicknamed Caine 'The Child of Heaven' because of his long curling locks. The Child of Heaven knew this was his big opportunity, the chance he had waited so long for.

Now it was all up to him.

However, there were still problems ahead. The rushes had to be sent back to England to be processed and so it was three weeks before Cy Endfield saw the first scenes that had been shot, including close-ups of Stanley Baker and Caine. When he did get to see them he wasn't pleased. 'Both Mike and Stanley looked awful. There was an exchange of close shots; and I kept running them and running them, and then it dawned on me. Mike's face had been lit from one side to give it shape, as otherwise it tended to get washed out; and Stanley's craggy features had been lit more square on, to flatten them out a little. So, of course, the shots didn't match!

'We were behind schedule, but I asked for all those close-ups to be re-shot. Of course there had also been a lot of first-day tension, so this was a most beneficial thing from Mike's point of view, because by now he was much more into the picture.'

Caine had heard about the problems too. He had become friendly with one of the secretaries on the shoot who had told him that after seeing his first scenes the big shots back in London had sent Stanley Baker a telegram saying that they wanted Caine replaced. 'I was distraught when she told me,' says Caine. 'This was the biggest chance I'd ever had and I'd only done a couple of scenes. Now I'd lost it. I didn't know what to do.

'The secretary told me to keep my mouth shut about that telegram otherwise I might make trouble for her. It was a secret between London and Stanley, I wasn't supposed to know. Nobody else did.'

For the next few days Caine wandered around in a daze waiting for Stanley Baker to tell him it was all over. But he didn't say a word. Every time Caine saw Baker he gave him a long look hoping to hear him say something. Nothing. In the end he couldn't stand it any longer. 'I went straight up to Stanley after I'd worked myself into a terrible state and said, "Listen. I know all about that telegram, so don't worry about it. I'll go home. I don't care. Just tell me outright because I know it's on your mind and I know you're trying to think of a way of telling me. Aren't you?"

'Stanley just looked at me and said, "No." There was a pause. I didn't know what to say. Then Stanley said, "Answer me this question. Who's the producer of this picture?" I looked him straight in the eye and said, "You are." He said, "Have I ever said anything to you about being replaced and going home?" "No," I said. "Well then, shut up and get on with your work," said Stanley.

'He let me have it for saying he'd be frightened of telling me. Stanley said that if I was bad for the picture then I'd be bad for everyone out there and in that case he would have no hesitation in sending me home. But Stanley didn't think I was bad for the picture. He'd been pleased with what I'd done.'

The turmoil in his mind, together with the different climate, were having another effect on Caine's well-being: 'I used to spend so much of the day in the toilet that I got bored. I would sit and stare at space through a hole in the lavatory door. That was my view of Africa.'

It became a familiar view. They spent three months shooting in South Africa during which time Caine had the grand total of 52 lines of dialogue to

99

perfect. Sometimes it wasn't even Caine in shot, leading to later confusion over certain aspects of his anatomy: 'I remember they had the Second Unit Director Bob Porter, run up a hill for me because the Second Unit were [in the right place]. He's got bow legs, and everybody thought I had bow legs for years. But I haven't; I have very good straight legs.'

Caine had been told by Endfield that 'The most important moment for an actor in a film is when he makes his entrance, and the most important moment in his career is the first film in which he makes that entrance.' But in fact in the very first shot in *Zulu* the person you see is not Michael Caine at all. 'I was meant to come round the side of a hill riding a horse,' recalls Caine, 'but the horse they chose was a Basuto pony which meant that it came from the flat lands of South Africa and had never seen its shadow at the same height. So when it came round the corner the sun brought the shadow up and the pony leapt about twenty feet with me on it. I could hear the propman on the radio saying, "I think Mr Caine's hurt, Guv." And the director said, "Leave him, take the cloak and get on the horse."

'So that first shot you see in the distance on *Zulu* isn't me at all, that's the propman. And I learnt a very valuable lesson—never do anything dangerous in movies. I still hate horses.'

Filming finally over, Caine returned home and waited for the opening of *Zulu*. In the interim he was summoned to see Joe Levine at Paramount. Levine had given Caine a seven-year contract at the start of *Zulu* but as Caine was about to find out he had had a change of heart: 'He said to me, "I'm sorry, Michael, you know I love you and I think

100

you're a really good actor, but I'm taking the contract away." And I said, "Oh", because actors are used to that. And then I said, "Can I ask why?"

'He said, "You look gay. And while there are a lot of leading men who are homosexual, they don't look it. You can't be like you, a very masculine man and look homosexual. So you'll never be a big star."

'And I said, "But they put false eyelashes on me." And he said, "Well, it doesn't matter. You haven't got them on now have you?" I said, "No", and he said "Well you still look gay today." He took my contract away ... and gave it to Jimmy Booth.'

Caine shrugged off the disappointment and continued to wait for the opening of the film. Finally, in January 1964, the evening of the première arrived. Liz Fraser, the actress from *Next Time I'll Sing to You*, and owner of the lucky mouse, found herself in the next seat to Caine: 'I asked him about my mouse but got no reply. At the end of the film there was a standing ovation, and only then did Mike turn round to me and say, "Here's your mouse back."'

Michael Caine had arrived.

The next day the newspaper reviews appeared and the praise for the new young actor was almost universal. *The Times* declared, 'There is one performance worth watching, that of Michael Caine as the untried lieutenant, cast right against type and proving conclusively that he can play something far other than his usual cockney joker roles if only someone will give him the chance.' John Coleman in the *New Statesman* commented succinctly, 'Michael Caine looks so staggeringly right as the foppish general's son.' Penelope Gilliat in the

Observer also singled him out for comment—'There is an interesting actor called Michael Caine who plays Stanley Baker's second-in-command: he is slightly wrongly cast as an upper-class officer but he does it very well.' And Ann Pacey writing for the *Daily Herald* added, 'Almost grabbing the film from [Stanley Baker] is Michael Caine as a young, aloof, arrogant Lieutenant who hunts game in a casual sort of way before the battle and fights like a lunatic before it has ended.'

Caine felt that he had at last made the vital transition from minor stage and slightly less minor TV 'face' to film 'face'. This was It. This was what he'd always wanted.

Almost the only dissenter was Alexander Walker, critic for the *Evening Standard* who commented, 'Michael Caine as a languid lieutenant gets nowhere because Mr Caine can't keep up the accents and attitudes of an aristocrat.'

Caine was distressed by the review and it was, as Walker says, 'the cause of serious comic arguments whenever we met for months afterwards'. Walker stuck by his comment and Caine by his opinion, but across the years Walker has remained one of the few critics whose views Michael Caine respects.

Caine, however, had the last laugh, courtesy of the officers of H M Forces, as Cy Endfield recalls. 'After *Zulu* Stanley Baker and I were courted by the upper-class military, and invited to the Army and Navy Club and to all sorts of soirées. They all liked the character of Bromhead and thought the actor who played him was "marvellous, absolutely marvellous". I got great pleasure from telling them that the actor would be along later. And Michael would show up, I'd introduce him and as he started to speak I could see them thinking, "Oh God, I thought he was one of us!"'

The effect Caine's performance had on some others, though, was quite unforeseen: 'Michael Caine was very bad for me,' claims TV chef Keith Floyd, for instance. 'I saw *Zulu* and the next day I went out and joined the Army.'

*   *   *

Even before *Zulu* went out to the cinemas on general release, word had already leaked out about the new young talent appearing in the film. While Cy Endfield was still busy editing the picture, the co-producer of another project asked to see a couple of reels featuring Caine. Endfield thought about the rather unorthodox request, and then agreed.

The new film was to be called *The Ipcress File*. The producer was Harry Saltzman who had made such a box office success of the James Bond movies starring Sean Connery, the man who had shot to TV stardom in 1957 in *Requiem for a Heavyweight* while Caine literally waited in the wings as an extra in the same play. This time, in the nicest possible way, Caine was to get his own back.

The Ipcress File was an antidote to the Bond films. It would feature an anti-hero, who, unlike the shaken but never stirred Bond, would have to do his own shopping at the supermarket and take his own suits to the dry cleaners for invisible mending after a dust-up. The screenplay was by Len Deighton, taken from his book of the same name.

If Caine had the long bar in the Prince of Wales Theatre to thank for his chance in *Zulu*, it was *The Sound of Music* that was responsible for him getting the lead in *The Ipcress File*. The role had originally been due to go to Christopher Plummer, who subsequently received a more lucrative offer to star with Julie Andrews in what was to become the all-time family favourite. Plummer decided to see if the hills really were alive with the sound of music, and Caine got his second big break.

Unlike Bond, with his constant stream of adoring females, *The Ipcress File* spy would have far less success with the opposite sex, although he was still to be allowed one leading lady. The girl chosen was Sue Lloyd, a young actress who was later to become a household name in the soap opera *Crossroads*. 'I was twenty-fifth in a line of twenty-five actresses auditioning for the part in *The Ipcress File*,' she remembers. 'I think by the time Michael got to me he was extremely tired. In fact, I think that's probably why I got the part.'

In the book the detective had been nameless, and so producer Harry Saltzman, director Sidney Furie and the executives of Paramount Pictures called a special meeting in Wardour Street to decide on a name for their new character. Caine too was invited: 'They were all the top guys connected with the film, and the big topic was "What are we going to call him?" Harry Saltzman said, "We need a name that means absolutely nothing, a common or garden name that means nothing at all." Without thinking I said, "Harry." I was so embarrassed, it just came out naturally. "Thanks very much," he said. "Just for that we'll call him Harry."'

Most significantly of all, though, Harry Palmer was to wear glasses, until then seen as the ultimate antidote to tough-guy macho status. Caine was pleased: 'I was the first leading man since Harold

104

Lloyd to wear glasses. And he was a comedian. The glasses were a psychological advantage—when I took them off people knew there was going to be action.'

However, not everyone involved in the project could come to terms with the new-style hero. 'When we were filming, one of the producers got dead worried,' recalls Caine. '"Who is this bum with the glasses?" he said. "He isn't even good looking." But I was good at the part because I liked it. I understood Palmer's frame of mind.'

Caine did indeed love the part. He identified strongly with the Palmer character, a guy who doesn't look like a winner but manages to come out on top—a dictum that had also seemed to hold true in his own life. It was a witty, perfectly paced performance, one that even impressed another James Bond, Roger Moore. 'I loved *The Ipcress File* and what Michael did with the character of Harry Palmer,' says Moore. 'Michael could never have been a Bond, though. As good an actor as he is, we're all limited when it comes to physical things. Michael is not an athlete. Not that I am, but I can sometimes look as if I am.'

The critics were also impressed with the new-style hero when the film premièred in March 1965. 'Michael Caine's performance installs him as the first mod conman of the new British crime wave,' wrote the *Sunday Telegraph*'s Philip Oakes, and *The Times* was unequivocal in its praise of 'Palmer', and Caine:

Michael Caine in the central role of the insubordinate conscript spy Harry Palmer could hardly be bettered . . . he is too good an actor for

105

that. What he gives here is not a bland generalized star performance, but a real actor's interpretation of a particular man in a particular situation and he does it superlatively well. He has the matinée idol good looks too, and could no doubt just coast along on them if he chose, but long may he be spared from that: as a real actor he is too good to be wasted.

Of course there were the inevitable comparisons between Palmer and Bond, and some decided they still preferred the traditional style—the *Sunday Express*, for instance: 'In the central role of the blundering hero there is Michael Caine giving the most dreary and colourless performance I have seen in years. In fact the whole thing looks like an emasculated James Bond story, alas without Mr Connery.'

But Caine must have been delighted to win over Alexander Walker. 'Michael Caine who plays Harry Palmer is the new style secret agent: everything that James Bond is not and all the better for it . . .' wrote Walker in the *Evening Standard*, adding, 'Mr Caine has undoubtedly made his mark.'

And all this despite the fact that Harry didn't even do his own stunts—'The omelette was doubled for me—the hand that broke the two eggs at once was Len Deighton's', confesses Caine.

*   *   *

Next came the role that would stay with Caine throughout his career: 'I made *Alfie* in 1966 and he still won't lie down and die. Alfie was never me. He was based on a very good friend of mine who used

106

to go through women like a dose of salts. I certainly couldn't keep up with him.

'I've had every man in the world tell me he is Alfie, from Ravi Shankar to the Chief of Customs in Taiwan. There's no doubt that the film struck a chord with guys.'

Alfie is the archetypal rogue male. Immoral but irresistible, he treats women like a commodity, once he has acquired the product he is no longer interested in possessing it. For Alfie the chase is everything and commitment is a dirty word. Only an Alfie could wriggle out of the prospect of marriage to his pregnant girlfriend with the immortal words, 'Look at it this way: if I was to marry you you might gain a husband but you'd lose a bleedin' good friend.'

Ten years later Alfie would have been lynched by feminists, and twenty years on the spectre of Aids puts him firmly in another time span. In the mid-sixties, though, Alfie caused an immense stir. Women were drawn to Alfie, safe in the knowledge that they could enjoy his attractiveness on the screen without the risk of having their hearts broken, and men couldn't help but secretly admire the modern-day Casanova, who seemed, at least for most of the film, to be having his cake and eating it too.

Caine's Alfie succeeded because he took an ostensibly unpleasant character and managed to show his insecurities. The film is a moral tale. At the end Alfie is left with nothing to show for his conquests; in fact, his situation has worsened. Not only is he left with nothing, he has lost the devil-may-care attitude he once possessed. He has begun to realize that there must be something more to life than the kind of relationships he's enjoyed up till now. The tragedy is that he has no idea what that something might be.

Alfie started life as a radio play by Bill Naughton, broadcast on the BBC's 'cultural' Third Programme as *Alfie Elkins and his Little Life*. With Bill Owen in the title role, it got such good reviews it was repeated a few weeks later. Naughton adapted it as a stage play, and Joss Ackland (who had recently been involved with another Naughton play) put forward several ideas for the lead. 'I suggested John Neville, Bernard Cribbins and a new young cockney actor called Michael Caine . . .' he wrote in his autobiography, *I Must Be in There Somewhere*. 'I think now it would have been beyond the capabilities of the young Michael Caine, who got his break in the movie where he played the role superbly.'

Caine might have lost out to John Neville for the stage version, but not long afterwards Lewis Gilbert bought the film rights to *Alfie*, and started considering who to cast as the lead. Among those he approached were Terence Stamp (who had played the role on the New York stage, where the play had not been well received), Tony Newley, Laurence Harvey and James Booth. They all turned it down. The reason is reputed to be the abortion scene, which was highly controversial in the mid-sixties. By the time the script finally got to Michael Caine it was covered with other people's fingerprints.

But Caine had no qualms about the role. He read the first page, which read 'Alfie turns to the camera and says "Never mind about the titles"', and realized instantly that here was something that could work brilliantly on film. He said 'Yes' before he got to page 2.

Director Lewis Gilbert cast six women as the victims of Alfie's seduction technique: Julia Foster, Jane Asher, Shirley Ann Field, Vivien Merchant, Millicent Martin, and from America, Shelley Winters. 'I agreed to make *Alfie* as a favour to Lewis Gilbert,' says Winters, 'thinking it was a small-budget black and white movie that no one would see. I didn't even bother to tell my agent. My fee was the minimum Equity payment plus two weeks at the Dorchester and a Rolls to take me around. As a joke I insisted that no filming would start until I got my car. It arrived engraved with an SW crest, all mod cons and a uniformed chauffeur. It wasn't until two days later that I realized that the "chauffeur" was actually my new co-star, Michael Caine. Caine must have been acting his part well because at that time he couldn't drive at all!'

'The first morning of shooting,' recalls Caine, 'Shelley Winters had only been in for a few minutes when she came rushing into my dressing room. She stopped and said, "Good morning", and I said "Hello, Shelley, how are you?" and then I naturally waited to see what she wanted.

'Finally I asked her, "What do you want?" and she said, "Nothing. I just thought someone had put me into one of the extras' dressing rooms out of some sort of disrespect or because they were trying to insult me. So I thought the best thing to do is to check up and see what the leading man has got and yours isn't as good as mine." I said, "No, you've got the best one because you're the lady."'

Caine would soon find out what Winters meant, when he arrived in Hollywood to make his first American film, *Gambit*. As he says, 'I had a bungalow on the Universal set which was better than the flat I lived in in London at the time.'

Julia Foster was thrilled to be cast as Gilda, and couldn't wait to find out who would be playing Alfie. 'When they said Michael Caine,' she says, 'I said, "Michael who?" Michael was still virtually unknown at the time. *Zulu* hadn't made a huge impact and *The Ipcress File* hadn't come out then. It was such an extraordinary part that I think I was expecting them to say that Robert Redford would be playing it. At the time I think I was quite disappointed.'

Denholm Elliott, who was cast as the abortionist, was none too sure who Michael Caine was, either: 'He was suddenly an enormous star and I'd never even heard of him. But there he was with secretaries buzzing around and phone calls, and the big number on the set, and I'd never even seen him. He'd done *Zulu* before. He was suddenly rocketed to fame.

'I was the abortionist, a role which pushed me into all those loser parts, and finally the press put me into one of those categories which they'd been trying to do for years—sleazy. Now of course everything I do is sleazy, even if I'm the most clean-cut character in the world.'

Lewis Gilbert was amused by Caine's evident enjoyment of his new star status. 'One day Michael asked me if he could bring the President and Vice-President of his fan club to lunch,' says Gilbert. 'I said sure, we'll all have lunch together. Two girls arrived and Michael, lording it a bit, went off to the bar. I said to them, "Are there a lot of people in your fan club?" and the two girls said, "Oh no, just the two of us!"'

Alfie was predominantly a night owl as he went on his rounds of rendezvous and roistering; this meant plenty of night shoots which made it possible for Millicent Martin, then starring in *That Was The Week That Was* to join the cast as Siddie. 'The first time I met Michael was in a fogged-up car in a coal yard somewhere near Victoria Station,' she recalls. 'They had to use some special device to keep the windows all steamed up. It was about three o'clock in the morning and Michael and I just sat there talking about all sorts of things; he was so easy to talk to. All of a sudden Michael wound down the window and shouted to the director, "'ere, Lewis, I thought all the girls in this film were going to put out for me!"'

Jane Asher had already met Caine socially at the Pickwick Club where her brother played in a group, and she and her friends thought he was 'very dishy, very chirpy and charming'. She was cast as the innocent young Annie who is picked up by Alfie in the less than romantic surroundings of a lorry-drivers' caff and taken to London by him.

Filming on the A1 for the scene where Annie is hitching a lift took far longer than anticipated as real lorries kept screeching to a halt to offer their services, forcing the camera car to keep going round to try and shoot the scene again.

Asher was very nervous at the prospect of one particular scene. 'In the scene where Alfie and Annie are in bed I wasn't suppose to wear anything,' she remembers. 'I was too shy though, and couldn't bear it, so in the end they let me wear a man's shirt, one of Alfie's, which worked very well, I think. Michael thought it was all very funny and couldn't understand my shyness. He was very

111

friendly and put everyone at their ease.'

Caine, always comfortable in female company, seems to have got on well with all his female co-stars in *Alfie*. Once she got over her disappointment about Redford Julia Foster soon began to enjoy working with Michael Caine and was even more impressed when she saw the results on screen. 'When I first read the script I thought the idea of Alfie talking to the audience would never work,' she says. 'It had never been done before, and we spent a lot of time talking about it. We started filming, and after about three days Lewis Gilbert invited us to view the rushes. I sat right at the back and watched. Suddenly, on the screen Michael turned full-face to the camera and said, "She's bleedin' 'opeless, she is," and it completely took my breath away. I thought, this man is a star. He had such magnetism on the screen, he just filled it. I still feel the same about him.'

As the filming got under way Shelley Winters began to feel differently about 'the small-budget black and white film' she had agreed to appear in: 'When we started filming I realized that it was going to be a much bigger film than I had thought. Paramount had spotters on the set and Michael told me that I couldn't change shoes between takes because it was in colour!

'When Michael invited me to a screening of *The Ipcress File* I began to get really annoyed. He was obviously hot property, the film was going to be a hit and I was being got for free.

'I got on very well with Michael, though, and he was very sweet to me. I was embarrassed about the groping scene and would blush every time we filmed. Michael took me out to lunch to calm me down and we completed the love scenes with cushions between us.'

Filming for *Alfie* took place all around London, from Waterloo to Victoria, in a disused hospital and along the Embankment, during the autumn and winter of 1965–6. It wasn't without drama as Millicent Martin recalls. 'One night we were filming by the river, near the tube. All of a sudden there was an almighty racket and people ran past us, over the barriers and down the escalators. Afterwards someone told us that it was one of the great train robbers with the police chasing him. I think Lewis Gilbert had to hand over our film to the police in case the man could be spotted in the background.'

A lot of the scenes between Caine and Martin involved 'dawn and dusk' shoots, which meant they both had to sit around for the rest of the night in full make-up waiting for sunrise. Sometimes they would go and have a late supper at the Pickwick, but for much of the time they would just sit around in the caravan talking. 'It was about the time that *Ipcress* was due to open in America,' says Martin, 'and one night at about 4 am Michael said to me, "How do you think it will go over there, Mil?" and I said to him, "Remember where you are at this moment because this time next year you'll be a huge international star."'

When *Alfie* opened in March 1966 it hit exactly the right note. 'The sixties were a wonderful time,' says Julia Foster, 'and *Alfie* epitomized everything about it. I think the *Alfie* première was one of the most exciting evenings possible. Everyone was there, the Beatles, the Stones, everyone. I think it crept up on us early on that we were making a very special film. It summed up that whole time.'

'It was just so right for the times,' adds Millicent Martin. 'It was the Swinging Sixties, people were much brighter about what was going on, the fantasy land of movies was a thing of the past and the audiences were much more canny.'

The timing was perfect for the critics as well. 'Without Caine *Alfie* would still be a rich, ripe, randy portrait of a cockney Casanova, bang up to the minute and a marvellous opportunity for any actor. But with Caine it becomes a ribald parable of our times ... Caine, cool, self-contained, very much his own man, dominates absolutely: sure of his style—star style!' wrote Margaret Hinxman in the *Sunday Telegraph*.

'From Michael Caine as the randy cockney lad of Bill Naughton's play comes a performance of such king-sized stamina and tight-packed skill that he makes all the other anti-heroes of the screen look like catchpenny bargains,' said Alexander Walker in the *Evening Standard*, adding, 'It is a performance that tops everything else on the London scene. If Goliath were a cockney his name would be Alfie.'

Michael Thornton in the *Sunday Express* once again reserved his judgement: 'The film is not, one feels, as successful as it should be, and that, I think, is because it depends too entirely on Michael Caine. As Alfie Michael Caine is a very very funny man. But not in my book a star, not yet.' Dilys Powell in the *Sunday Times*, on the other hand, was convinced. 'I must say that the self-admiring little swagger and the natty self-confidence combined with the air of indiscipline and insolence which one remembers from *The Ipcress File* to make as good an Alfie as one could hope for. Everything an actor can do for the cheerful callous sexual athlete, Mr Caine

114

does.'

The film's publicity posters proclaimed: MICHAEL CAINE IS ALFIE IS WICKED! and, awake to the benefits of keeping in character, Caine gave a wide selection of Alfie-style interviews. On arriving in America for the *Alfie* publicity tour, for instance, he told the *Sunday Express*: 'The birds. They're dollier here than anywhere else I've been. They come strictly under the Strong Men Sobbed category. They're like unbroken horses—very independent. They've never been controlled by anybody, you see. If you do break them, they're grateful, as all women are. After that, all they need is to be fed three times a day and shown who's master. Just like horses.'

'What's it all about, Alfie?', the theme song sung by Cilla Black on the British release and by Cher in the USA, became a big hit. The phrase caught on everywhere.

Millicent Martin's prediction came true. Eighteen months after their night-time conversation in the caravan Caine was sitting in Hollywood as a nominee for Best Actor of 1966. Also nominated were Richard Burton for *Who's Afraid of Virginia Woolf?*, Steve McQueen for *The Sand Pebbles*, Alan Arkin for '*The Russians are Coming, The Russians are Coming*, and Paul Scofield for *A Man for All Seasons*. Paul Scofield took the Oscar, but for Caine at that time just being there was more than enough. It was only his third film in a leading role. It was also probably the most important role of his entire career. It made him a household name in Britain and brought him to public attention in America too.

As Caine says, though, 'You couldn't make a film like *Alfie* now. Alfie existed in a moral climate

115

where girls didn't do it. And I suppose nowadays poor old Alfie would have to have a medical certificate saying he was HIV negative.' But as Alfie in 1966, Michael Caine hit exactly the right moral note for the Swinging Sixties; his final soliloquy in the film aptly summing up the philosophy which reverberated around the spirit of the age:

You know what, when I look back on my little life and the birds I've known, and think of all the things they've done for me and the little I've done for them, you'd think I'd had the best of it all along the line. But what have I got out of it? I got a bob or two, some decent clothes, a car. I've got me health back and I ain't attached. But I ain't got my peace of mind and if you ain't got that then you ain't got nothing. I don't know, it seems to me if they ain't got you one way then they've got you another. So what's it all about, that's what I keep asking myself, what's it all about? Know what I mean?

CHAPTER SIX

'I'M NOT REALLY STAR MATERIAL':
1966–1969

'If I work fast enough and pack enough bleedin' pictures in, I'll be a star before anyone realizes I'm not really star material.'

Michael Caine

Caine spent the rest of the decade working at 'packing in the pictures'. Between 1966 and the beginning of 1969 he made ten films, and built on his initial burst of success to become an established star. It was a work ethic that became ingrained, and the pace has never really slowed since.

But with a background like his, it isn't surprising that Michael Caine worked as hard as he did. A working-class lad who had struggled for years, suddenly presented with all the trappings of stardom, wasn't going to believe it was anything other than temporary. And if it was only temporary, he'd better be careful with the money now finally—to his and the taxman's pleasure—rolling in.

Caine invested his money and, typically, his investment portfolio included a measure of self-improvement as well as blue-chip certainties. He bought art—often modern painters like John Piper—so he could watch his money grow and study the subject at the same time. Other investments were more orthodox, like endowment insurance policies. From the very beginning of his success, Caine was insuring his future. As he said in 1967, 'I realize it's not going to last, all this. That's why I'm working so hard ... the other night on TV I saw four girls blasting the Beatles and I thought, "If they can turn on them, what hope have I got?" I depressed myself so much I rushed out next day and bought myself another insurance policy.'

His caution, however, never extended itself as far as his confidence. He would tell journalists—in much the same way as he'd told his friends he was going to be a film star—that he was definitely going to make a million, 'and maybe a little more!'

He was determined to enjoy himself too. With the *Alfie* reputation preceding him, any appearance he made with a girl was a source of interest. Caine made the most of it. The 'Birdman of Grosvenor Square', as he became known, was often seen around town squiring a number of good-looking ladies, like Swedish actress Camilla Sparv, and a young student called Bianca de Macias later better known as Mrs Mick Jagger. But the minute marriage was mentioned, he ran a mile. At this stage of his life, his career came first. If becoming a star had been a long fight, remaining at the top was going to be almost as much of a challenge.

Part of that challenge was America. *Alfie* had been successful in the States, but only after some of the dialogue was changed. 'Fag', for example has disastrously different meanings on different sides of the Atlantic. 'In the scene where I'm examined for tuberculosis,' recalls Caine, 'the woman doctor says, "Do you cough much?" and I say, "Only after the first fag in the morning, but doesn't everyone?!"'

'We changed "fag" to "smoke".'

Later he got his American break from Shirley Maclaine, both as her leading man in *Gambit*, and from her introduction to Hollywood social life. It wasn't long before he was observed escorting the likes of Natalie Wood and Nancy Sinatra. The Americans took to Caine, and he to America, but his heart and his life were in London.

Back home, he adroitly played the working-class-lad-made-good angle, realizing that he'd be daft not to exploit what had now become very fashionable. He'd had a front seat on the sixties bandwagon of working-class heroes, but by now it was beginning to rankle occasionally. Working-class actors, models and photographers had now been dubbed The New Aristocracy, but as Caine told *Esquire* magazine in 1966, 'It's so "in" now to have a working-class background that any actor, painter or writer who is working class is automatically assumed to be great.'

It was around this time that Michael Caine, working-class film star, wrote out the now famous shopping list: 'Razor blades, Bread, Butter, Cornflakes, Rolls-Royce.' Cautious Caine had waited until he'd made his first million before awarding himself the traditional symbol of success, an unthinkable dream just a few years earlier. The trouble was, the doorman at the nearest Rolls-Royce dealers still believed it unthinkable. Instead of being shown the latest model, Caine found himself being shown the door. He can still remember the incident vividly: 'I said to the doorman, "How much is a Rolls-Royce?" And he said, "How many do you want?"

'I said, "Are you mucking me about?" And he replied, "I've got a feeling you're mucking *me* about, son. Clear off!"'

Seething with anger at such prejudice, Caine strode off to another dealer, where he purchased the instrument of his revenge, a rather nice Rolls convertible. After taking delivery, and with the top down, his chauffeur drove him slowly past the first showroom where, in full view of the astonished commissionaire, Caine sailed past regally—demonstrating a broad grin and the full two-fingered salute.

Success was beginning to suit him, whether he thought he was star material or not.

After *Alfie* Caine felt he needed a change, and, in the spring of 1966, he ran into his old friend from the Under Thirties Club, Bryan Forbes, who was now developing a career as a director. Forbes' latest project, which he was also producing, was *The Wrong Box*, a late Victorian black comedy based loosely on a story written by R L Stevenson and his stepson, Lloyd Osbourne, on a visit Stevenson made to America in 1887.

The script had been written by ace TV writers Larry Gelbart and Burt Shevelove, the pair who had written the hit musical *A Funny Thing Happened on the Way to the Forum*. Gelbart, of course, later went on to create *MASH*.

Caine eagerly accepted the part of Michael Finsbury as a complete contrast to Alfie. Unlike the womanizing rogue, Finsbury is a shy, naïve young man who can scarcely bring himself to speak to the girl he worships from afar, played by Forbes's wife, Nanette Newman.

The star-studded cast included almost every top name in British comedy. Peter Sellers appeared as a back-street doctor who lives alone amidst a colony of cats (and uses a kitten as blotting paper), and Tony Hancock was an incompetent policeman. Peter Cook and Dudley Moore played Caine's cousins, one obsessed with his egg collection and the other obsessed with women, and Wilfrid Lawson appeared as the aged and decaying butler, Peacock.

Working with Lawson was a memorable experience, and one particular story remains a favourite with Caine. Lawson was due to travel from London to Bristol for some filming and an assistant had been detailed to collect him from the station as it was a certainty that the alcoholic charms of the dining car would prove too much for Lawson during the journey. Caine takes up the story: 'The train came in, everybody got off and there was no Lawson. It was the end of the line; the train hadn't stopped anywhere, hadn't even slowed down. "Where the fuck is he?" said the assistant. The train pulled out. Sitting on the other line with his suitcase was Wilfred Lawson. 'Wheersa platform?" he said. He'd got out the wrong side.

'I'm sure all those actors got pissed in the sixties as a homage to Wilfrid Lawson.'

The two central characters of the film, played by John Mills and Ralph Richardson, are brothers who are the last surviving members of a tontine, worth £100,000. One definition of a tontine (named after one Lorenzo Tonti) is 'A legacy left among several persons in such a way that as any one dies his share goes to the survivors, till the last survivor inherits all.'

It naturally follows that the survivors have a vested interest in each other's demise, and the comic value stems from the attempts on the life of

121

the unsuspecting Ralph Richardson by the murderous John Mills.

For Caine it was a marked contrast to the last time he had worked with John Mills, sixteen years earlier, when Caine had taken on the less than memorable role of teaboy on the set of *Morning Departure*.

One incident, during location filming on Englefield Green in Berkshire, firmly cemented the friendship between Caine and Bryan Forbes, as Forbes recalls: 'Michael and Nanette were sitting in a Victorian hearse about ten feet off the ground and pulled by four horses, and Nanette was wearing very tight Victorian clothes.

'The second unit cameraman made them go too fast and these four large dray horses took off. Everyone was shouting to Nanette to jump off and if she'd done that she would have been killed. Michael held on to those bolting horses for well over two miles and finally managed to stop them. I was shooting a distance away and I could hear the screams, I thought I was going to find my wife dead. Michael needed a very large brandy after that. He literally saved Nanette's life.'

Caine, who already had a strong dislike of horses after his experience on *Zulu*, also recollects the incident: 'The camera car was in front of us and suddenly it backfired . . . we were two miles away before I could stop those horses. We could have been killed. I always remember we were going across this ploughed field at about 50 mph and Nanette was screaming and the camera was on us. So I said, "Stop screaming, otherwise you'll have to post-sync it!"'

When the film opened in May 1966 the critics

122

agreed that they preferred individual segments to the whole. 'This is a film in which the whole is considerably less than the sum of its parts. Fortunately, several of them are very good parts indeed,' said Kenneth Tynan in the *Observer*, while Dilys Powell in the *Sunday Times* commented:

Michael Caine as the young lover—well, Mr Caine is better in gravelly roles; he fails to catch the glaucous accents of the period (circa 1900), the mood (spoof romantic) and the class (top-hat); but then if one didn't know how well he can do, as Alfie, say, he would seem pretty good here.

By mid-1966 Shirley Maclaine was looking for a director for her new film, a comedy thriller to be called *Gambit*. Someone suggested Sidney Furie, and so a screening of *The Ipcress File* was arranged. It turned out that Furie was committed elsewhere, but while watching the film Maclaine had made a decision; she wanted the actor who played Harry Palmer as her new leading man. Caine received a call and was offered his first Hollywood film role. He was delighted.

Caine played a confidence trickster, Harry Dean, who meets a Eurasian girl Nicole Chang (Maclaine) and realizes that she bears a startling resemblance to the late wife of the fabulously wealthy Ahmad Shahbandar (Herbert Lom) who is said still to be in love with her memory. Harry then devises a plan to steal a priceless sculpture from Shahbandar's apartment, using Nicole as his bait.

This was Caine's first experience of working in America, and he was impressed with everything he

123

saw. Above all he was thrilled to be working in Hollywood, the centre of the film industry. There was only one problem. He didn't know anyone, and he was left feeling very isolated in his suite at the Beverly Hills Hotel.

Shirley Maclaine came to his rescue. As soon as she hit town she telephoned Michael and told him she'd arranged a party in his honour. Caine, knowing that he was virtually unknown in Hollywood, was convinced the party would fall flat. 'Don't worry, honey,' said Maclaine, 'they'll come.' Filled with trepidation, Caine turned up at Chasen's a few days later to discover a huge ballroom, a band, and 20th Century-Fox picking up the bill. The only thing missing were the guests. Caine waited nervously: 'The first person to walk through the door was Frank Sinatra. I nearly fainted. The second person was Judy Garland, then Dean Martin, Kirk Douglas . . . all these famous people, and they said, "Welcome to Hollywood. We hear you're doing swell!"'

Eventually the party wound up and Cary Grant invited Michael and Shirley back to Danny Kaye's kitchen for dinner. Still reeling from the shock of mingling with all the Hollywood idols he'd admired right through his boyhood, Caine arrived at Danny Kaye's, only to discover the place crawling with Secret Service men, all of whom looked (and were) heavily armed. Strange, thought Caine, I didn't know Danny Kaye or Cary Grant or Shirley Maclaine were *that* important.

However, sitting in the kitchen of Danny Kaye's home was the man the security was really intended for, Prince Philip. 'Hullo,' said His Royal Highness. 'It's old Ipcress, isn't it?'

Caine regained his composure enough to discuss the niceties of playing Harry Palmer with the Prince. Finally, he and Shirley left at about 3 am, Caine offering to drop Maclaine at her home on the way back to his hotel. As they drew up at her house Caine was surprised to see steam rising all around the back of it. 'Oh Christ,' announced Maclaine, 'I left the pool on!'

Caine's first sojourn in Hollywood was more remarkable for the people he was meeting than the film he was making, for it introduced him to some of those who would become his lifelong friends. *Gambit* turned out a likeable if perhaps not a memorable movie. As the *Daily Mail*'s critic wrote, 'You could call it perfect type-casting—Michael Caine as a glib, Cockney opportunist, and Shirley Maclaine as the hard-boiled dumb-belle who lets him tarnish her golden heart with crime.' He referred to Caine putting on his 'dead-eyed look—or as the women would no doubt prefer to call it his bedroom-eyed look—and his slack-lipped Alfie accent.' Derek Prouse, in the *Sunday Times* expanded on this:

Exercise for an actor: Express your feelings when your accomplice in crime, with only a few minutes to spare, is threading her way through a battery of electric burglar alarms in an effort to carry off a priceless bust of a Chinese Empress. How do you express your inner panic? Michael Caine's solution is to wear a completely dead-pan expression and simply observe—and the result is both tense and hilarious.

Not all of *Gambit* is on this highly accomplished level but there is an unforced air about the proceedings that makes the film unusually pleasant entertainment.

Before he left Hollywood, Caine came across another of his boyhood heroes. 'I was walking through the lobby at the Beverly Hills Hotel,' he remembers, 'when I heard a helicopter outside, and in came John Wayne in the full "Hondo" kit and the sideways walk. He saw me and said, "Kid?"

'I said, "Yes, Mr Wayne?"

'He said, "You're doing swell! You wanna piece of advice?"

'I said, "Yes, Mr Wayne."

'He said, "If you wanna last in this business, talk low, talk slow and don't say too much. Goodbye, kid."

'John Wayne was always very nice to me, and I've never forgotten his advice.'

★   ★   ★

Before *Gambit* was released in Britain at the end of 1966, Michael Caine began work on the second Harry Palmer film, happy to be reunited with the secret agent who was turning insubordination into an art form.

This time the story was set in Berlin, adapted from Len Deighton's novel *The Berlin Memorandum*. The plot centred around a Russian intelligence officer's bogus plan to defect, with a sub-plot concerning a Nazi war criminal being pursued by a Zionist group.

Many of the technicians on *Funeral in Berlin* had also worked on the first Harry Palmer film, among them lighting cameraman Otto Heller and production designer Ken Adam. This time the director was Guy Hamilton who had just finished making *Goldfinger* for Harry Saltzman.

Since his previous incarnation as Palmer, Caine had had time to dwell on the essential differences between his own character and that of Bond. In April 1969 he told *Films and Filming* magazine, 'I think that James Bond, as he was written by Ian Fleming, would never have mixed or come into contact with anybody like Harry Palmer. If they had ... Palmer would have regarded Bond as a bit of a toffee-nosed twit; at least that's the way I see it. Rather like a cockney tearaway who hasn't had any boxing training coming up against the heavyweight champion from Cambridge. He would think of him as a bit of a twit but, at the same time, he'd have been a bit worried. I think as Sean Connery played him he's a much bigger, tougher man than Fleming originally conceived ... I've always imagined Bond being played by a 35- or 40-year-old Rex Harrison.' Palmer's one-liners were as good as ever. On being given his covering identity he retorts, 'I'm sorry, I just don't feel like an Edmund Dorf ... can't I be Rock Hunter?'

Generally, the critics liked the new Harry Palmer film, but some of them felt that this time the plot was simply too convoluted, with the Berlin scenery adding to the drabness. Dilys Powell, writing in the *Sunday Times*, clearly felt that the film owed everything to Michael Caine:

It is difficult to imagine the first film without Mr Caine's mastery of the techniques of insubordination. In the case of the second it is impossible: the actor makes the film ... even the

127

fondest enthusiast can barely keep pace, as the story of a plan to smuggle a defector out of East Berlin zigzags along, with the variety of cross-actions and cross-purposes, and double-crosses.

Robert Robinson, in the *Sunday Telegraph*, commented, 'As the trendy cockney who spies for money Michael Caine seems rather vague, and I place the film in the 40-watt category'; but Felix Barker, in the *Evening News*, was more enthusiastic: 'His fans will be delighted to hear that Michael Caine succeeds brilliantly in making Palmer a highly individual hero. Poker-voiced, deadpan, and paid only £30 for appalling risks, he is as phoney as the sybaritic Bond, but Mr Caine gives him a wonderful off-beat quality.' And Alexander Walker, critic for the *Evening Standard*, was fast becoming a firm Caine fan:

> There are so many tarnished anti-heroes in the spy business nowadays, it is no wonder that Harry Palmer, who was meant to deglamorize James Bond's high life now looks as bright as an Army button-stick.
> It says a lot for Michael Caine, who plays the ex-fly boy turned Secret Service messenger boy, that *Funeral in Berlin* still distils its own brand of astringent bitters. Caine is an actor-star whom it's becoming a connoisseur's pleasure to watch in action . . .

The review continued in similar vein, Walker's only reservation being the lack of reference to Harry's well known culinary skills. One thing was certain.

Harry Palmer was now as much of a sex symbol as Bond. In the *Observer* Penelope Gilliatt analysed his charms:

> Michael Caine is an interesting actor to watch. He is the new pin-up: instead of a cleft chin or great legs, wiles and repartee. Intransigence and opportunism are as central now to sex-appeal in English male acting as charm and height used to be. Make a crack, cheat the boss, expect nothing, go for the lot, and never commit murder except on expenses. The girls fall like skittles.

Caine was delighted at Palmer's success, for personal as well as professional reasons: 'Someone once said of Harry Palmer that he is a winner who came on like a loser. I liked that—you could say the same of me.'

★　　★　　★

The year 1966 was a busy time. Before the year was out, Michael Caine was starring in another, very untypical role. Set in the Deep South, *Hurry Sundown* was a story of racial prejudice and land grabbing in the Mississippi delta in 1946. Caine played Henry Warren, a southern businessman determined to buy out a Negro whose farm stands in the way of his plans for a business venture. Jane Fonda played his wife who supports the plan until she finds her husband has lied to her about a serious accident involving their retarded son.

Filming took place in Baton Rouge in Louisiana and the cast, which included Diahann Carroll, faced many of their own problems with the colour prejudice that still existed in the area. At first the hotel where they were staying refused to allow the Negro actors to use the same swimming pool as the whites. When director Otto Preminger threatened to move elsewhere the thought of the lost dollars caused them to back down, at least in part. One swimming pool would be reserved exclusively for the film unit, black and white. The other swimming pool would remain segregated and be used only by white hotel guests.

The whole unit felt the presence of the Ku-Klux-Klan. Right at the start of shooting, the tyres on the company's cars and vans were slashed; and members of the cast, black and white, were harassed. Caine recalls standing in a village with the journalist David Lewin who was asking him if there was racial tension. 'I said yes, we had the Ku-Klux-Klan after us,' says Caine. 'They shot at our motor homes when they realized they were empty! They don't pull their hoods down because it's illegal to [cover] their faces, but they wear them.

'I told him my driver was their leader, and he said, "Come on, Michael, you're pulling my leg!"

'At that moment the Sheriff came walking along the street and he said to me, "You're from the nigger picture, aren't you?"—we were known as the nigger picture—and I said, "Yes." He said, "I told you sons-of-bitches not to come here, so get the fuck out of here." And he looked at David Lewin and he said, "And take the fucking kyke with you!"'

In the end, armed Louisiana State troopers were assigned to the picture to protect the cast and crew from harassment.

Director Otto Preminger, who once played the

prison camp commandant in *Stalag 17*, had a fearsome reputation for instilling terror into actors and crew alike. Caine was well aware of this and by the time of their first meeting had already worked out his tactics: 'When I met the director Otto Preminger, I said, "Listen, I hear you've got a reputation for shouting and screaming at people. Don't ever shout at me because I'm a very sensitive little flower. If you shout at me, I burst into tears and I go into my dressing room and then I go get dressed and I go home."

'And Otto, who was a tyrant, looked at me and said, "I would never shout at Alfie," and I said, "Why?" And he said, "Because that's me!"'

By all accounts he never did.

As well as having to deal with Preminger Caine also had the notoriously difficult Southern accent to master. However, he did receive some coaching from someone who had had detailed experience of mastering the Southern drawl, Vivien Leigh. 'I met Vivien Leigh and I said, "How do you learn the Southern accent?" She said, "I'll tell you, Mike, you say Four Door Ford—for-a-dor-ford—all day long." And in Georgia they said I really got it; but it's typical, the only place I got bad reviews with my Southern accent was in England, and they didn't know what they were talking about.'

The Americans did indeed applaud his accent. 'Caine is believable, showing no traces of an English accent, but a facility with his Dixie dialogue,' said *Variety*, while the *Hollywood Reporter* commented 'He has affected an almost flawless regional accent.' But back in England, the *Sun*'s Ann Pacey was scathing:

131

It is not Michael Caine's fault. He apparently studied hard to get the accent right by listening to tape recordings of the real thing. Still he neither looks, nor sounds, nor acts like a ruthless Southern boy ... He behaves more like an uncomfortable 'Alfie', out of his own time and environment, whose voice keeps trailing off into London vowel sounds.

The *Monthly Film Bulletin* thought that 'Michael Caine, despite a fair shot at a Southern drawl, is way out of his depth', while in the *Daily Mail* Cecil Wilson declared, 'It takes an adventurous producer-director like Otto Preminger to cast Michael Caine as a Southern go-getter in this spacious saga of industrialized Georgia. For I fancy that to Mr Caine the Deep South has hitherto meant somewhere near Clapham Common.' But he went on, '... the strange thing is that in no time it seems the most natural thing in the world for our cockney wonder boy to drawl lahk thet.'

Caine's final verdict on the experience: 'Louisiana is incredible. Until I went there I thought Tennessee Williams was one of the most imaginative writers in the world. When I got to Louisiana I realized he was a newspaper reporter; he just wrote about the people next door.'

*   *   *

Once the hectic pace had started, Caine found it difficult to stop. In the early spring of 1967 came the third movie of the Palmer series, *Billion Dollar Brain*. Now running the none-too-successful HP Detective Agency, ex-secret agent Harry Palmer accepts an assignment to deliver a package to Helsinki. He is then blackmailed into rejoining MI5 by Colonel Ross, who is also interested in the package and threatens to implicate Harry in a murder connected with it if he doesn't co-operate. With a shrug of his raincoated shoulders Harry agrees.

The package proves to contain eggs infected with deadly viruses stolen from a government laboratory. Their theft has been plotted by an obsessive anti-communist oil millionaire, General Midwinter, who plans to use them in an attack on Russia. Midwinter is using Latvia as the centre of his operations and issues his orders from a massive computer, the Billion Dollar Brain. After infiltrating the General's organization Harry bumps into his old adversary Colonel Stok and the film climaxes on the frozen Baltic Sea.

The film was a 'first' for at least two people. One was Caine's brother Stanley Caine, making his acting début as a postman. The other was director Ken Russell, making his feature film début. Russell was relieved to have Caine with him. 'Michael was great fun. He was also the most helpful star I've ever worked with. It was my first feature and he did everything he possibly could to help me. I can't speak highly enough of him.

'Some actors are intuitive, like Oliver Reed and Glenda Jackson. I think Michael is of that breed. He had Harry Palmer in his bones by the third picture and I was very fortunate in having his input and that of the other directors before me.'

The scenes at the end where Caine jumps from ice floe to ice floe were shot in Finland and Ken Russell's frequent use of the telescopic lens meant it was impossible to use a stunt man. Starting on a long shot and gradually zooming in for a close-up didn't allow for a stand-in to be substituted—it had to be Caine and no one else. Caine innocently but nervously obliged. 'We were right out on the sea, and the ice was melting. The catering van was about to go through, and we had to do the stunt fast,' he recalls. 'I wasn't thinking. My mind was numb with frost, and I just did it. Afterwards this Finnish guy said to me, "Where are your ice knives?" I said, "What ice knives?"

'He said, "You haven't got any ice knives? You could have died!"

'I said, "What do I want ice knives for?"

'He said, "Well, if you fall in, how are you going to get out?"

'I said, "How *would* you get out?" and he had these two [knives] on either side and he showed me how to stick them into the ice—CHOP!—and you pull yourself out.

'I'd done it without ice knives, and no one had told me. Ken Russell didn't know—what does Ken Russell know about ice knives?'

'He was very brave,' says Russell of the stunt. 'I wouldn't have done it. There is a scene at the end where the American fascists are bombed and the ice floe splits up. A lot of it was done in the studio but when it came to the day we were actually out on the Baltic.

'Michael had to jump on to an ice floe and then jump off it. If he had slipped he would have been gone; the water was minus 50 degrees Centigrade! But he made nothing of it. He just got on the ice floe and jumped. We were three miles out on the Baltic, with ships passing behind. One slip and he would have had it. But he did it and then he trooped off across the endless ice towards Trafalgar Square!'

When the film opened in November 1967, the critics found Ken Russell's visual style hard to cope with. The general feeling was that the story had got lost somewhere. Patrick Gibbs wrote in the *Daily Telegraph*: 'I liked much of *The Ipcress File*, something of *Funeral in Berlin*, but little of this scarcely comprehensible rigmarole except, perhaps, the snow-covered Finnish scene and Oscar Homolka as a genial old communist.' In *The Times*, John Russell Taylor said, 'Caine survives as ever and Oscar Homolka is his usual flamboyant self as the chief of the Russian secret police. Everyone else sinks with the ship.'

Caine was impressed with Russell's direction but felt that the time had come for him and Harry to part company. The next film which had been planned in the Harry Palmer series, *Horse Under Water*, was never made. For a time Harry Saltzman toyed with the idea of finding a new Harry, but in the end it was decided to let the character slip away. Ken Russell has the last word: 'Harry Palmer was so totally fictitious. I think if anyone other than Michael Caine had played him it would have been far less convincing. A lot of Harry Palmer was Michael Caine.'

Two years later, according to Caine, he was nearly cast in what would have been a most unexpected role: 'Ken Russell, who's a great friend of mine, offered me *Women in Love* before he offered it to anyone else,' Caine told *Film Comment* in 1980. 'He said, "Choose which part you want." So I said, "Fine, thank you." I read the script and

135

decided on the Oliver Reed part. "We'll just cut the nude wrestling scene," I told Ken. He said no. So I said I couldn't do it. Because I couldn't. I would never appear nude in a picture. And I certainly couldn't appear nude and wrestle with a nude man. I find it repulsive. I told Ken I wouldn't appear nude standing still by myself, let alone wrestling another naked man. Not even with the set closed off and black velvet all around me. My own view on that is that I find nude women very beautiful. But I find nude men ridiculous, and ridicule is the arch enemy of the actor. Plus the fact that when you're naked you're no longer in control of the situation because people are not looking where you want them to, or listening to what you want them to. They're looking at other things—at your genitals—and the interest has gone out of what you're doing. Therefore you lost the control which is the actor's basic weapon. He must control the audience every single second he's on screen.'

*   *   *

Next came something of an oddity. *Tonite Let's All Make Love in London* originally set out to be an impressionistic examination of the phenomenon of 'swinging London'.

While he was shooting *Billion Dollar Brain* Caine gave an interview on film to Peter Whitehead, who then cut it together with other interviews to make a full-length film. Other ingredients included shots of mini-skirted girls dancing in a disco, performances by Eric Burdon and The Animals, Pink Floyd, and Allen Ginsberg, interviews with Edna O'Brien and David Hockney, and Vanessa Redgrave singing a

136

revolutionary song at a protest meeting at the Royal Albert Hall.

The end result was a confused jumble of unrelated snippets and Caine, who had not known that the interview he had given was destined to end up in a film, was not best pleased.

*   *   *

Caine had deeply appreciated Shirley Maclaine's generosity on his first visit to Hollywood, and he was more than happy to accept a cameo role in her new film, *Woman Times Seven*, as a favour to her.

The picture, directed by Vittorio De Sica, was a vehicle for Maclaine. It took the form of seven vignettes, all set in Paris, in which Maclaine plays seven different female characters. Caine was in good company; Peter Sellers, Philippe Noiret and Rossano Brazzi had also accepted supporting roles.

Caine appeared wordlessly in the last of the seven vignettes as a man who follows Maclaine home, causing her mind to wander over possible romantic reasons for his pursuit. When she gets home to her rather dull husband she looks out of the window and is delighted to see the young man sitting on a park bench below. Convinced he is keeping a vigil for her she does not hear the telephone ringing. It is the young man, a private detective, relating her movements during the day to her husband.

Shot after *Billion Dollar Brain*, it was released in the UK first, in June 1967. The critics seemed to feel they would have preferred to see a little less of Maclaine and a little more of the supporting cast. *Time* magazine commented:

137

Most of the blame, however, must fall on De Sica, who has wasted such talented actors as Arkin, Sellers, Michael Caine, Philippe Noiret and Vittorio Gassman in a ponderously directed, flaccid work. Better than anyone else, he should know that a tour de force is like a striptease: there is no point in the performance if the material does not come off in style.

The *Daily Mirror*'s Dick Richards wrote that most of the supporting cast 'looked as bored and uncomfortable as I felt', while the *Daily Sketch* complained that 'Michael Caine appears in a silent part, which seems an insolent way to treat an actor whose main charm is the gift of the cockney gab.'

His return to Paris to make *Woman Times Seven* was significant for Caine. During his last visit to that city he had been sleeping in the air terminal and hoping for the occasional free cup of coffee or a sandwich. This time he was in residence at the George V Hotel with everything he could possibly want laid on. What a difference eleven years could make!

*　　*　　*

After the frenetic activity of the previous eighteen months, Caine slowed down a little—at least for him. Early 1968 brought him back together with Bryan Forbes who had last directed him in *The Wrong Box* two years earlier. This time Forbes had also written the screenplay for his new film, a thriller called *Deadfall*. Caine played a jewel thief, Henry Clarke, who becomes involved with a married couple in a master plan to rob a villa belonging to a multi-millionaire. As their relationship progresses, Clarke discovers that the husband is gay and embarks on an affair with the wife. The story progresses through lust and incest to its final conclusion, the robbery at the villa.

The film, shot in Spain, showed shades of Hitchcock, especially in the first robbery sequence when shots of the theft were interwoven with a classical concert.

The critics felt the film began well but was eventually swamped in a labyrinthine script. The *Daily Sketch* was not impressed:

Michael Caine, with the sullen indifference of a conscript soldier who can't buy himself out, strolls through *Deadfall* in utter bewilderment.

I am not surprised, for this is a film which seems to be in need of psychoanalysis. Caine, a freelance jewel thief, teams up with Eric Portman, who is a homosexual married to Giovanna Ralli, who eventually turns out to be his daughter.

Caine is thus immersed in a sexual situation that might have delighted the late Dr Kinsey, but is utterly perplexing to the rest of us.

Having saved Bryan Forbes' wife, Nanette Newman, after their horses bolted on *The Wrong Box*, Caine found himself involved in another life-threatening situation with Forbes himself on *Deadfall*. 'Michael and I were coming in to Madrid on a flight from Majorca,' says Forbes, 'and I said, "We're never going to land at this angle. We're not going to make it!" I'd done some flight training during the war so I knew something about it. If

139

they'd had to dig us out of the wreckage, it would have set a few people thinking, because we were holding hands as we came down. We hit the ground with one wing touching and went up the runway with smoke trailing. When we finally stopped, one of the Spanish passengers went up to the cabin and knocked the captain out.'

Forbes's admiration for Caine the actor is complete: 'He's a dream to direct, very professional. He always knows his lines and he has no ego on the floor. I'd work with him anytime.'

Caine has always remembered and frequently used one particular line from the film. Eyeing up a wealthy man, Nanette Newman asks Caine, 'Is he anything to do with films?' 'No,' replies Caine, 'he's just rich enough to keep you out of them!'

*   *   *

Caine's next film, *Play Dirty* was based loosely on the activities of the Long Range Desert Group who worked behind enemy lines during the North Africa campaign of 1942.

Shot in May and June 1968, the film was originally to have been directed by René Clement, who had shot to fame in the fifties with such classics as *Les Jeux Interdits* (1952), but he left the production shortly after shooting began, and the experienced André de Toth, with whom Caine had recently worked when de Toth was executive producer on *Billion Dollar Brain*, took over.

Caine played Captain Douglas, leader of a group of assorted criminals and mercenaries who are given the task of blowing up a German oil terminal on the North African coast. While they are engaged in the operation the British command change their mind and decide that the terminal will not be blown up, but captured instead by Montgomery's troops.

Out of radio contact, Douglas's group are unaware of the change of plan and are betrayed to the Germans by their own side. The oil terminal is still blown up but most of the group are killed. Caine and his No 2, Nigel Davenport, still wearing their decoy enemy uniforms, give themselves up but are shot down by their own side, despite waving the white flag.

Richard Harris had originally been cast in the role of Caine's No 2, and Nigel Davenport was to play a much smaller part. But Harris failed to arrive at the location because, Nigel Davenport thinks, of a dispute with Harry Saltzman, who was producing the film. Davenport was called upon to take over: 'I suddenly found myself with my first leading film part. No one could have been more supportive and encouraging than Michael. He was tremendously helpful. If you are the star of the film it almost behoves you to take leadership of the unit. Not everyone does it, though. Michael does, and he does it better than anyone I've ever seen.'

Caine was able to draw on his experience in Korea for the filming, remembering vividly how he had felt when men around him were being killed. 'My whole idea was let's not be film stars with dying speeches,' he said afterwards. 'Let's prove to people that people who are there one minute who you know quite well, aren't there the next minute. And they don't say, "Give this to my mother ... Tell my sister I love her ... Pat the dog for me ..." and all that Family Favourites stuff. It was decided at a discussion at the time as to what should be done with the ending. No one was ever satisfied with the ending. And my whole idea was that what struck me, having been a soldier myself, was that one minute someone was there, then the next minute they weren't.'

Filming took place in Almeria in Spain, known then as 'Spain's answer to Hollywood'. As well as resembling the African desert, the dunes around Almeria were in heavy use, doubling geographically for Utah, Arizona and Mexico.

There were seven Westerns shooting at the same time as *Play Dirty*, two Yugoslav, two Italian, two French, and one Spanish. The dunes were crowded, to say the least. At one point de Toth used bulldozers to cut trenches in the sand to stop another unit getting into his stretch of dune!

That atmosphere led to confusion which didn't please Caine. 'The one thing that Michael can't stand is inefficiency,' says Nigel Davenport. 'If he feels people have fallen down on what they're meant to do, that to him is unforgivable. Not that it happens often because he's the sort of personality that makes people want to do their best. There were two occasions on *Play Dirty* when things hadn't been worked out properly, logistically. On those two occasions Michael shouted at the top of his voice, said he wasn't going on until it was put right, and then walked off into the middle distance. Those are the only two times I have seen him furious.'

The cast were staying in a hotel called The Grand which had only recently been built, cashing in on the spaghetti westerns that were at that time being made in the region at the rate of about three a week. Nigel Davenport remembers it as 'large and brassy, with an absolutely enormous lobby in palatial

142

Spanish style'.

'It's quite extraordinary,' Caine told *Photoplay* Magazine. 'Our hotel in the evenings is packed with the weirdest assortment of character actors you ever saw. They all look like villains. They all seem to have black beards. One day I'm going to shout "Injuns!" at the top of my voice, and watch 'em dive for cover.'

The hotel lobby was to become very familiar territory. 'We hit a run of very bad weather,' says Davenport, 'and in total we lost twenty-three shooting days, which you don't expect in southern Spain. There was rain, gales and even snow, so we spent a lot of time in the lobby, playing Scrabble, talking and waiting to work.

'At the end of the huge lobby was a bar and the waiters would bring you cigarettes and coffee and vodka tonics. In those days when you wanted a waiter you would shout "Oiga" and clap your hands. A free-lance journalist in a battered old car came out from London to spend a few days on the set and like the rest of us he spent a lot of time in the lobby. He was very intrigued by this "Oiga" as various people called for waiters. Michael leaned across to him and said, "Sometimes we have to sit for so long in this lobby that we get through eight sets of Oigas a day."'

During shooting Caine celebrated his birthday; Harry Saltzman sent him some sausages, Nigel Davenport gave him a copy of *Alfie* in Spanish, and someone else sent him a stuffed flamingo with a note attached saying: 'This is the only tall slim bird we could find around here'.

However, things did look up. Also in Almeria at that time were Sean Connery and Brigitte Bardot, making *Shalako*. BB caused a big stir, not only because of her beauty but because of her retinue, which included a secretary and a hairdresser and a black chauffeur who would drive her around in a splendid white Rolls-Royce.

As Nigel Davenport remembers, they were all very interested in Miss Bardot, and determined to overcome the fact that she couldn't speak English. 'When we were introduced I thought I could speak French,' says Davenport, 'but by the time I had thought about my pronunciation and constructed my sentence, the conversation had moved on.

'I was fascinated to hear Michael chattering away to her in fluent French, with a strong cockney accent. He didn't give a damn what it sounded like; I learnt a lesson from that.'

Caine too was delighted to find BB in the sandy wastelands. 'When I first got here I was having a drink and wallowing in despond because the place was so horrible, when in came Brigitte Bardot, who was filming nearby. She came straight up to me and said, "Hello, I've always wanted to meet you."

'Well, I tell you I just didn't know what to say. I was absolutely knocked out, meeting her. I started falling over chairs.'

As a cinematic experience Caine did not enjoy Almeria, and had it written into future contracts that he wouldn't have to work there again.

The critics' view of the film did nothing to change his opinion. 'It's the sort of film that tries to be heroic, but trips over its conscience and ends up in a tangle', said Robert Ottaway in the *Daily Sketch*, adding, 'It mainly worried me because I think Mr Caine, whom I admire as an actor is misjudging his own star appeal, and throwing it away in a casual off-hand performance.'

And *Time* magazine declared:

Play Dirty plods across the screen like a camel in a sandstorm. In that desert in 1942 a martinet officer (Michael Caine) is assigned to blow up an oil depot of Rommel's desert rats. But the officer has rodents of his own—junkies, homosexuals, thieves, who compose his squadron. Only proper, announces his commandant, since 'war is a criminal enterprise'. So is *Play Dirty*, which leaves no oases of taste or drama along its route. There is also no room for Caine as a skilled actor to display his talents in a war picture that could give hell a bad name.

Michael Caine's next role was very different. *The Magus* was the second of John Fowles's novels to become a film. The first had been *The Collector*, in which Caine's old friend Terry Stamp had starred. Caine had seen *The Collector* and decided that he would like to appear in a Fowles work, so when he heard that producer John Kohn had the option on the next book—before it was even written—Caine told him 'I'll do that, no matter what it is.' It was agreed that Caine would do *The Magus* in the late summer and autumn of 1968 as part of his two-picture deal with Fox, the other film having been *Deadfall*.

When Caine read the novel he was fascinated by it. 'It's a very personal thing and I suppose *The Magus* can really be taken by each individual for what it means to them,' he says. 'There are some lines from T S Eliot which feature heavily in the screenplay, I think they're from the end of "Little

Gidding":

> We shall not cease from exploration
> And the end of all our exploring
> Will be to arrive where we started
> And know the place for the first time.

And this is really the central theme, at least for me, of *The Magus*.'

The film told the story of a young man called Nicholas Urfe (Caine) who runs off to an obscure Greek island to forget his past and find himself. He meets a Greek called Conchis (Anthony Quinn) who plays games with his mind, leading him in and out of reality. Also starring in the movie was the twenty-two-year-old Candice Bergen. Sometimes appearing as Conchis's dead lover and sometimes as his schizophrenic patient, she greatly impressed Caine with her intelligence and maturity.

During shooting Caine and Bergen attended the wedding of Roman Polanski to Sharon Tate at the Playboy Club.

Despite the fact that Fowles himself had adapted his Chinese puzzle of a novel and simplified it for the screen, it still left the critics confused. 'John Fowles' novel could have made a very jolly film in the hands of a Fellini,' said John Russell Taylor in *The Times*, adding:

> Unfortunately it has been directed by the eminently capable, businesslike Guy Green, who does a straightforward, professional, completely unmagical job on it. The phantoms may be all actors dressed up, but they should never look like it; the borderline between reality and illusion

146

should remain hauntingly hazy. Instead, Michael Caine as the teacher and Anthony Quinn as his tormentor look as uncomfortable as only those who have wandered lounge-suited into a fancy-dress ball can.

By contrast, *The Italian Job* was very much Michael Caine's personal project. After writer Troy Kennedy Martin showed him the initial synopsis for a comedy revolving round a bank robbery in Turin, Caine decided that this was the sort of film he wanted to be involved in and set about helping to raise the finance needed for the project. Peter Collinson, who had just made *Up The Junction*, would direct.

They scored a coup in persuading Noël Coward to return from his self-imposed exile in Switzerland to play the leading role of Mr Bridger, a big-time crook who has not allowed imprisonment to interfere with his operations and treats prison in the same way as he would a hotel, complete with room service and private bathroom facilities.

Caine played Charlie Croker, a minor villain who is released from the same prison and then breaks back in again to take an idea to Mr Bridger. Croker's plan, left to him by a deceased former associate, is to trap a bullion van in a huge traffic jam in Turin and make off with the gold.

The day of the gold delivery coincides with an England *v.* Italy football match, so Croker disguises his crooks as football supporters. Included among them was Benny Hill as the computer expert Professor Peach, whom Croker has freed from a lunatic asylum, where his lust for fat ladies had landed him!

The highlight of the film is the spectacular car chase through the jammed streets of Turin. The three Mini Cooper getaway cars show a wonderfully anarchistic contempt for any Highway Code by driving over roofs, and down sewers and subways to get back to the rendezvous on time. Boiling after them come the Italian police in three Fiats.

Included in the car chase is a sequence of three cars chasing across the top of the aircraft museum in Turin, 180 feet high and shaped like an egg. Permission for this extraordinary feat was gained by a fortunate linguistic confusion. As Caine explains 'The way we got up there was luck—the Italian for car is *machina* and the same word also means camera. So when we asked for permission to put a *machina* on top of the building they thought that we were going to position a camera up there, and the whole sequence was shot before anybody quite realized that the camera was on the ground, and the three motor cars were roaring over the top of the building.'

The Minis are driven at speed into a specially converted coach, accompanied by the song 'Get a Bloomin' Move on', in which the words 'This is the self-preservation society', sung by the entire heist team, feature heavily. (This may, incidentally, be the only time that Michael Caine has actually sung anything in a film!) The music was by Quincy Jones, the highly respected composer, arranger and producer who has worked with almost every famous name in the world of music from Ella Fitzgerald, Ray Charles and Frank Sinatra to Michael Jackson. Nothing could have prepared him for Michael Caine and cockney rhyming slang, though. 'When we did *The Italian Job* I was on the phone to Quincy Jones,' says Caine, 'and I was explaining cockney rhyming slang to him because he wanted to do a song for the film. He had never heard of cockney rhyming slang and he went off and investigated it. Then he rang me and said, "Listen, man, you're all spades, the cockneys. You're the only people over there with soul talk."'

'I had so much fun with that,' says Jones. 'I didn't know what I was talking about but I just got fascinated with the cockney slang.'

Jones describes himself and Caine as 'celestial twins'—they were born at the same hour, on 14th March 1933—and now they make sure that, wherever they are, they congratulate each other on their birthday. One year, as Jones recalls, Caine appeared at his house, accompanied by Henry Mancini and carrying a single candle. 'It's a beautiful relationship,' says Jones. 'To me he's one of the greatest dudes in the world and a great friend.'

The twist at the end of *The Italian Job* is as neat as it is now famous. The bus, safely away from Turin and traversing the Alps, takes a corner too fast and see-saws perilously on the edge of a cliff, gold at one end and thieves at the other. The film closes with Croker's words, ''Ang on a minute, boys—I've got a great idea!' But that wasn't the only possible ending. Originally, writer Troy Kennedy Martin had taken the plot on to Switzerland, where the boys get the money safely stashed away in a numbered Swiss bank account. Unfortunately, the Mafia manage to top the only two people who know the number, and the film ends with Charlie Croker's girlfriend sticking a pin into a list of numbers, hoping to hit the jackpot.

The script was also re-written as a novel, which ended with Bridger reaching an agreement with the Mafia, and Croker being told to take the gold back to Italy! And a sequel was planned to the film, starting with the coach hanging over the cliff with the engine running. The fuel tank being at the rear, when the coach ran out of fuel the balance tipped back in the gang's favour, and they retrieved the loot.

The Italian Job made its public appearance in June 1969, and the critics took it at face value as just another criminal caper movie, Dilys Powell writing in the *Sunday Times*:

No straight faces, no straight characters either, just some happy small-part playing (Michael Standing as an asthmatic crook, John Clive as an obsequiously bent garage manager, Irene Handl as the genteel sister of a sexual enthusiast); a little cheerful vulgarity; and a car chase which ought to do something for the export of Mini Coopers, at any rate to customers who like to make their cars behave like ski jumpers.

The film was, however, a bigger hit with the public, whose love of the car chase in particular has never diminished.

During the past three years Michael Caine had chosen his roles widely, and he'd set a pace which he was to keep up right into the nineties—two or three movies a year, on average. The public liked it, the tycoons liked the box office returns, and

Michael Caine liked it. He had made his mark with *Zulu, The Ipcress File* and *Alfie*, and now he'd consolidated his victory. He'd made it, but underneath he still couldn't quite believe it.

CHAPTER SEVEN

'WITH OLIVIER I CAN'T LOSE': 1969–1972

'If you make enough pictures then two or three of them must work out as something special.'
Michael Caine

Caine's choice of roles over the next three years was certainly eclectic. Among the characters he would play were a seventeenth-century German mercenary, an RAF fighter pilot, a pulp fiction writer and a hairdresser of Italian extraction.

His work would take him from the Philippine jungle to the Highlands of Scotland by way of Austria and Malta; but his domestic life began to reflect his increasing desire to settle down.

Tired of London pieds-à-terre, no matter how lavish, he decided the time had come to move to the country, and to buy a house with a garden; somewhere that would be more than a stopping-off place between locations. Finally, in 1971, he found exactly what he was looking for in The Mill House, a 240-year-old converted mill in the village of Clewer near Windsor, Berkshire. Best of all, it had the Thames running close by, the river Caine would later call his 'umbilical cord', linking his old world in the East End with his new world in Berkshire.

Not very long after he bought The Mill House, Caine met the woman who would become his second wife. Shakira Baksh was a former Miss Guyana who had won third place in the 1967 Miss World contest. In the early seventies Shakira, then a model, appeared in a commercial for Maxwell House coffee, set in Brazil. As soon as Caine saw the coffee girl he was intrigued, but assumed she was Brazilian and ensconced in Rio de Janeiro. One night he mentioned the sultry beauty to a friend, who informed him that, far from being on Copacabana beach, Shakira shared a flat with some other girls in the Fulham Road. Caine phoned her and within days they were an item in the gossip columns. Soon, they began living together, and within three years they were married.

After years of staying determinedly unattached, Michael Caine had finally met his match.

Imperceptibly, but permanently, Caine's life changed. Having attended his fair share of parties over the years, he now developed an enthusiasm for staying in. He became a keen cook, and cultivated an extensive knowledge of wine. He also developed a passion for gardening.

On matters horticultural, Caine got sound advice from a somewhat surprising quarter—Lord Olivier. The co-star of one of Caine's most important films, *Sleuth*, Laurence Olivier was an experienced gardener and would send Caine choice examples of flowers and trees, among them a flowering cherry; and later an orchid plant on the birth of his daughter Natasha.

By the time he made *Sleuth*, in 1972, Caine's life had become very different from the ritzy existence just a year or so before, when he was making *Zee and Co*. Of that time he says: 'I went up to fifteen and a half stone and was getting through up to two bottles of vodka a day. We were all like madmen. What surprised me was the swiftness with which I snapped out of it after meeting Shakira.'

After *The Italian Job*, Caine's next role was in *Battle of Britain*. A project of Harry Saltzman's, it was to be a meticulous re-creation of the events of 1940, when the Luftwaffe constantly attacked British airfields in an attempt to clear the path for a German invasion.

Initially there were problems over the funding of the film. Rank were the original backers, but pre-production was slow and costly. Just as Harry Saltzman joined the wartime Polish air veteran Benjamin Fisz as co-producer in September 1966, Rank pulled out. Paramount Pictures were briefly interested but, according to Saltzman, they wanted the film to tell the story of how the Americans won the Battle of Britain. Paramount denied this, but, whatever the case, United Artists finally stepped in to fund the project. By late 1968 they were ready to start making the film.

The British stars who accepted roles, among them Laurence Olivier, Trevor Howard and Ralph Richardson, agreed to accept far less than their usual fees to keep the film an all-British production. Said Saltzman at the time: 'The film would have cost us fifty per cent more if these stars had demanded their normal fees. But they felt this was an important story that should be told—and they agreed to do it at a fraction of their normal pay.'

Caine happily joined them, agreeing that an accurate recreation of such a historic story was important, and because 'we didn't want a couple of actors winning the Battle of Britain the way Errol Flynn won Burma'. He played Squadron Leader

Canfield, an air ace who is shot down and killed while defending a British airfield.

Great care went into the re-enactment of the airborne battle scenes that were at the heart of the film. Group Captain Hamish Mahaddie, a veteran of the original campaign, was responsible for finding and acquiring the planes, among them the only remaining Spitfire to have fought in the original conflict. A team of ex-service fitters travelled from as far afield as Poland to reassemble the planes and restore them to their former glory.

Among the advisers to the film were many of those involved as pilots and command in 1940, including Sqn Ldr Ginger Lacey and Wing Cdr Robert Stanford Tuck. To Ginger Lacey, Caine voiced his fear that, at thirty-six, he was too young to be playing a squadron leader. Lacey assured him that he was actually too old—in the war he'd have been flying at nineteen and a Squadron Leader at twenty-four; if not, there was either something badly wrong with his flying or he'd have been dead.

Caine was also given some tips on making manoeuvring of the Spitfire look as realistic as possible. 'Ginger Lacey told me to taxi the Spitfire as if I was going to take off,' he remembers. 'Then he said, "Put the brake on and it will stop."

'It's very very cramped in a Spitfire cockpit. Just as we were ready to go, Ginger said, "By the way, keep that knee in."

'I said, "Why?" He said, "Because if you hit that red lever there you could take off." I thought, "Bloody hell!"

'Bob Shaw went so fast in his Spitfire, he put it on its nose.'

Group Captain Brian Kingcome, also an adviser

on the film, told Caine how he had been accidentally shot down by another Spitfire over Maidstone. At the time he was in the habit of wearing a German Mae West because they were more comfortable than the British issue. As he drifted down from the skies he began to worry as he saw a crowd gathering below. 'Shot down by a Spitfire and punched up by the populace!' remarked Caine, amused by the story.

Representing the Germans as adviser was General Adolf Galland who, at the time of the Battle, was reputedly the youngest general in Europe since Napoleon. 'With my background of growing up in the war, it was very odd to watch Harry Saltzman, the Hollywood producer, and Adolf Galland, a genuine German fighter pilot who was advising on the film, having a screaming match over who won the Battle of Britain,' says Caine.

Air Chief Marshal Lord Dowding also visited the set and watched Laurence Olivier at work portraying him.

Duxford airfield in Cambridge was used for many of the ground scenes and the town of San Sebastiane in northern Spain doubled for Berlin. But a location was needed in which to re-create the bombing of London. As it happened, the Bermondsey streets around Caine's childhood home near the Old Kent Road were due to be knocked down for development, and the authorities agreed to let the film-makers in. Those houses that had suffered so badly during the war, when Caine was a seven-year-old evacuee, faced the onslaught again for the film.

Residents in the surrounding area awoke in the middle of the night to the flashing of searchlights and the unmistakable sound of bombs falling. Some even thought they were in the midst of the blitz once again, among them a Mrs Ivy Pain who complained to the *Daily Mirror*: 'It was a bit much at one in the morning. Surely it could have been done at some other time?'

When the film was released in 1969 it was generally praised as a faithful and authentic depiction of a crucial episode in British history. 'The authors, like the actors, have wisely realized that in this film the planes are the thing, and a beautiful thing they are as they weave through the sky with all the precision of Tiller girls and all the grace of a grim ballet,' wrote Cecil Wilson in the *Daily Mail*, continuing, 'When you see what a price they paid for their valour you wonder how we ever survived. But somehow we did and there could be no prouder homage to that survival than *Battle of Britain*.'

However, some critics felt that the characterization had suffered at the expense of attention to detail, like John Russell Taylor in *The Times*.

Take any five minute of dog-fights over the Channel and the film looks marvellous ... But five minutes is long enough: one plane going down in flames is very much like another, the people inside the planes are unrecognizable behind their masks, and though possibly to the expert eye the pilots perform prodigies of daring, to the uninitiated it all looks much the same ... Meanwhile, on the ground, an impressive assemblage of stars appear and disappear. But that is about all they are given a chance to do. In the cause of discretion, good taste and all that plot, mere human interest is kept to an absolute minimum.

Time magazine wryly commented:

> Once they are airborne and covered with goggles and oxygen masks, it is impossible to distinguish between any of the actors. A possible solution for future projects: the flight helmets should have the names of the performers, rather than their characters stencilled across them. One could then immediately tell the difference between Caine, M; Plummer, C; and Shaw, R.

Although they had fought on opposite sides during the war, Wing Commander Robert Stanford Tuck and Adolf Galland had since become firm friends. 'After filming,' says Michael Caine, 'Stanford Tuck told me he was going on holiday. So I asked him where he was going and he said, "I'm going to Hungary. There's lots of shooting there; we shoot deer and everything." I asked him why on earth he wanted to kill animals—I haven't shot anything since I was a soldier—and he said, "Well, Adolf and I are going together—we're best friends."

'I said, "What, even after the war?"

'He said, "Yes. We're two old killers—no one understands us. We understand each other, and we're going off to Hungary to kill everything in sight." And that's what they did!'

*   *   *

War films have liberally peppered Michael Caine's

career, right from his first ever film appearance as a cockney private in *A Hill in Korea* in 1956. On that occasion he had made a fleeting appearance and delivered just four lines of dialogue. Now, thirteen years later, he was to play a cockney private again, but this time he would rarely be off the screen.

The film was *Too Late the Hero*. Harry Andrews, who had played the sergeant in *A Hill in Korea*, was also in the cast, now playing a colonel, and joining him were Denholm Elliott, Lance Percival, Ian Bannen and Ronald Fraser.

They played a disparate group of British soldiers stationed on a small island in the South Pacific during the Second World War. The British occupy one end of the island, the Japanese the other, and between them is an area of no man's land. The soldiers are sick of war, bored and cynical, and none too pleased when they find out they are being sent on a mission to blow up the Japanese radio transmitter. Co-opted to join them is Lieutenant Lawson (Cliff Robertson), a Japanese-speaking American, who shares their dedication to the art of self-preservation.

The leader of the mission is Captain Hornsby (Denholm Elliott), a nervy soldier with no natural charisma, who has difficulty in motivating his reluctant troops. His disastrous tactics during an ambush by the Japanese result in several of his men being shot by each other. A particular thorn in his side is Private Tosh Hearne (Caine), a cockney with a quick line in wisecracks, a well-developed cynicism and very little respect for his leader. When, after a mine explodes, Hornsby asks, 'Where the hell is Rogers?', Hearne surveys Rogers' landmined remains and quickly retorts, 'You might

159

say he's all around here—as a matter of fact you might even say he's got us surrounded!'

However, Captain Hornsby eventually demonstrates his bravery and is killed while blowing up the transmitter. As they make their way back to the camp, the survivors come across a secret Japanese air base. Pursued through the jungle by the Japanese, they are offered fair treatment if they give themselves up. While Lawson and Hearne are asleep the others do so, but Lawson is determined to return to the camp and report their findings, in part motivated by the guilt he feels at not having helped Hornsby destroy the transmitter.

Finally they reach the no man's land and make their bid for home. Only one of them survives.

Too Late the Hero was directed by Robert Aldrich, who had made *The Dirty Dozen* a couple of years before. The presence of Cliff Robertson was designed to make the film a success in America, but unfortunately the Americans didn't take the bait; despite the fact that Robertson had just won an Oscar for his role in *Charly*.

The location shoot was the longest that Caine would experience in his career, and conditions were less than ideal. 'Filming in the Philippine jungle for *Too Late the Hero* was twenty-four weeks of absolute purgatory,' he declared later. 'The temperature was 120 degrees Fahrenheit and very muggy. There wasn't even anywhere nice to stay. There was this brothel being built and they ran out of money after completing only two floors. They let us take those two floors so we all had a brothel room each. Now, if you live in a place for twenty-four weeks you need plenty of room to move about in. But in a brothel the rooms are designed to spend about an hour in!

'And as we paid our weekly fee for living there they gave it to the builders, who came back and started building another two floors. All in all, that really was the worst location.'

Lance Percival too has vivid recollections of the Philippines. 'It was still the time of the Vietnam war and Subic Bay was the biggest American naval base in the Far East,' he says. 'When we came over that hill there were more ships in that bay than in the entire British navy.

'Olongapo was like a pimple on Subic Bay. Out of 15,000 inhabitants, 12,000 were prostitutes there for the American naval base. It was a very dangerous place and we stayed away.'

However, the naval base would finally prove their salvation. Decent food was in short supply until the group found a way of getting a good meal. 'We formed ourselves into the Olongapo patrol under the captaincy of Michael,' recalls Lance Percival. 'Being the star, he had a car and he would be invited out to various houses on the American base for drinks and dinner.

'He would only accept if he could bring the Olongapo patrol with him—me, Ronnie Fraser and his gofer. If Michael got any invites, the idea was that we went *en bloc*. We went round to people's houses for a good square meal. The American wives were doing their best to entertain film star Michael Caine and getting us three into the bargain. They were very good about it, though.

'By the end, the film company were flying tinned food in for us from Los Angeles. It would have been fatal for the film if we'd fallen ill. It was the Olongapo patrol that saved us.'

161

As well as the problems with food there was also the oppressive heat to deal with. 'The first day they put sticky stuff on us to make us look sweaty,' says Lance Percival. 'After half an hour we didn't need it, though—we were sweating pretty naturally. At least, we all had a shower in our rooms . . . intended for another purpose later.

'We only had two make-up guys and at 7 am you would see a stretch of jungle with a lot of actors in army gear putting on eye make-up!'

Despite the agonies that had gone into making it, the film did not generate any particular excitement among the critics. In *The Times* Trevor Grove wrote:

Robert Aldrich's *Too Late the Hero* is a war film with a vengeance, which is to say that anyone rash enough to put on a uniform, British or Japanese, and come within twenty yards of Aldrich's cameraman can enjoy a life expectancy of a further five minutes before being blown, spectacularly, into a thousand tiny pieces . . . I will not deny that *Too Late the Hero* generates a deal of excitement in the course of its 144 excruciatingly noisy, action-packed minutes, but it is strong meat and pretty fly blown at that.

But there was enthusiastic praise of Caine in the *Sun*, where the reviewer declared 'What takes this picture out of the ordinary is the true to life, yet larger than life, acting of all concerned. And this film does prove that Michael Caine is one of the top screen actors in the world.'

Time magazine, on the other hand, warned that:

Caine, an extraordinarily good performer [has] an apparent weakness for taking any role that comes along. Despite his mighty skills both as a dramatic actor and comedian (*Alfie*, *The Magus*, *Gambit*), his talent is in danger of being blunted by too many appearances in too many hapless exercises like *Too Late the Hero*.

The final word on the whole experience goes to Caine: 'I spent twenty-six weeks in the Philippine jungle. When we got back [we realized] we could have shot it in the tropical garden at Kew, because it was just all of us looking out from behind a load of palm leaves.' Caine clearly did not relish the experience; perhaps it was just too close to home and brought back ghosts of Korea that he'd rather forget.

★   ★   ★

Caine's next role was far less demanding. *Simon Simon* was a thirty-minute mimed comedy about a couple of incompetent Council workers who, having wrecked their hydraulic platform truck, use the new one to save animals, battle a fire-engine, and catch a thief. It was written and directed by Graham Stark, who had played Julia Foster's dull bus-conductor boyfriend in *Alfie*. Julia Foster also appeared.

Caine's appearance, a favour to Stark, was not so much a cameo as a lightning flash. He appeared in the film for just 10 seconds, playing himself and seated in his Rolls-Royce.

★   ★   ★

The Last Valley remains a mystery to Michael Caine. He regards it as one of his finest performances and yet the film made hardly any impact.

Set in 1641 during the Thirty Years War in Europe, *The Last Valley* starred Caine as the captain of a group of mercenaries who come upon a virtual Shangri-La in Austria, a quiet valley which the war seems to have left untouched. Rather than ravage the inhabitants and plunder the valley, the mercenaries are persuaded by a scholarly Omar Sharif to winter there instead.

A warm respect grows between Vogel (Sharif) and the Captain (Caine), until news of the approaching enemy drags the Captain reluctantly back into the war. Eventually he returns to the valley, mortally wounded, from a siege in which he has lost almost all his men. As he dies he whispers to Vogel, 'If you ever find God tell Him we created ...' the implication being Paradise, not because life in the valley was perfect but because it had held wars, both public and private, in abeyance for a while.

Producer, director and screenwriter was James Clavell, who had already written the successful novel of life in a Japanese POW camp, *King Rat*, and would later go on to write historical novels like *Shogun* and *Tai-pan*. His *Last Valley* is a mixture of thought and action, covering subjects as diverse as religious bigotry, idealism, and pragmatism, as the soldier and the scholar begin to see each other's outlook on life.

Also in the cast was Nigel Davenport who had last worked with Caine two years before, in 1968, on *Play Dirty*. Each night, after the day's shooting was finished, Caine, Sharif and Davenport would go out to dinner together. 'The Austrian restaurants always had a rather elegant string quartet,' recalls Davenport, 'and every time we walked in with Omar Sharif they would stop whatever they were playing and strike up the famous theme tune from *Dr Zhivago*, which had come out about two years before.

'One night we went to a restaurant and the usual procedure took place. We sat down and suddenly a lot of thickset Austrians headed for us waving menus. They were only interested in Omar and they were very rude, pushing everyone else out of the way.

'Michael and I retired to one side and Michael looked at me and said pensively, "Do you know, Nigel, I'm beginning to think I'm not a bleedin' film star at all."'

Reviews of *The Last Valley* were mixed. In the *Sunday Times* Dilys Powell wrote:

What at the start looks like a moral duel between the scholar and the man of war turns into a rationàl alliance; the captain recognizes the virtues of peace, though he does not embrace them. And this brings me to the contribution of the film—the rediscovery of Michael Caine. I have long admired his portraits of the callous, the savage, the insolent; I had begun to think he could not extend far beyond them. *The Last Valley* shows us a player of cool, measuring authority, formidable in reflection and in decision. The part is decently written. Mr Caine makes it seem excellently written.

165

But in the *Financial Times*, David Robinson commented:

> Short bursts of action, effectively staged in the tiny arena of the mountain village, come as a relief from talk which might, given a ruthless editorial purgation, have been coherent and persuasive, the sort of parable for our times which Mr Clavell quite clearly intended. The scholar is played rather well and modestly by Omar Sharif: but Michael Caine (as the Captain) has adopted a disconcerting new acting technique of uttering words in arbitrary groups of two or three regardless of syntactical point.

Despite the lukewarm reception, the film did impress some of those in the film world, winning Caine the accolade of Best Actor of 1970 from the magazine *Films and Filming*.

'I think it's one of my best performances, and it was a wonderful picture. I've made some films that failed because they were rubbish, but I'll never understand the failure of this film.' Michael Caine does, however, have a theory as to why the film failed, going on to say, 'I wanted to play this irreligious mercenary because of the things he said about people who were fighting each other for religious reasons, which were valid then and even more so today. I think up until the time I made that film I had a very lightweight image, and I guess the people who wanted to see me didn't want to see me playing a sixteenth-century German.'

* * *

The difficulty in accepting Michael Caine as a sixteenth-century German in *The Last Valley* may have been partly due to the timing of the film's UK release, in April 1971. Just five weeks earlier Caine's latest and most controversial movie, *Get Carter*, had hit the screens.

Jack Carter was a very different character—a new type of hero, a man who used violence mercilessly whenever he felt it was needed, abiding only by his own unconventional moral code. Unlike the heroes of the sixties—men like James Bond and Harry Palmer—Carter would not dream of drinking a Martini and would never enter a kitchen of his own free will, let alone attempt to cook. In short, Carter was a hard man, a seventies character who owed more to the Kray Twins than to Philip Marlowe for his inspiration. Men like Carter paved the way for the heroes who came later, like Clint Eastwood's Dirty Harry; men who dispensed their justice without remorse.

Made in the autumn of 1970, the film was set in Newcastle, where Jack Carter returns to investigate the mysterious death of his brother. As he unravels the catalogue of underworld violence and exploitation, he sets about disposing of those who have been involved.

The producer was Michael Klinger, an experienced deal-maker whose last film had been *Cul de Sac* with Roman Polanski. In the early seventies he was offered the galleys of a book called *Jack's Return Home* by a first-time author called Ted Lewis. 'Immediately I could see there was a film there,' recalled Klinger. 'I had also just seen the work of a young TV director called Mike

167

Hodges who had made a TV film called *Suspect*. Then a friend of mine, Robert Litman, was made Head of European Production for MGM and he asked me if I had anything I wanted to get made. I told him about *Jack's Return Home* and he said, "We'll do it."'

Klinger hardly knew Caine at the time (although Caine had collected a prize on behalf of Klinger and Polanski at a film festival in Acapulco) but he could immediately see him in the part of Jack and approached Caine's agent, Dennis Selinger. 'Dennis asked, "Who's directing?"' said Klinger, 'and I began to explain about this new young director and told him that Hodges' second TV film *Rumour* had gone out the night before.

'"He did that?" said Dennis. "Michael and I saw that. If that guy's directing I'm sure Michael will want to do it." And so the whole thing came together, hey presto. Sometimes it can take years.'

Selinger's instincts were, as usual, correct. As Caine himself said at the time, 'Carter is a subtle combination of private eye and ruthless gangster. It's the strongest, most fascinating character I've played since Alfie.'

Caine found a role-model for the character of Carter: 'I modelled him on an actual hard case. I watched everything he did and once saw him put someone in hospital for eighteen months. These guys are very polite but they act right out of the blue. They're not conversationalists about violence, they're perfectionists.'

The author of the book, Ted Lewis, came from Scunthorpe and had written it with his home town faintly in mind. But when Klinger and Hodges saw the town they felt it lacked the strong identity they

168

needed.

Hodges had done his National Service in the Navy, and began to think back to the places around the coast he had seen on the minesweepers. One place which had made a strong impact on him was North Shields. 'It was visually extraordinary with a physically strong, separate quality,' he says.

Once he had decided on Newcastle, Hodges began to investigate actual stories that had taken place there. 'I remember there was a night club, appropriately called La Dolce Vita, where there had been a murder,' he says, 'and someone told me about a character very similar to Jack Carter who had been sent up there to get rid of the man.

And the house we filmed in had belonged to a man who had lined his fruit machines with false bottoms, and then disappeared. It was very spooky; no one wanted to buy it, and so we were able to use it.'

Also appearing in the film was Ian Hendry, and producer Michael Klinger soon foresaw a potential problem: 'At the end of the film Michael has a very heavy confrontation with the Ian Hendry character. Hendry was a fine actor but he had a bad drinking habit. Michael had made *Alfie* and Ian had made a film called *Live Now Pay Later* which had been quite successful, but nowhere near an *Alfie*.

'The night before shooting began we all arrived in Newcastle and were having a drink together. Ian very quickly drank too much and it became apparent that he really hated Michael because he was such a big success. It was a smouldering situation and I thought, "How am I going to handle this? We haven't even begun shooting yet."

'Michael said to me, "Don't worry, he hates me

169

and that's good, I'm going to make this work for the film." He really did, that edge between them comes over very well.'

Get Carter caused great controversy when it opened. Some critics felt the use of violence was gratuitous while others praised the film for showing villains in a realistic light. 'At any time this would be a revolting, bestial, horribly violent piece of cinema,' wrote Felix Barker in the *Evening News*, adding 'It is all the worse for being given a quasi-realistic setting and because Caine (who should really know better than to stoop to this sort of thing) is a horribly effective smiling killer.' Whereas Ian Christie in the *Daily Express* declared:

> The result is a tremendously exciting thriller that gives Michael Caine the best part he has had in years. He carries off his role as the super-tearaway with great style and considerable humour, plunging knives into people, punching others about their person and blowing holes into more of his enemies. Carter you will gather is not a nice person to know ... It is a cruel, vicious film, even allowing for its moments of humour but completely compelling nevertheless.
>
> I'd get Carter if I were you. He certainly got me.

Alexander Walker says of the film: '*Get Carter* showed a side of Michael which I found very interesting. There was a British trend in criminal films showing that anything Hollywood could do, Britain could do more violently. Michael played the hard man in *Get Carter* and showed he's not a man you should mess with—a bit like Sean Connery in

170

that respect. You can't imagine Roger Moore being attracted to a real knuckle-duster match, but Michael you can. He was brutal, and suddenly I saw a side of him I wouldn't like to meet as a critic.'

The film had given Caine his first sight of Newcastle and it had made quite an impression. Ian La Frenais, a friend who would later involve Caine in the comedy film *Water*, bumped into him in a disco back in London some time later. 'He said, "I've just been up to your neck of the woods,"' recalls La Frenais. '"Do you know," he said, "I've always gone on about this working-class image I've got and so on; but now I've been to Newcastle I realize I'm middle class."'

The unit had filmed in a slum area 'and wherever we went there were thousands of kids following us around, little snotty-nosed kids,' recalled Michael Klinger. 'One day we were shooting in one place and of course lots of these kids came rushing up for autographs holding scrappy bits of paper, toilet paper and all sorts.

'One eight or nine-year-old came up clutching his piece of toilet paper, which Michael duly signed.

'"What does it say?" said the kid.

'"Michael Caine," replied Michael.

'"Never heard of ya," said the kid, and ripped it up.'

No wonder Caine remembered Newcastle so vividly.

★   ★   ★

After the gritty realism of Newcastle, Caine returned to London and a rather more glamorous assignment. *Zee and Co* was the story of an eternal triangle, with Elizabeth Taylor cast as the central character of Zee. Caine was to play her husband Robert, and Susannah York his mistress, Stella.

As with most feature films the actors who finally took the roles were not necessarily those who had initially been envisaged in them. Elizabeth Taylor had agreed to play the wife at an early stage after reading Edna O'Brien's screenplay, but the character of Robert Blakely had been offered to Peter O'Toole before it went to Caine. The first choice for the part of the mistress had been Anouk Aimée; but as one of the producers had once been her agent and they had not parted on the best of terms, that plan was abandoned. Next the role was offered to Faye Dunaway who was too busy and then to Lee Remick who agreed to play the role but then backed out. Romy Schneider was also considered before Susannah York was finally signed up to play Stella.

York, who had first seen Caine in his TV *Hamlet* and who had also appeared in *The Battle of Britain* but had had no scenes with Caine, was pleased to be working with him. 'Michael has technique to a superlative degree, like Gary Cooper,' she says. 'He managed to achieve a total oneness with everything around him, with the furniture, everything. He seems to look totally at ease.'

Elizabeth Taylor and Richard Burton were together at the time of *Zee and Co* and the on-set joke was that if the Burtons' huge retinue alone went to see the movie it would be enough to ensure box office success. Caine perfected an impeccable imitation of Richard Burton, although, perhaps surprisingly, the two actors never became close friends.

172

As always with the Burtons the fictionalized image of showbiz life and the reality seemed entwined. One weekend Caine flew to New York with them to see the Clay-Frazier boxing match. Later, after he had met Shakira, they both attended Elizabeth's fortieth birthday party in Budapest.

However before shooting began in January 1971 both Caine and Taylor had been apprehensive. Caine later explained: 'When we began this film both Elizabeth and I were nervous of each other, and it was difficult because we had to go right into fights and love scenes rolling round the bed and we never even knew each other.

'But after the first couple of days we admitted that we were nervous and I gave her a bit of a hug—you know, not being familiar, but just to make human contact and we were fine after that.'

Caine felt that the tremendous publicity constantly surrounding Elizabeth Taylor provided a lesson to him and all other actors. 'The thing to do is to get less publicity,' he says, 'and then people will take you for what you are when you come on. I went to see *Zee and Co* afterwards and for the first ten minutes when Elizabeth Taylor came on everybody was going, "Oh, she looks good doesn't she? I think she's lost some weight ... has she got the ring on? Look she's got the ring on!" And she's an expert actress playing this character but they were all thinking about something they read in *Woman's Own* all the time. Publicity can hurt in that way.'

Caine also had to defend himself against the constant furore surrounding Taylor. On American TV critic Rex Reed apparently said to him, 'I can't stand the thought of our Elizabeth Taylor being in love with you in *Zee and Co*. You look like soggy oatmeal.'

'Well, that's better than looking like sugar-coated cornflakes,' retorted Caine.

Robert and Zee are a well-off couple, he a successful architect and she something of a social dilettante. Their marriage appears to work, even though it is built on a foundation of verbal sparring and game playing. Neither, it seems, has seen fidelity as of paramount importance in the past, but no fling seems to have become serious enough to intrude significantly into their private relationship.

Then at a party Robert meets Stella, a woman who is the complete opposite of Zee. Stella is controlled where Zee is extreme, discreet where Zee is flamboyant, and Robert is attracted by the contrast. Stella is also a widow with two young sons whereas Zee and Robert's marriage is childless.

At first Zee seems to take a masochistic delight in Robert and Stella's affair. She teases him with it and is triumphant when she manages to invade one of their trysts. But after Robert declares he is going to leave her, Zee changes. She becomes desperate and attempts suicide.

While in hospital she asks Stella to visit her. Apprehensive at the prospect, Stella is deeply relieved when Zee is gentle and friendly and the two begin to confide in each other. Stella tells Zee that she was expelled from her convent for falling in love with a nun.

Unwittingly, Stella has given Zee her weapon. A few days later Zee arrives at Robert and Stella's new home while Robert is out. Robert returns to find Stella in bed, having been seduced by Zee.

The director of the film was Brian Hutton, who

had also directed *Where Eagles Dare* and *Kelly's Heroes*. Edna O'Brien was furious at the treatment her screenplay received, as Hutton added and took away scenes at will. In the original script there had been no hint of an affair between Stella and Zee, which was added later.

Susannah York was not disappointed in her expectations of Caine as a co-star. 'Michael is thoroughly professional, and very open and easy about the way you work too,' she says. 'He is always very supportive and never betrays any temperament. He is a thoroughly nice guy and always very popular with the crew. Roger Moore is someone else who's like that. Michael has absolutely the right touch; there is no side with him, never a hint of any kind of snobbery, inverted or otherwise.'

When *Zee and Co* opened in January 1972 the critics agreed that Elizabeth Taylor dominated the film but that Caine and York had held their own. Margaret Hinxman in the *Sunday Telegraph* wrote

If I have made it sound a little loony, well it is ... But that said, it is still a rich slice of bravura entertainment. Brian G Hutton directs with a discretion that is entirely proper. No need after all to embellish Elizabeth Taylor's gorgeously garish performance as Zee; Susannah York's correct underplaying of the girl in the middle and, above all, Michael Caine's subtly intelligent portrayal of that desperately unstuck character, the man at the mercy of the woman who loves him not wisely but too well.

And in the *New Yorker*, Pauline Kael wrote, 'One

can take pleasure in Taylor's brute triumph especially since she's working with two of the best screen performers of our time. (Michael Caine does all he can with a role that requires him to be mostly exasperated, infuriated and exhausted.)'

But *Zee and Co* was definitely a child of its time, and Caine has his own view as to why it now appears dated: '*Zee and Co* is underrated because the period, the early seventies, went right out of fashion, even more than the sixties,' he told *Time Out* in 1988.

★   ★   ★

Director Delbert Mann had already adapted two classic novels for the cinema, *Jane Eyre* and *David Copperfield*. Now he turned his attention to Robert Louis Stevenson's much-loved books, *Kidnapped*, and *Catriona*, and decided to combine them into one film. Originally the production was intended for US television and cinema release in Britain, though in the event it also appeared in US cinemas.

The summer of 1971 saw Caine playing the Scottish rebel Alan Breck, trying to escape from Scotland (where he is a wanted man) and reach France. Lawrence Douglas, a new young Scottish actor, played David Balfour, and Vivien Heilbron, Catriona.

It was an unusual role for Caine and he had a very particular reason for accepting it. 'I made *Kidnapped* solely for my daughter [Dominique was then fourteen]. She has never been able to see my movies because they've all been rated as not suitable for children. At last I have one rated OK for her.'

Caine found himself enjoying the variety, and a

beautiful Scottish summer. On one occasion they were filming in the grounds of a stately home when the old gardener came up and asked what they were doing. 'We're filming *Kidnapped*,' replied Caine. 'Well, you can't film up there,' he said. 'Who are you playing?'

'Alan Breck,' said Caine.

'Well, you can't film there,' repeated the old man.

'Oh yeah?' said Caine, 'there's the Assistant who's got the permit.'

'Never mind about the permit,' said the gardener, 'you still can't film there.'

'We can film anywhere we like!' said Caine.

'You cannot film there.'

'Why not?'

'Because you've got Alan Breck standing in front of the rhododendrons,' the gardener retorted, 'and they never came out until a hundred years after he was dead.'

For Caine, filming the hale and hearty outdoor life was something new, and Lawrence Douglas remembers him occasionally yearning for 'a film set with white plastic telephones and settees'.

Half-way through shooting, though, the production ran out of money. After a struggle the picture was finally finished, but the experience tainted the film for Caine. After keeping such a close and watchful eye on his own financial affairs he was more than irritated when others couldn't do likewise.

Caine looked good in the part but his southern English accent collided on more than one occasion with his otherwise valiant attempt at the lowland Scots. 'I offered to help him with his Scottish

177

accent,' recalls Lawrence Douglas, 'but he said that only about two per cent of the market was Scots so it didn't matter too much!'

Caine's own verdict on the subject of accents: "All you have to do is put two million dollars up front and I'll do any accent you want.'

Delbert Mann had taken severe liberties with plot and time-scale in combining the two novels, but nevertheless the end result seemed to attract gentle approval from the critics. 'Where other actors might settle for a swashbuckling impersonation, Michael Caine's Alan Breck is a genuine characterization: reckless, warm-hearted, insufferably proud, a born rebel with no talent for peace,' wrote Margaret Hinxman, in the *Sunday Telegraph*.

And the *Guardian* added:

Michael Caine plays Alan Breck, the Highland hero, with a certain amount of presence but some trouble with his consonants (loch is pronounced lock throughout). Otherwise it is all pleasant scenery, cameos (Trevor Howard, Donald Pleasence, Jack Hawkins and Freddie Jones) and very basic story-telling. Perhaps the fact that everyone eats so much porridge renders the script so constipated.

After *Get Carter* the three Michaels involved in that film, Klinger, Caine and Hodges, formed their own company. They called it 3M. Not long afterwards they received a letter from the giant 3M Corporation inviting them to change the name forthwith. Not wishing to face a giant legal suit, they quickly complied.

In *Pulp*, their second collaboration, Caine played a former funeral director, Mickey King, now enjoying a new career as a writer of pulp fiction and living in the Mediterranean.

King is invited to ghost-write the memoirs of an actor called Preston Gilbert (Mickey Rooney), who in his heyday had been well known for gangster roles. Gradually King realizes that Preston Gilbert is mixed up with a real-life underworld, and after he is killed King finds himself caught up in a thriller of exactly the kind he churns out for his readers.

The film, a comedy thriller, was a very different proposition from *Get Carter*, and deliberately so. 'Before *Get Carter* came out I never had the chance to see it with an audience,' says director Mike Hodges. 'The first time I ever saw it on the big screen I was utterly stunned by the violence. Not that it should have been done any other way; up until then violence had always been rather romantic, but we had attempted to make it as realistic as possible. Until then people thought gangsters were rather nice people played by Michael Balfour. But I was still fairly stunned. The film was immensely successful and I realized that audiences wanted to see it. It made me want to make a film about why people want to go and see violence, and about the commercialization of violence. I wanted to make it funny, too. That's how *Pulp* came about.'

'When *Get Carter* came out it was acclaimed,' said producer Michael Klinger, 'and a man called David Picker, President of United Artists, said, "Jesus, I'd love to do a picture with you three guys." Hodges wrote the script, which he based on a true story that happened near Naples. I originally

179

wanted to call the film *Scandal* but I was overruled. It was a good title . . . as we know now.'

The film was shot on the island of Malta in the winter of 1971–2. 'We were filming in Malta at the time the British were being kicked out by Dom Mintoff,' Michael Klinger remembered. 'There were lots of stories in the paper about it, never true. We became very friendly with Mintoff, a tough little man who gave us a lot of help.

'One Sunday he invited us out to his country house for lunch. Well, Malta is like a postage stamp so it didn't take us long to get there. When we did it was a terrible little house, everything was broken, all the crockery was chipped and so on.

'It was December and freezing cold. "The PM is swimming," we were told and we were led over the headland to this little cove. There was Mintoff in the middle of five or six guys who were all treading water. Mintoff had a ball which he threw as hard as he could at them and then they gently lobbed it back to him.

'"Hello Michael," shouted Mintoff, "come in and have a swim." Michael, who is not the type to go in swimming most of the time, let alone in December, declined.'

On another occasion journalist Jack Bentley of the *Sunday Pictorial* (now the *Sunday Mirror*) called Michael Klinger in search of a story and asked how the cast and crew were spending their spare time. Klinger told him they were all off the next day to play football against a local team and he was welcome to cover that if he wanted. The match was not a great success: 'I was the referee,' said Klinger, 'Michael was the linesman and our secret weapon was Stanley Matthews who had gone to live on

Malta ... We still lost 6–0.'

Malta was another location Caine took a dislike to and made a mental note never to visit again. When an interviewer from the *Maltese Times* asked him what he liked most about Malta, Caine's reply was instant: 'The plane out.'

When the film opened it failed to achieve the commercial success of *Get Carter*. Says Klinger: 'Hodges finished the whole thing in mid-air. That's how it is in real life but not how you finish a movie. At the end people felt cheated, but the critics loved it.'

Time magazine's critic, Jay Cocks, wrote:

> Hodges has not only got his distance in *Pulp*, he has also found a style and voice of his own.
> He is constantly, ebulliently inventive, whether in the scrupulously outrageous dialogue ('I expected the place to be crawling with cops like maggots in a Camembert') or in one of the many dazzling visual jokes, like a group of Italian priests squirming through the humiliation of a police line-up ... Always an adept actor, Caine is splendid here. His King, quintessentially seedy, strikes just the proper note between calculated mediocrity and droll detachment.

Ian Christie in the *Daily Express* was more reserved, though:

> It tries too hard, for one thing. Michael Caine, plying his craft somewhere in the Mediterranean, has only to step into any vehicle for it to be involved in a crash. The humour of such

181

accidents soon palls ... The film is by no means a total disaster. The commentary by Michael Caine is often wryly funny, and there is a splendidly extravagant performance by Mickey Rooney as a retired film star in love with his image as a screen gangster. A pity that Mike Hodges ... didn't exercise more self-discipline.

Director Mike Hodges had put some subtle references to his last working collaboration with Caine into *Pulp*: 'In *Get Carter* there had been a scene where I'd said to him, "Right, just get into the car and drive off.' There had been a stunned silence and Johnny Morris, Michael's stuntman, took me aside and said, "Michael can't drive."

'"Can't drive?!" I said. "But he played Alfie—a chauffeur!"

'"Yes, but he was towed everywhere," said Johnny Morris.

'So when we made *Pulp* there's a scene where Michael is chased by a gunman. The guy he is with is gunned down, and his last words to Michael are, "Can you drive?"

'"No," says Michael, as the car kangaroos across the beach.'

★　　★　　★

Caine's next project was perhaps his most challenging to date. Any leading actor would have been flattered by an offer to star opposite Laurence Olivier, especially when the film involved just two major characters for almost all its length. At the same time, though, many would be daunted, and even terrified, at the prospect of exposing themselves so openly; fearing the critical annihilation that could follow if they failed to acquit themselves adequately.

Not Michael Caine. He looked at the problem and dismissed it with impeccable logic. 'With Olivier I can't lose,' he said before shooting started. 'If I am not as good as he is—and he is the best actor in the world—that won't be news, so no one will be surprised. If I do give him a run for his money—and I will—people will say, "Fancy Michael Caine being able to do that", so I'll come off well either way.'

In fact, Michael Caine had been one of Olivier's own suggestions for the role of Milo Tindle; others had included Alan Bates and Albert Finney. Availability had made the part Michael Caine's.

Anthony Shaffer had adapted his highly successful thriller for the screen, and the director was to be the Oscar-winning Joseph Mankiewicz, whose distinguished record had encompassed *All About Eve*, *Julius Caesar* and *Guys and Dolls*.

Milo Tindle is a hairdresser of London-Italian stock who is having an affair with Marguerite Wyke, the wife of famous novelist Andrew Wyke (Laurence Olivier). Wyke invites Tindle to his sumptuous country home, where he offers to do a deal with him; if Tindle would break into the house and steal Marguerite's jewellery it will give him a source of income with which to keep her in the lavish style to which she is very accustomed. Meanwhile Wyke will be able to claim the insurance money on the jewels.

But the plan is really a game which Wyke uses to humiliate Tindle, before shooting him.

In the second 'act' of this very theatrical film, a

183

policeman called Inspector Doppler arrives at Wyke's home. He claims to be investigating the disappearance of Milo Tindle who was last heard of visiting Wyke. Unnerved, Wyke explains that Tindle had fainted after a game in which he pretended to shoot him by firing blanks. After his recovery, Wyke tells the inspector, Tindle left the house.

But Doppler finds Milo's clothes in a cupboard, blood on the stairs, and newly dug earth in the garden. Wyke breaks down in terror, and Doppler rips off his disguise to reveal himself as Milo Tindle.

In the final act, Tindle convinces Wyke that he has murdered his mistress and left clues around Wyke's home to incriminate him. Wyke sets off to find the clues in the fifteen minutes Tindle sets him and completes the task just in time. Tindle then explains that the murder was a complete fabrication and, unable to face losing the game, Wyke shoots Tindle—just as the sound of a police car is heard outside.

The filming schedule was intensive and demanding. The two characters each had long and involved soliloquies and there was no other action to break up the intense exposure. As Caine put it, 'you can't cut to an Indian falling off a horse.'

But before shooting began, in April 1972, one thing was uppermost in Caine's mind: how was he to address Lord Olivier, whom he had never met? As the rehearsals approached Caine was still considering the problem when a letter arrived from Olivier. 'Dear Mr Caine,' it began, 'it suddenly occurred to me that you might be wondering how to address me as I have a title; well, I think we should introduce us by our own titles which would be Mr Caine and I would be Lord Olivier the first time we meet. Forever after that I hope it will be Larry and Michael.'

Caine's problem was solved.

With such a demanding schedule, Caine was completely exhausted at the end of each day. 'Remember it was just the three of us, Joe Mankiewicz, Olivier and me for sixteen weeks,' he told *Film Comment* in 1980. 'Only two of us in front of the camera, so we had to cover everything to make it interesting. We had to shoot it close up, long shot, eyes, nose, fingers; we shot everything around the room, pictures to cut to. There were no days off, because everybody was in every scene. It's all one set; it really was an extraordinarily difficult film to make.

'It was incredibly tiring. I'd have six-minute monologues at a time. I used to get home in the evening and say to Shakira, "I really can't talk now. I'm sick of the sound of my voice. I don't want to hear it again. You tell me everything but don't ask me any questions. Let me just sit here and listen."'

Scenes like the one where Milo Tindle believes Andrew Wyke is about to shoot him were emotionally draining too. 'You see actors on the screen about to be shot and they don't do anything,' says Caine. 'I thought, someone who's going to have his brains blown out must be in abject, snivelling terror. He'd do anything to stop them pulling that trigger. It's a difficult, humiliating thing to do, to burst into tears, plead, beg, sob, especially for someone like me, who's not at all like that. But I thought, if you do it half-heartedly, you embarrass the audience. Better to go right into it, and take the risk of overdoing it, because actually there's no way of overdoing it. People in certain situations will scream themselves to death.'

But there were some moments of relaxation too. Wimbledon took place during the filming—it was the year Evonne Goolagong won—and Caine had a television installed in his dressing room to keep up with the action. Olivier, whose own dressing room was completely bare but for his script and a few papers, was very taken with the idea—needless to say, Caine had cigars and refreshments on hand too—and soon took to joining Caine to watch a few sets between takes.

Caine had every respect for the way Joe Mankiewicz was directing his performance. 'Mankiewicz is bloody marvellous,' he said in an interview on set. 'He knows what you should want and he also knows when you've got it. He's one of those directors who says nothing if he likes it, but if he starts going on and starts to ask you questions, you know you haven't got it right.'

Finally, the film was finished and the day of the Royal Première approached. The Caines weren't keen on going. Shakira Caine was pregnant with their daughter Natasha at the time, and Caine felt that it should be Olivier's night as he had been doing all the publicity whilst Caine awaited the birth. It was Roger Moore who persuaded him to attend. 'I encouraged Michael to take me (this is before *Dressed to Kill* and *Deathtrap*, otherwise I might not have been so keen),' says Moore. 'It was a charity do and Princess Margaret was the Royal in attendance. She came over to Michael and said she was interested in his dialect—where exactly was it from? "Oh, Somerset," said Michael. Then, turning to Olivier, she asked, "And do you do dialects as well?"'

The critics agreed that Caine had managed to pull off the difficult task of giving Olivier a run for his money. In the *Guardian* Derek Malcolm wrote, 'It gives us a chance to confirm what some had already suspected—that Michael Caine can act a great deal better than his screenplays generally allow.'

And George Melly in the *Observer* agreed.

There is a great deal to relish. The main protagonists gave excellent performances, not only individually, but in relation to each other. Olivier, with his braying laugh and his self-indulgent rather empty delight in hedonistic correctitude, his veneration for the aristocracy and his contempt for any class below his own has Evelyn Waugh-like echoes. Caine's tight-arsed dandyism, his po-faced insecurity and sentimental exasperation at his Italian immigrant father's acceptance of the world is exactly judged.

There were some reservations, though. In *The Times* David Robinson commented, 'The pleasure lies in the skill with which it is done. The casting in itself is a clever trick, opposing the dexterity of Laurence Olivier to the much more stolid and limited personality playing of Michael Caine.'

Dilys Powell in the *Sunday Times* added:

Mr Caine, with the help of spectacular make-up, shows a range which one had not expected from this excellent player of layabouts and secret agents. There are one or two moments, though, when the role, no longer a parody, becomes

187

disagreeably stagey—the blubbing under threat, for instance, is surely out of character; and there one needs the kind of theatrical playing in which Mr Caine is not experienced.

Alexander Walker's view is that 'In *Sleuth* Michael was not only holding his own against the great actor, but doing a cinematic performance that is in some ways more skilful than Olivier's. Michael was the long-distance runner and Olivier the cameo.'

Both Caine and Olivier were nominated as Best Actor in the 1972 Oscars for their performances in *Sleuth*. Caine attended the ceremony and was disgusted when Marlon Brando won the award for his role in *The Godfather*, not because he had any doubts about Brando's talent, but because the actor hadn't bothered to collect the award himself, sending instead an Indian girl to make a political speech. Caine was appalled. 'He should have been there. Doesn't he owe that town *anything*?' he is reported as saying.

That issue aside, the film had been a crucial one for Caine. His logic had paid off, and the result had won him new admirers. He and Olivier had developed a warm relationship based on mutual respect in spite of their vastly different backgrounds, both personal and professional. Caine found himself advising Lord Olivier, though not strictly speaking, about acting: 'I remember we talked about money. I said, "Listen, you're out of the National now, so what do you get—about £150 a week?" I said, "You can't have any money; stay in movies and don't give a packet what they are, get some money together." And he did; I don't know whether it is my fault he made *The Betsy* or *The*

Seven-Per-Cent Solution ...

'He said, "Do you really think so? Do you think I should make pictures and earn a lot of money?" I said, "Of course you should. Go out and do it; they can't take your Lordship away from you." ...

'I planted the seed of avarice in him.'

At Lord Olivier's memorial service in 1989, Caine was one of the actors invited to join the procession through Westminster Abbey carrying mementoes of Olivier's career. Caine told *The Times*: 'He was a unique man and undeniably irreplaceable. I will always remember him as a very funny man and a very good friend.'

CHAPTER EIGHT

'LIMEY DUDE, OR THE NEW CARY GRANT?': 1972–1976

'When I open a script and it says, "Nome, Alaska. Our hero is walking in the blinding snow with a dog sled. It's December 25th", I close it again. Quickly.'

Michael Caine

Sleuth was a difficult act to follow. Between 1972 and 1976 Caine kept busy, but most of his films were makeweight titles, like *The Marseilles Contract*, *Peeper* and *Silver Bears*; films that in the main passed the audiences and critics by. Some, however, like *The Romantic Englishwoman* won him a modicum of critical attention; and one, *The Man Who Would Be King*, was destined to become a true classic, a film in a class of its own. But none he worked on came as close to British hearts and critical minds as had his performance with 'Larry' in *Sleuth*.

Domestically, though, the stage was set for a long-running and very successful performance. Since taking up with Shakira Baksh in 1971, Caine had settled very quickly into a new, more home-loving, life and when Shakira became pregnant he decided to marry her. After his first unhappy experience Caine now felt ready for the responsibility of marriage and parenthood again.

Any plans he had for his own future career had

now, of necessity, to take his new family into account. That he adapted admirably is in no doubt—his family, including his first daughter Dominique, is now the cornerstone of Michael Caine's life and more important to him than ever before.

Natasha Halima Micklewhite, Michael Caine's second daughter, was born on 15 July 1973. The name Karim had been decided upon if the baby turned out to be a boy—with half an eye as to how 'Karim Caine' might look, up in lights, in years to come. Now, of course, Michael Caine believes he can see Natasha following in his footsteps and becoming an actress. 'She used to come on set just to see what her dad was doing,' he says. 'Now I've noticed her watching the actresses instead, which is a sure sign. Natasha Caine's a good stage name—though I didn't think of that when I named her. Mind you, I didn't call her Doris or Doreen.'

Providing for his family encouraged Michael's business mind into diversifying his interests outside movies, although he was astute enough not to diversify too far. Obviously it made sense to be able to capitalize on his public profile; ownership of Burke's Club, for example, by Michael Caine, film star, certainly didn't stand in the way of it being the fashionable haunt of *other* famous film stars.

The wine trade, though, wasn't so susceptible to fame—when Caine attended the Hotel Exhibition in his capacity as partner to wine merchant Michael Druitt, he discovered that no one he shook hands with recognized him at all, including his Worship the Lord Mayor of London!

Business activities brought up the thorny subject of taxation, and Caine joked that for every movie he

191

made he had to make two more for the taxman. This was the period when Chancellor Denis Healey had sworn to soak the rich, and the top tax rate was hovering around 90 per cent. Pressure from his accountant forced Caine to think seriously about becoming a tax exile, although he spent several years protesting loudly he'd never go. 'I want to live in England and sod it I will stay here. But I can understand the people who do leave,' he told the *Daily Mirror* in January 1975.

In the end the decision to leave came for two reasons—Caine's worry that taxes and inflation together would wipe out his fortune by the time retirement came around, and the feeling that his career was getting nowhere in Britain anyway. He decided he needed to get right into the swim in Hollywood if he was ever going to make headway as a truly international star.

After his declarations that he wouldn't leave England under any circumstances, the press gave Caine a rough ride when he finally decided to go, quoting back at him statements he had made in previous years. At a time when many home-grown movie and music stars were deserting Britain for easier tax laws elsewhere, the whole subject had become a huge hornets' nest.

In September 1977, the Caine family finally announced their official departure for Beverly Hills. Leaving his beloved Mill House, where he had spent so much time up to the top of his wellies in mud, tending his rhubarb and roses, was a personal wrench for Caine, but the practical side of his nature overruled his feelings and determined the direction of his next career move, for good or ill.

Caine's US press agent Jerry Pam (by

coincidence, like Caine an ex-pupil of Hackney Downs Grocers' School) remembers the turning point: 'I was always encouraging him to come over, but I finally won the battle when Michael rang me about a script he adored. The film had in fact opened the week before, and Michael finally got the message that if he wanted the best roles he had to be on hand.'

★　　　★　　　★

Back in 1973, the possibilities in Britain weren't looking quite so bleak for Caine. American director Don Siegel was in England to make *The Black Windmill*, and Caine was eager to work with a director whose earlier credits had included *Riot in Cell Block Eleven*, *The Killers* and *Dirty Harry*.

The Black Windmill was a spy story in which Caine played Major John Tarrant, a Government agent in the department of subversive warfare who has a tendency to Harry Palmer-ish rebellion. The department uses an auction room for its cover, from where Tarrant and his boss Cedric Harper (Donald Pleasence as a twitchy creature forever fiddling with his moustache and holding paper tissues to his nose) operate.

In the midst of an attempt to infiltrate a gang of gun runners Tarrant learns from his estranged wife that their son has vanished. Shortly afterwards they begin to receive mysterious phone calls from someone calling themselves simply 'Drabble'. However, there seems to be more than one 'Drabble', as each time the caller has a different voice. 'Drabble' demands a ransom for the return of Tarrant's son—the diamonds which his boss has

193

recently purchased for another operation.

The story unfolds across locations in England and Paris, with Tarrant finally running the gang to ground at the black windmill of the title and exposing a mole in the Government.

Originally the film was to be called simply *Drabble*. The title was changed, but director Don Siegel had already had jackets made up for everyone with 'Drabble' emblazoned on the back. Many, including Donald Pleasence, Caine's co-star, felt 'Drabble' was a better title anyway. One day, Pleasence recalls, he was coming out of Harrods and about to get in a taxi when he heard someone behind him speak. 'A voice said to me, "Excuse me please, are you Drabble?" It was Michael.

'I turned around and said: "Yes. Are you Drabble?"

'"Yes I am," said Michael and we both got in the taxi, whereupon the taxi driver said, "No one ever bothers to ask my name"—thereby proving that he had no idea who either of us were!'

Also appearing in the film was one of Britain's favourite actors, Joss Ackland, who shared Caine's tendency to 'corpse'. 'We were about to start shooting a particularly sad scene when Michael and I got the giggles,' Ackland writes in his autobiography *I Must Be In There Somewhere*. 'So did the director Don Siegel, so he left the room. "Action," he yelled from afar and we played the scene. After a while from the next room came Don's voice, "Have they finished?" "Yes," called the first assistant. "Okay," boomed Don, "cut!"'

The critics felt the film lacked the usual Siegel tension and often seemed to be re-working the motifs of his earlier movie *Charley Varrick*. In the

194

Evening Standard, Alexander Walker, referring to the track records of producers and director, felt that 'all such talents succumbed to the English virus of dud script, type casting and general woolliness'.

Caine had his own theory as to why *The Black Windmill* didn't live up to its promise, as he said later: 'I think the gentility of England rubbed off on Don Siegel and he was out of his own atmosphere. It became too sentimental and convoluted and we didn't know it at the time but the spy thing was over then.'

*   *   *

Caine accepted his next role for one reason only—the location. Having served his time on the ice floes in *Billion Dollar Brain* and in the Philippine jungle for *Too Late the Hero* he had decided that in future he would rather not suffer for his art.

So when, in the middle of the freezing English winter of 1973–4, producer Judd Bernard called to ask him to take on a role in a picture to be shot in the South of France Caine didn't hesitate. 'I was offered a part which started in Nice, went on to Cannes, then St Tropez, Marseilles and ended up in Paris,' he remembers. 'They said, "Will you do it?" and I said, "Yes", so they said, "Right, we'll send you the script." I said, "Don't bother; I'll do it." I just enjoyed myself.'

The picture in question was called *The Marseilles Contract*, starring James Mason and Anthony Quinn; Quinn working with Caine again after *The Magus*. Caine's role was as an assassin hired by US Embassy official Steven Ventura (Quinn) to dispose of Mason. The film never came to very much but at least Caine had had an expenses-paid winter break.

The critics were not impressed. Tom Hutchinson wrote in the *Sunday Telegraph*:

The Marseilles Contract is a thriller that throws most of the current clichés—crashing cars, bouncing motorbikes, vigilante cops—into one uneasy story and comes up with not very much apart from ... the sad realization that Michael Caine and James Mason cannot walk away from the story-shambles with any credit.

The *Daily Mirror*'s Arthur Thirkell commented:

Michael Caine is paid a vast sum of money by Anthony Quinn to bump off James Mason in *The Marseilles Contract*. They are three good actors bogged down in a boring yarn of drug smuggling in France. The plot chases between Paris and Marseilles and allows Mr Caine to make love and shoot a few people.

But judging by his one expression, I'm not sure which he preferred.

Caine was quite happy to take the flak. He has one of his pieces of irrefutable Caine logic worked out for just such situations: 'I remember talking to Sheila Graham, the Hollywood columnist, and she said, "You people just coming up. What about Clark Gable, you know, the great movies that Clark Gable made." I said, "I happen to know that Clark Gable made 122 movies, name me ten," so she said, "Well, *Boomtown*, *It Happened One Night*, *Gone With the Wind*, er, er ..." and she got to about eight, and this is a person who *knows*. Just try it.

Ten Clark Gable movies.

'What happens is you wait until people die and then you say, "Christ, that wasn't bad, that wasn't bad", but in the meantime you've got to live; which is what I've done, obviously, to the hilt.'

★　　　★　　　★

Mid-1974 found Michael Caine, unusually for him, doing a film partly for political reasons. Directed by Ralph *Soldier Blue* Nelson, *The Wilby Conspiracy* was an anti-apartheid film and action yarn combined. Caine played Jim Keogh, a mining engineer whose defence lawyer girlfriend Rina (Prunella Gee) wins the acquittal of a black revolutionary leader. Almost as soon as they leave the court to celebrate, the revolutionary, Shack Twala (Sidney Poitier), is involved in a brawl over his identity pass and Keogh is persuaded by Rina to accompany Twala to Johannesburg where he has friends who will help him leave South Africa.

In hot pursuit is Major Horn of State Security (Nicol Williamson), hoping that Keogh and Twala will eventually lead him to the congress president, Wilby Zaba, encamped just beyond the South African border. Horn's plan follows its course as Twala collects a cache of diamonds from an Indian dentist, Mukerjee (Saeed Jaffrey), before heading for the border. When they finally arrive at the encampment they are surprised by the arrival of Horn who tells Shack, Keogh and Rina they are free, as he now has the person he really wanted, Wilby Zaba. Before Horn can leave, though, his helicopter is attacked by Twala and the villagers, his men are killed and after being persuaded to hand over Zaba, he is shot dead by Keogh.

Because of the issues involved, Kenya stood in for South Africa on location. Caine had become especially conscious of the issues of apartheid since his marriage to Shakira and was pleased to be involved in a film which would highlight the problem, although disappointed at the box office response. 'I thought it would be more of a success,' he said afterwards. 'What we did was a very serious theme in an entertainment framework in order that a lot of people would go and see it. What it actually proved to me was that the mass of people agree with apartheid because they didn't bother to see it. In fact, the film was quite good, but it fell between every stool you could possibly have. The general public couldn't care less about the black plight anyway, and the black Americans couldn't care less about apartheid because they're too worried about their own problems.'

Some critics were impressed, however. 'Michael Caine has never been better, carrying off his role with a sense of humour that never interferes with the seriousness of the escapade,' wrote Ian Christie of the *Daily Express*; 'I urge you to see it.'

David Robinson in *The Times* had some reservations, though:

This lusty and violent entertainment might force on people's attention the brutality of the South African situation ... But the argument is fairly tenuous, when the blacks of the case are painted so black and the whites so white; and when you know that it is Poitier the audiences love to love, and the villainy of Nicol Williamson they love to hate, rather than being helped to any assessment

198

of a political or moral system.

'But it was a lead-up to *The Man Who Would Be King* in a way,' says Caine, 'because the chemistry was right. Maybe two years earlier, or two years later, the film would have been a success. I've made some good films with bad timing—*Get Carter*, *The Last Valley*, *The Wilby Conspiracy*. Now would have been a good time to make *The Last Valley*. I must say I've usually been ahead of my time, not behind it.'

There was also another link with *The Man Who Would Be King*. Saeed Jaffrey, who played the Indian dentist Mukerjee, would later be cast as Billy Fish in John Huston's epic. 'It was on *The Wilby Conspiracy* that I first met Michael,' says Jaffrey. 'I remember Michael said to me, "I know a lot about curry, you know, Saeed. It was the cheapest food down where I lived."'

*   *   *

Following the usual form, Caine's last role in 1974 was completely different from his previous two. In *The Romantic Englishwoman* he was cast as author Lewis Fielding, suffering from a severe case of writer's block. His wife Elizabeth, played by Glenda Jackson, leaves him in their comfortable middle-class Weybridge home to go on a trip to Baden Baden, where she meets a drug smuggler posing as a poet, played by Helmut Berger.

Back in Weybridge Fielding imagines his wife having an affair, or is he simply manipulating the situation to try to jolt his creativity back into action? Unfortunately the drug smuggler doesn't stay in Baden Baden, and back in England the secure, predictable lifestyle enjoyed by the Fieldings is shattered by his unwelcome intrusion. Or has Fielding set up the whole scenario?

Joseph Losey's direction of Thomas Wiseman's complex novel, adapted by Wiseman and Tom Stoppard, found little favour with either critics or audience.

'Joseph Losey's *The Romantic Englishwoman* is the most complicatedly trivial film in London: a highly polished humbug,' wrote Russell Davies in the *Observer* and added, 'Intuition suggests that the best of the chi-chi life jokes are Stoppard's.'

In the *Standard* Alexander Walker commented, 'Caine does well, very well indeed, as the sarky husband, considering that he's fairly well limited to looking continuously irritated, exasperated and infuriated', and Dilys Powell in the *Sunday Times* pointed out: 'The element of fantasy, when the husband struggles to translate his suspicions into the stuff of a film script, fails because the visual images he calls up are neither satirical nor passionate; if that is the best he can do he won't be able to afford that Weybridge house for long. All the same, *The Romantic Englishwoman* never bored me.'

For Caine, though, the film represented the chance to play a character very different from anything he had done before, someone with whom he had nothing in common and with whom he found it hard to identify. In real life, Caine later remarked, he would have disliked and despised a man such as Fielding.

Unable to draw on his own experience Caine had to invent a different 'background' to draw on, and

200

his success gave him some not inconsiderable professional satisfaction. He was also very impressed with the professionalism of his co-star, Glenda Jackson, who had, he felt, unlike many stage actors and actresses, the ability quickly to adapt her performance and voice projection to the demands of the screen. Caine said at the time that she reminded him of Jane Fonda, except that in Fonda he could see the vulnerability, whereas in Jackson he could see the femininity but not vulnerability. Glenda Jackson had, in turn, been observing Caine: 'Michael is like all English actors; they pretend that they're only an actor because they can't think of anything more interesting to do. It's all a front, of course. I thought Michael was marvellous in *The Romantic Englishwoman*. He took a lot of risks. But he likes to pretend it's all a great big club with his cigars and everything.'

Caine had enjoyed the experience of making *The Romantic Englishwoman*. 'We knew it wasn't going to be *Jaws* but an esoteric little piece and that was that. I did that purely for my personal satisfaction.' And he also enjoyed working with Joseph Losey. 'I liked old Joe Losey,' says Caine. 'He lived round the corner from me in London, and I used to see him every now and then. I mean, we weren't close friends or anything, but we got on.

'I had a £10 bet that I would be able to make him laugh. I can make anyone laugh, but not him. I lost that bet—he was my only failure, was Joe Losey!'

* * *

John Huston, on the other hand, was a better bet. Caine and Huston were about to team up for *The*

201

Man Who Would Be King, a pet project of Huston's. For twenty-five years the veteran director had dreamed of making a film of Rudyard Kipling's classic story set in the India of the 1880s. Originally he had planned to cast Humphrey Bogart and Clark Gable in the roles of Peachy Carnehan and Daniel Dravot, but the project had never come to fruition during their lifetimes.

Now at last the film was going to be made, and Huston had his Peachy and Danny: Michael Caine, stepping into the shoes of his hero Bogart and Sean Connery as Danny. Also in the cast was Christopher Plummer taking the role of Kipling.

Told entirely in flashback, *The Man Who Would Be King* is the story of two former British Army sergeants in India who devise a plan to venture beyond the North-West Frontier into Kafiristan— the first Europeans to set foot there since Alexander the Great—and make their fortunes by setting themselves up as kings. But, enmeshed in power and legend, Danny tries to make the stuff of fiction into reality, and fails. Peachy lives to tell the story, and another legend is born.

From its beginnings as a parable of British imperial attitudes ('Strewth, I look like a Chelsea pensioner in this,' said Caine to costumier Monty Berman the first time he tried on his uniform), an exploration of human ambition, and a rattling good yarn to boot, Kipling's story became a terrific adventure film without losing the spirit of the original moral tale. It has become a cult classic, possessing the rare capacity to be seen over and over again and still offer something new every time. As Jerry Pam, Michael Caine's US press agent points out, it is consistently the most requested film on two of the American cable TV networks.

And in making it, everything just clicked.

Caine and Connery were delighted to be working together. 'Our two characters were really different aspects of the same man,' says Connery, 'so being close friends with Michael in real life made it much easier to portray that in the film.' And Caine agrees: 'I think I'm right in saying the camera picked up how well Sean and I worked together. That was very easy for us because we were already into that relationship—not as those characters, of course—but the warmth between us was there.

'You can get a situation like that where each actor can be edging around trying to get more screen time or getting up to tricks behind one's back with the director. But Sean and I decided that we'd play absolutely everything together for the benefit of the picture.'

Caine and Connery share very much the same approach to their craft. They both see themselves, and behave, as consummate professionals, always knowing their lines and ready for their cues; although Caine is generally credited with being more gregarious on set. Needless to say, the similarity in their upbringings contributes greatly to their friendship. Both are men who embarked on rigorous courses of self-improvement in their local libraries and created the people they wanted to be. They also share a very healthy respect for money. After the film was completed Connery complained that he had only been paid enough for *The Man Who Would Be Prince*. He and Caine jointly sued Allied Artists for a £109,146 discrepancy in the five per cent of the gross receipts they had been promised on top of their $250,000 fees. Allied

Artists countersued for defamation and malicious interference, and lost.

During shooting on *The Wilby Conspiracy* Caine had mentioned to Saeed Jaffrey, playing the part of the Indian dentist, that he might be hearing from the producers of *The Man Who Would Be King*, and Jaffrey still feels that it is Caine he has to thank for suggesting him to John Huston. Jaffrey was cast in the role of Gurkha Billy Fish who acts as Carnehan and Dravot's interpreter and becomes involved in the deception of the tribesmen.

Caine made sure that Jaffrey, despite his relative newness to the world of film-making, was treated in the way Caine felt he should be. 'On the set there was a chair for John Huston, a chair for Michael Caine, a chair for Sean Connery, and a chair for Christopher Plummer while he was there,' recalls Jaffrey. 'And Michael would say, "Where's the bloody chair for Saeed?" He was very vociferous on the subject. I remember he used to say, "I've said it once, I've said it twice, I've said it three times! I mean, he is the third fucking lead on this picture!"'

Working on only his second feature, Jaffrey felt he had a lot to learn from Caine: 'I remember Michael being displeased with me one day. It was a scene towards the end where we're escaping. It was a heavy day, and several cameras were capturing the scene. I stopped somewhere over the hill, thinking that was the end of the shot, and Michael really shouted at me: "Saeed, never bloody stop until the Director says *cut*!"

'I was unaware that one of the cameras was over the hill where I thought the shot had ended. We had to do the scene again.

'I learned a tremendous amount from him.'

Filming took fourteen weeks in the country around Marrakesh, which doubled for the Afghan foothills. It was a beautiful spot, but the nightlife left a lot to be desired. 'We were in this dumb little town on the edge of the Sahara desert,' remembers Caine, 'and there was nothing to do at night except go to this disco place. But it was all men dancing with men because women weren't allowed out at night.

'So we're standing at the bar watching all these guys dancing when Sean leans over and says to me, "Do you mind if I dance with your driver? Mine's too ugly."'

Compensation came later in the picture when Caine fulfilled a long-held ambition to stay in the Churchill Suite at the famous Mamounia Hotel, where Churchill had escaped from affairs of state to come and paint. The day Caine moved in heralded a double celebration: Saeed Jaffrey's chair had finally arrived—with his name correctly spelt—and the two men celebrated these small triumphs in the comfortable surroundings of Churchill's suite.

Filming became virtually a family affair. Not only were 'blood brothers' Caine and Connery cast together, but Shakira Caine also joined the production to play the role of Roxanne, the beautiful girl Danny takes to be his queen.

Originally, Tessa Dahl, daughter of Roald Dahl and Patricia Neal, had been signed up for the role, but when John Huston saw her against the Berber tribesmen who were to play her 'family' he realized that the skin differences would not work, and the darker-toned Shakira was persuaded to step in.

Naturally Caine was concerned for Shakira; a film set is a daunting place for any new actor, let alone an inexperienced one suddenly co-opted onto the production. 'A couple of times when we were rehearsing John Huston told Michael to get off the set because he was loitering around! He was very nervous for me, but very helpful,' says Shakira, and Saeed Jaffrey adds, 'Michael used to stand right behind all the extras so he wouldn't make her more nervous, watching to see how she was getting on. He had total trust in John Huston to teach her.'

And teach her Huston did, acting out the part for her and telling her, as Saeed Jaffrey remembers 'to move like a pantheress'.

So when Peachy Carnehan mentions Roxanne to Daniel Dravot, it's with genuine feeling that he says, 'I must admit, she really is an eyeful.'

It was Shakira's movie début *and* farewell performance wrapped up in one role. The strain of playing a minor but pivotal role—even though she has to say only one line, the film naturally depends on her looking convincing—in front of the legendary director John Huston *and* her movie-star husband, decided for Shakira that one actor in the Caine family was enough! Caine, perhaps unsurprisingly, agreed with her decision.

There were only two problems for Caine on the picture—the exotic location which would lead to his usual stomach upsets, and his recurring nightmare problems with animals, this time in the shape of a recalcitrant camel. 'I got to the stables first and got the good camel and Sean had the rotten one,' says Caine. 'We were just getting ready to do the first shot, but I was suffering from diarrhoea by then and Sean switched the camels while I was in the toilet. I came out and I didn't even notice. Then suddenly I thought, "This bloody camel is pulling a bit!"'

Sean Connery can also recall Caine's stomach problems: 'I never get stomach upsets on location. I stayed at the Saadi in Marrakesh, and Michael stayed at the Mamounia Hotel, getting neurotic about the food hygiene and the water. Everything had to be boiled for him.

'His daughter came out to visit him, but was sent home because he was so worried about the hygiene.'

'One day I rushed to the "honey wagon", as they call it in the movies,' says Caine, 'and it was smothered in a black cloud of flies. So I said to the Moroccan fella, "Why don't you put some disinfectant down?"

'And he said, "We left it in Marrakesh and it would take three hours to get there and back." And then he added, "I'll tell you what, come back at lunchtime—all the flies will be in the kitchen then!"'

Like a fine wine, *The Man Who Would Be King* seems to improve with each passing year, but even at the beginning the critics were already well disposed. In the *Monthly Film Bulletin*, Tom Milne wrote:

The film is beautifully served by the performances of Sean Connery and Michael Caine (very funny as twin incarnations of typically endearing Kipling ranker-rogues, identical in their sharp-witted, foul-mouthed opportunism but with just a hint that Celtic mysticism *might* have caught fire had it not been banked down by Cockney pragmatism.

The *Sunday Times*' Dilys Powell added:

207

Everything works logically—the victory of the British adventurers, their acceptance by the people as sons of Alexander, the gradual assumption by the more ambitious of the pair of the status of God. Sean Connery gives him power, a fine display of hubris. Michael Caine shows a nice discretion as friend and lieutenant. And Huston has caught the essential of the original story, the feeling for the enterprise and bravado which the author saw in the British soldier in India.

The *Daily Mail* declared:

The ending has an element of Greek tragedy and indeed this is the quality that elevates a remarkable film. Huston, as always, allows his actors to do their own thing but urges them to dig a little deeper into themselves than they ever have before.

Caine's quirky cockney characterization has never been so succinctly employed.

From the beginning John Huston had looked after his cast and crew like a father. 'What broke the ice was the very first scene we shot, where the natives bring some arrows for Michael and Sean,' recalls Saeed Jaffrey. 'John Huston said, "Tell the guys to bring a few more arrows to give the kids confidence."

'I remember Michael looking at Sean and Sean looking at Michael, and both of them looking at me. It was the first time we'd been called "kids" by anybody for a very long time. John loved them, he really loved them.'

'John Huston only gave me two directions,' Caine told *Stills* magazine in 1984. 'The first came at the very beginning of the picture. He said, "Speak faster, Michael; he is an honest man." He believes, you see, that people who talk slowly are dishonest!

'And there's a line in which Chris Plummer as Kipling says, "But you can't go off to Kafiristan, just the two of you!" And I had a line which was, "We are not little men." John just came over and said, "I never give actors inflections, Michael; but would you please say, 'We are not *little* men'?" Meaning we are *big* men.

'And, if you saw the three of us—Sean, John and me—on the set, it was true: we were definitely not little men.'

'There's one scene where we capture a fortress,' remembers Saeed Jaffrey, 'and all the noblemen are sitting down, and Sean Connery says, "Go tell them that we'll not loot their treasure, nor rape their daughters." Then I had to translate into the local language.

'I said, "Just a minute—let's go see Big John." And John Huston was there, squatting Mexican style and smoking his cigar, and I said, "Big John, in the Indian sub-continent the word 'rape' is a very sensitive word. There are a lot of euphemisms for it, like 'forced entry' or 'to take away pride', and so on. Perhaps we should use one of those?"

'So Big John puffed away at his cigar and finally said, "Well, Saeed, I don't think a honest-to-goodness Gurkha soldier would use high-falutin words like that. What's the word for fuck?'

'I said, "Chodna, C-H-O-D-N-A."

209

'"That's the one I want you to use," he said; and I said, "Be it on your own head, because we'll have all sorts of reactions to that."

'When the film came out I went to see it incognito, and there were usually embarrassed giggles, because it was the first time in the English or US film industry that the Indian word for fuck had been used. I said it without batting an eyelid, as the soldier would. John was absolutely right—it was the word Billy Fish would have used there.'

Looking back on the film, the critic Alexander Walker comments, 'Sean Connery and Michael Caine are, saving Roger Moore, the only two names who came out of the sixties, made an impact on the international scene, and have never needed or wanted to return to the stage. *The Man Who Would Be King* is the perfect demonstration of their strengths—character roles that are also star vehicles.'

And Caine's own verdict is as succinct and pithy as ever: '*Educating Rita* is the best performance I ever gave. *The Man Who Would Be King* is the film people will remember after I've gone, if they remember any of them.'

*   *   *

Caine followed *The Man Who Would Be King* with *Peeper*, a film that was intended to be at once a spoof of and a homage to the private-eye thriller film. Unfortunately though, an overcomplicated plot ends up leaving the audience slightly adrift.

Michael Caine played a private detective hired to find his client's long-lost daughter in 1940s Los Angeles. He solves the mystery, but not before his client is murdered, blackmail is threatened, and Caine has to go into hiding, but with the wrong girl. The end comes not with the usual explanation of the mystery, but with Caine falling in love with the wrong girl and offering her the money that the right one should have inherited.

At least Margaret Hinxman, writing in the *Daily Mail* had a good word to say for Michael Caine:

It's worth looking out for, if only to see Michael Caine's knowing funny performance as an English opportunist who fetches up in California after the war as a private eye. Director Peter Hyams can't produce the pace to propel the preposterous plot along—something about the search for an adopted heiress. And it misses that sense of manic panic that made *The Black Bird* so enjoyable.

But Caine is always good value and so too is Natalie Wood as the inevitable shady lady.

Monty Smith, writing in *Street Life*, did not agree:

It would be a whole lot funnier were Michael Caine not the eponymous private eye. His distinctive Englishness works against him from the start . . . and he doesn't begin to look the part of a down-trodden detective: 'Blimey, I hate this job,' he says—and one believes him—and when Natalie Wood says, 'Don't get cute, it clashes with your face,' she's too near the mark.

Caine's own verdict is uncompromising: 'It was a disaster. It was fine to make; we all went down to Mexico on a ship, and we called at all the Caribbean ports. It was like a lot of films; you have the time of your life making it, but it didn't work at all.

'One problem with some films is not that they're bad; it's just the timing. I think *Peeper* is an example of a film which came out at exactly the wrong time.'

★   ★   ★

Harry and Walter Go to New York brought Caine together with James Caan and Elliott Gould in a period romp set in the 1890s. Caine played master safe-cracker Adam Worth who finds himself in jail as the result of a tactical error. His attitude to imprisonment strongly resembles that of Noël Coward's 'Mr Bridger' character in *The Italian Job*—when incarcerated he occupies a suite of cells made more attractive with opulent furnishings, and acquires a couple of factotums in the shape of two other convicts Harry (Caan) and Walter (Gould).

But the prison scenes were rather more realistic than those in *The Italian Job*. 'We did some filming in an old penitentiary in Ohio,' says Caine, 'and all the guys you see in the picture are prisoners. Very depressing. Particularly when you consider we were shooting a nineteenth-century scene and didn't have to change anything.'

Harry and Walter escape and use photographs of Adam Worth's blueprints of a bank to set their own bank robbery in progress. Worth also plans to rob the bank, of course, and the race is on with Harry and Walter finally winning. Worth accepts his defeat graciously.

The idea promised much, but the film actually delivered little. Similar in style to *The Sting*, it was photographed by the same cameraman, Laszlo Kovacs. Caan and Elliott were criticized for overplaying their characters, and Caine praised for the underplaying of his. The *Daily Mirror*'s Arthur Thirkell wrote:

It's not the fault of Michael Caine that *Harry and Walter Go to New York* is a four-star flop. The blame for the unfunny shambles rests with director Mark Rydell and Caine's co-stars James Caan and Elliott Gould, who must be in line for the ham acting awards of the year ... Caine and Miss Keaton do their best to salvage something from the chaos, but they are clobbered by the crude fooling of Caan and Gould, who are about as subtle and comic as an elephant stampede.

Alexander Walker in the *Evening Standard* agreed:

I defy you to find two riper hams, whose narcissism is only equalled by their clumsiness with pacing of dialogue. They handle wit like coalmen making a delivery. By contrast Michael Caine, as the gentleman cracksman, comes out with some dignity and a few smiles. Not enough, though, to save a film which incidentally looks as if it was photographed by the kind of illumination you find in vandalized telephone kiosks.

In the *Sunday Telegraph* Tom Hutchinson declared, 'The timing seems all wrong', and Derek Malcolm in the *Guardian* decided 'What is missing ... is simply a sense of humour.'
The sense of humour was there all right, but
213

unfortunately it stayed firmly behind on the set. The working atmosphere was very enjoyable, with Caan and Gould ad-libbing before takes, and keeping it up when they started filming the scene. Caine's difficulty was to insert the essential lines into these ad libs while not destroying the tone of the banter. He did it, and it should have been terrific; but unfortunately the magic evaporated on its way to the celluloid, and the end result bore little relation to a movie that was so much fun in the making.

*   *   *

Since early 1974 Caine had been globe-trotting almost continuously, but May 1976 saw him filming in his own backyard. The location of *The Eagle Has Landed* must be the easiest Caine has ever had to contend with—just ten minutes from his home in Berkshire.

Adapted from Jack Higgins' novel, the film was the story of a supposedly real-life German plot to kidnap Winston Churchill during the Second World War.

The director was the experienced John Sturges who had adapted the classic Japanese film *The Seven Samurai* into the equally classic Western *The Magnificent Seven*; so he should have been used to directing a war scenario set in a small village. But *The Eagle Has Landed* posed its own particular problems.

For a British audience there was always going to be some difficulty sympathizing with Caine's character, a Nazi officer sent to kidnap Churchill. And Caine himself faced an almost impossible task in trying to portray a supposedly 'good' Nazi forced by circumstances to help shorten the war by non-pacifist means. As he says: 'It's a difficult film because I play a kidnapper. In *The Day of the Jackal* you never felt sympathy for the assassin, and you knew de Gaulle wasn't assassinated, and in this case you know Churchill wasn't kidnapped but you've got to feel sympathy for the kidnapper. How are you going to get sympathy for a German paratrooper colonel without encouraging children to become Nazis? It works in the book and that's the actor's great problem and responsibility.'

The problem was never really overcome, as the critics pointed out. *Newsweek* commented:

Since most moviegoers probably know that German forces did not kidnap Winston Churchill during World War II *The Eagle Has Landed* is in the unenviable position of being a thriller without thrills ... It is also a war movie without sympathetic protagonists because non-Nazi viewers may have trouble wishing the would-be abductors good luck in their endeavour.

Tom Hutchinson in the *Sunday Telegraph* had some kind words, though:

Good portrayals from Caine, Duvall and Donald Pleasence as Himmler, while the final confrontation between the German commander and Churchill has a neatly ironic twist. But for the rest, this Eagle has landed with a rather dull thud.

And in the *Financial Times*, Nigel Andrews

declared:

The film manages the remarkable feat of being both far-fetched and dull at the same time. Far-fetched in its painstakingly silly and Miniver-ish recreation of English village life c.1944—every pub and cottage looks as if it has been freshly visited by the set designers—and dull in its singular inability to suspend the audience's disbelief, even for a history-defying moment, about the possibilities of Churchill's abduction. Caine, Sutherland and a host of stalwart British character actors go through their paces with unblenching professionalism.

That perfect English village caused some problems for the cast too, as Jean Marsh, who was playing the traitor Mrs Grey remembers. 'We were filming in a gorgeous village; they built extra bits on, though. I remember one day I didn't have my glasses on, and I thought I would go into the pub to get a drink of lemonade or something. I walked into the pub, but it wasn't a pub; the river was on the other side and I fell straight in.'

Caine did rather better with his German accent this time, though of course on this occasion he was playing a German playing an Englishman! He had had experience in German or German-type parts from *A Foxhole in Cairo* and *The Last Valley*; and his professionalism in listening to language records as preparation took care of some of the pitfalls likely to trip many actors.

He applies the same approach to accents that he does to playing drunk—if an actor tries to act drunk by walking crooked and slurring his words it won't work; he has to be someone who tries desperately to walk straight and speak clearly but cannot. In the same way, an actor will only master a foreign accent if he plays it like a foreigner trying to speak perfect English.

How to speak with a foreign accent is only one of the problems facing actors when shooting a film. Filling in time between takes requires a technique one has to learn, as Jean Marsh recalls. 'I was very impressed with the way Michael adjusted [to movies]. I remember moaning one day, saying I preferred the theatre to films because I didn't know what to do with myself during all the gaps in filming. Michael said to me, "Why don't you bring in all your mail to go through?" I said, "But it would only take me about ten minutes to go through *my* mail!"'

★ ★ ★

Caine's next offer came from Sir Richard Attenborough, who was keen to involve him in his latest project, *A Bridge Too Far*, an epic war film on the grandest scale imaginable. At $45 million (over £25 million), it was at the time the most expensive British film ever made. It set out to tell the complex story of Operation Market Garden, in which 35,000 British, American and Polish troops were parachuted 64 miles behind German lines in the Second World War. Their objective was to capture five bridges, culminating with the bridge at Arnhem.

Richard Attenborough was to direct, and the producer was Joe Levine, whose commercially astute mind had envisaged the huge African

217

warriors on the publicity hoardings for *Zulu* thirteen years earlier.

This time he had another trick up his sleeve. Gathered together for *A Bridge Too Far* were virtually all the major box office stars of the mid-seventies: Robert Redford, James Caan, Gene Hackman, Sean Connery, Dirk Bogarde, Elliott Gould, and, mixing happily in the distinguished company, Michael Caine.

'Joe Levine had decided that he needed the largest canopy of stars that he could possibly assemble,' says Richard Attenborough. 'My belief that major figures were involved was based on very different criteria. The subject matter of the whole "Market Garden" operation was immensely complex, with Germans, Poles, Dutch and Americans as well as British involved. If you were writing a piece of drama you would never contemplate keeping so many storylines on the go.

'I felt that the only way to overcome this was to place in the major commanding roles faces with whom the audience were already familiar, so that when they saw a particular person they immediately clocked "that's Michael"—or Sean Connery or Bob Redford.

'Equally a pre-requisite was that they had to be superb actors, and there's no question that Michael steps with the greatest of ease into that bracket. He is a British screen actor par excellence. It is very difficult to think of someone you would put ahead of him. He not only has the virtue of versatility, he also has an immense degree of concentration. If you are a true screen actor, the cavalry could come charging up behind you and you would just keep acting.'

The huge $45-million budget had certainly helped when it came to persuading so many stars to accept parts in the production. One reviewer, the *Sunday Mirror*'s Bernard McElwaine, even suggested that the size of Laurence Olivier's cameo was such that he could have phoned it in!

Many of those whose real-life stories were being told on celluloid acted as advisers to the production. Among them was Lt-Col (now Brigadier) J O E Vandeleur, whose character Caine would be responsible for portraying.

In one scene Caine, in command of a huge column of tanks and military vehicles, was supposed to signal them into battle. As Vandeleur was standing next to him, Caine asked him what he actually said at the time. The answer impressed Caine, and he used the exact words. On film, as in real life, the entire mile-long column set off to war in response to their commander gently picking up the microphone and saying, quite normally, 'Well, get a move on, then!'

Brigadier Vandeleur was impressed with his on-screen counterpart. 'Michael Caine was first class,' he told the *Daily Express*. 'I think it will be a marvellous film. Dickie Attenborough is a great director.'

And Richard Attenborough too recalls Vandeleur's opinion: 'Michael and Joe are very different physically, but afterwards Joe Vandeleur said to me, "I would like to have been Michael Caine."'

Other participants, or their relatives, were less happy, though. Daphne du Maurier, outraged by the portrayal of her late husband, General Sir Frederick 'Boy' Browning as ineffectual and aloof,

219

commented to the *Daily Express* at the time, 'My God, they wouldn't have dared to do this if Boy had still been alive [he died in 1955]. He would have roasted them alive.'

It was in fact General Browning's phrase, 'We might be going a bridge too far' at the planning stages of the operation, which gave rise to the title of Cornelius Ryan's book on which the film was based.

The reconstruction of the battle scenes was impressive. Meticulously planned, they won universal acclaim. The sheer weight of detail involved in the story was immense.

The public was impressed, though the critics were divided. Unable to keep their eyes off the huge cost of the enterprise, it was Attenborough who came in for the heavy stick, not his stars. In the *Guardian* Derek Malcolm wrote:

By now you must all know it is the most expensive British production ever, for which Robert Redford alone, with scarcely more than a cameo part and no 1940s haircut was paid two million dollars . . . basically the trouble with the film is what you would expect—the logistics get in the way of narrative drive, observation of character and any real intimacy. Too often Attenborough and his team, having accomplished the noisy battle-scenes well, are reduced to little more than arty spasms elsewhere, once or twice seemingly culled from *Oh What a Lovely War!* . . . Somebody has already christened it *The Sound of Shell Shock*.

But Ian Christie in the *Daily Express* disagreed:

Just how historically accurate it is I wouldn't know, but under Richard Attenborough's direction it comes across as a vast, vivid, spectacular event, a catalogue of disasters, major and minor, and a tribute to the courage of the men who took part in it ... Nobody allows his ego to take prominence over his role ... It's an exciting story, brilliantly told—a military defeat turned into a cinematic triumph.

Alan Brien, in the *Sunday Times*, declared:

The thin irony of *Oh What a Lovely War!* has curdled into the heavy satire of War Is Hell. When celluloid death is so random and so spectacular, so mechanized and so grotesque, at an expense of Joe Levine's 45 million dollars and our 2 hours and 55 minutes, then it is impossible not to fill the screen, intermittently, with pictures which stun the mind and bruise the conscience. *A Bridge Too Far* has some marvellous moments—and some dragging quarters of an hour.

Caine was unperturbed, though: 'I enjoyed *A Bridge Too Far*. I was only on it for a little while, but I thought Dickie Attenborough did a marvellous job. I had a nice part: me and my tanks moving straight down the road, typical me—no finesse, nothing—just straight down the road, right at the front, being incredibly brave. Joe Vandeleur was in Holland, watching the filming. He said, "I'm glad you're playing me because you're taller and funnier than I am."'

221

And Michael Caine ended up with a 5-star review from his director: 'The Americans taught us that reaction and silent observation are just as powerful as speech; actors like Bogart and Tracy. Michael has that, the extraordinary ability to play reaction and concentrated observation of circumstances which are not part of the actor's bag of tricks.

'Michael was cast as a slightly upper-class gung-ho military officer, and a lot of people would say that casting him in that role was madness. But he was perfection. There isn't a performance to top him in the film.'

★   ★   ★

After the pyrotechnics of *A Bridge Too Far*, Caine finished off 1976 in the more discreet but equally vicious world of international finance with the comedy *Silver Bears*. He played financial wizard Doc Fletcher—'Doctor of what?' he is asked. 'Money,' he replies—who really just wants to retire to his own little bank in Lugano. To get it he becomes caught up in all sorts of shady deals with smuggler Iranians and Mafiosi, not to mention an epidemic of deceit, which is, by all accounts, normal in the world of money.

Caine joined an excellent cast, full of actors whose characterizations always give pleasure in a comedy, people like Charles Gray and Joss Ackland, and less well-known faces like Bruce Boa and Steve Plytas (both of whom turned up later in *Fawlty Towers*).

It also starred Caine's old friend Louis Jourdan, as well as Cybill Shepherd (later to find TV fame in *Moonlighting*), whom Caine found impressive.

Shepherd later commented that Caine was far more relaxed about doing love scenes when his wife was around. 'On location it was really uncomfortable,' she says. 'He wasn't a good kisser. Then we came to London and had this great love scene. He was wonderful—I couldn't understand it. It turned out that his wife was with him in London. He was much looser when she was there.'

And indeed it has been noted that Caine frequently takes Shakira round the set to introduce her on films involving love interest, thereby also subtly pointing out that with a wife as beautiful as his, there is going to be no danger of fiction and reality blurring during love scenes.

With a subject like international finance, the critics had no trouble in accepting outrageous fiction as reality; but they weren't sure what to make of the rest of it. The *Monthly Film Bulletin*'s John Pym derided the 'somnambulistic acting [which] heightens the inoffensive tone; humorous remarks are tossed about like leaden medicine balls, after which the characters look at each other expectantly, waiting for them to register.'

'Amusing people. Opulent houses. Vintage cars. Glorious settings. Lovely women. Pity about the story,' wrote Felix Barker in the *Evening News*, while the *Evening Standard*'s Alexander Walker said 'A gilt-edged cast—Caine the sharp-talking Cockney ... Cybill Shepherd just peachy as a zany young wife who keeps the strangest things in her handbag ... —seem to be having a lot of fun: more fun at times than the audience. But it is unquestionably entertaining.'

On the other hand, Alan Brien commented in the *Sunday Times*, 'I'm worried about Michael Caine. Is he going on forever as the red-eyed stiff-suited Limey dude, or will he someday fill the gap waiting for him as the new Cary Grant?'

For himself, Michael Caine was now appreciating comedy much more, as well as the difficulties associated with playing it. In the next decade he was to choose comedy increasingly as the area into which he could move as an actor, while at the same time using it to develop further his own inimitable techniques.

CHAPTER NINE

'WHAT THE HELL DO I KNOW ABOUT BEES?': 1977–1983

'If you have a very high standard of living you sometimes have to make a very low standard of movie.'

Michael Caine

In 1978 Michael Caine was facing his usual difficulty—how to make money *and* win critical acclaim. They appeared to be mutually exclusive; and, since his move to Hollywood, the money-making side of his career seemed to be in the ascendant. Often, it seemed, at the expense of quality.

It took a while before the Caines had time to settle into Beverly Hills. When they first announced their intention to leave Britain in September 1977, Caine was already busy with *The Swarm*, and diving immediately afterwards into the acclaimed *California Suite*, closely followed by location work on the dire *Ashanti*, meant that Hollywood wasn't really home for a while.

By the end of 1978, however, Caine was following the LA Rams and the Dodgers instead of Chelsea and the MCC, even though he and his family were still camping out (albeit very comfortably!) at composer Leslie Bricusse's place while they sorted out their own.

Finally, in January 1979, Caine found their new home; a house right on top of a Beverly Hill, four miles from the coast and, at 996 feet above sea level, well above the smog line. It also had a terrific view overlooking all their celebrated neighbours—Kirk Douglas, Gregory Peck, Louis Jourdan, Charles Bronson, Robert Stack and Robert Mitchum, to name but six. And at around £600,000, it was reckoned to be a bargain. Originally owned by Woolworth heiress Barbara Hutton, she'd given it to her son as a twenty-first birthday present in the same year that a twenty-year-old Michael Caine had been earning £2 10 shillings per week on the other side of the world.

Despite the security gate, armed patrols and the guard dog, Caine enjoyed the life. The tennis court, swimming pool and jacuzzi, and large garden kept him happy and healthy; though with the size of those hills, jogging was out. And it was conveniently close to Tinsel Town, very useful for life's little essentials—as Caine put it—'if you run out of handbags at 6 pm you can nip down to Gucci on Rodeo Drive. It's only six minutes by car.'

Needless to say, Caine still couldn't drive, though he bought himself a new Rolls-Royce in yellow and gold. There was no personalized number-plate 'for security reasons', but the opulence of the car itself didn't bother him. In Hollywood, Rolls-Royces are as common as Fords—no one takes any notice unless they know who is in them.

Michael Caine says he always missed the quintessentially English things while he was in California—sausages, Harrods, Sunday papers— and he was in the habit of occasionally serving a traditional English Sunday lunch to his fellow British exiles, complete with Bisto gravy, Yorkshire pudding and Colman's mustard.

But although he was firmly installed in America the British press couldn't let Caine go, and accused him of 'slagging Britain off'. Even the journalists who did make the effort to see him were agog at his lifestyle—one hack, having shaken hands with Michael Caine, was exhorted to let Caine's dog sniff his hand, so the dog would recognize his master's scent on the stranger and let him pass. The *News of the World* man was amazed and wrote in his organ 'It is probably the only dog on earth trained to recognize the smell of his master's wad.'

Although there is no doubt that Michael Caine missed Britain, he knew when he was on to a good thing. He was earning a fortune, and keeping most of it. When he went off on location, as for *Blame It on Rio*, he discovered it was his Californian home he got homesick for. And he had Denis Healey to thank for that. In 1979 Caine told the *Daily Express* 'Denis Healey said he was going to make the rich squeal, but he forgot that we all had money for the plane fare. So now we're all squealing in the South of France and Beverly Hills!'

*　　　*　　　*

Of Caine's turkey movies *The Swarm* is undoubtedly the best remembered ... and best loved. At the time of its release it immediately, and unintentionally, became a comic cult classic. Lines like 'I never dreamed that it would be the bees, they've always been our friends' and 'these bees are brighter than we thought' convulsed critics and audiences alike into bouts of collective hysteria. Critic and wit Clive James appeared on LWT's *Saturday Night People* each week wearing a *Swarm*

227

badge, all of which helped to make *The Swarm* the film to see, if not for the reasons the director originally intended!

The swarm of the title was a plague of killer bees threatening to kill the citizens of Texas. In fact, the concept was not quite as bizarre as it might appear. Killer bees do indeed exist in America, spawned from a lethal African variety which escaped during an experiment in 1956 and mated with a local species. Nervous natives were meant to be reassured by an end title which read 'The African Killer bee depicted in this film bears no resemblance to the industrious American Honey bee.'

In Irwin Allen's film, however, the killer bees became ludicrous rather than terrifying. Until then Irwin's pedigree as a disaster film maker had been impeccable. His formula of putting famous people in life-threatening situations for the audience to experience from the safety of their seats had worked to great effect in *The Towering Inferno* and *The Poseidon Adventure*. Now he was to use bees instead of burning skyscrapers and sinking ships. Olivia de Havilland, Henry Fonda and Richard Widmark took cameo roles, while Caine accepted the starring role of the macho-sounding entomologist, Brad Crane.

The peculiarity of his dialogue, coupled with the company he found himself keeping, led to a very strange moment for Caine: 'I had to give a very long speech using all sorts of entomological terms which were very hard to remember. Anyway, eventually I got it all off pat with the correct pronunciation, Irwin Allen said, "Action", and I began to give this lecture to all these other doctors. Then suddenly I became a film fan again because sitting there staring at me were Fred MacMurray, Henry Fonda, Olivia de Havilland and Richard Widmark. And I became the kid from the Elephant here with all these stars and I thought to myself My God, what am I doing here? And I dried up.

'When I was a boy these people weren't real—they were myths and legends. And here I was talking to them. It's the only time I've ever dried on a film set.'

Working with bees was a new experience for all the stars. In total there were some 22,000 bees used for the effects. 'There were Mexican illegal aliens sitting in little refrigerated caravans pulling the stings out,' says Caine. 'Of course they used to drop off and miss a few now and then, and they were known as "the hot ones"!

'It's only in Hollywood you get 22,000 bees with no stings in flying about.'

Although they lost their stings, the bees still had another secret weapon. 'We used to wear white smocks and they would keep the bees crated up until the last minute and then release them,' recalls Caine. 'But what we didn't realize was that bees never make a mess in their own homes! So they released all the bees and we had our smocks on and suddenly there's a sort of haze coming down and it was literally a haze of bee pong.'

During the recording of *The Trouble with Michael Caine*, Michael Aspel asked 'You must have realized quite early on, I suppose, that you were in the presence of an awesomely bad movie?' 'Well,' answered Caine, 'we had an inkling when the bees crapped all over us . . .'

Over the years Michael Caine has given various

229

reasons for why he took on *The Swarm*. For example, he wanted to do a special effects picture: 'What you don't realize when you do a special effects picture is this: if it works they say, well, it was the special effects; and if it doesn't they blame the star, they blame me. You know, what the hell do I know about bees?'

Or he needed the money to buy a house in America: 'You see, I treated my career the way you treat a job. I'd say, "I want that now"—like a new house or something—and I'd go out and do some films and get it.'

Or it was the only film he was offered at that time: '*The Swarm* was the only film offered to me. So what am I going to do? I did *The Swarm* and then they said, "Well, it's a dreadful movie". So what?'

Either way he survived the experience without any loss of stature, and mention of *The Swarm* still brings a wry smile to the lips of moviegoers. It gave the critics some fun too:

This disaster film—in spite of its budget of 12 million dollars and its cast of star names—is so dreadful that it is almost impossible to believe that it could have been made by an intelligent human being. All is not lost, however. The script by Stirling Silliphant is so absurd, the acting so wooden and the direction so clumsy that the combination is often enormously funny.

Wrote Ian Christie in the *Daily Express*; he also drew attention to Caine 'speaking the absurd dialogue given to him with all the passion and warmth of a railway station announcer.'

230

In the *Evening Standard* Alexander Walker commented, 'The general acting is abysmal, the cast seeming to hold themselves very still in case they split open with laughter. Even Caine seems only able to get his dialogue out in short bursts like 'What we need ... is every helicopter ... that you've got', while Eric Shorter in the *Daily Telegraph* declared, 'Mr Caine has never acted so badly. Mr Fonda has never acted better. And the film is so ill-written, and therefore so laughable, that it has the makings of a cult'; Richard Schickel in *Time* magazine lamented, 'It seems to be Caine's sad fate to go around being intelligent in dumb movies.'

Caine had a comeback to that one: 'Early on I did work that I was proud of and I got no kudos for it, so I thought to myself, "Now I've got to be artistic and wonderful and everything is going to be fine, and I'll get great reviews and get an award." And I did that and I got bad reviews and no award, so I thought I might as well do it for the money, so I did.'

Roger Moore has nothing but admiration for Caine's approach to his career. 'What I think sums up Michael is that he can do a film like *The Swarm*, be covered in bee shit and come up smelling of honey. I think it's absolutely bloody marvellous. Good on you, Michael!'

'Everyone keeps threatening to show *The Swarm* to me,' Caine told the *Sunday Mirror* in 1978, 'and I will see it one day. But I can tell you one thing. If it didn't work, it was all the bees' fault. I always knew they couldn't act.'

★　　★　　★

231

With his next film *California Suite*, those who accused Michael Caine of always playing himself were about to get their come-uppance. Whatever potential characters had been envisaged for Caine over the years the part of a bi-sexual antiques dealer was unlikely to have been among them.

California Suite was a series of four playlets adapted by Neil Simon from his Broadway stage production. All set in the plush surroundings of the Beverly Hills Hotel, each sequence involved major stars. The first featured Jane Fonda and Alan Alda as a divorced couple meeting up again to discuss their daughter, and the second starred Richard Pryor and Bill Cosby as two doctors on holiday with their wives. It was the third segment that cast Michael Caine as Sidney Cochran, the (closet) homosexual husband of nervous Oscar-nominated actress Diana Barrie, played by Maggie Smith; while the fourth focused on the trials of a middle-aged man (Walter Matthau) who finds a nubile young woman in his room just as he is expecting his wife to arrive.

The Sidney Cochran/Diana Barrie script is an exquisitely choreographed verbal dance between two people who are trying to step on each other's toes, while maintaining their perfect public poise as a well-matched couple. Caine was well aware of the potential difficulties. 'In *California Suite* the timing was everything,' he said. 'Doing that character was like walking on a razor blade. Very very difficult and enervating.'

Diana: What's the green slime you're eating? It looks like a dish out of Oliver Twist.

232

Sidney: I'm not sure, I think they ran the front lawn through a blender.

It has to be played with a straight face, and it gave Caine his best opportunity yet to prove himself in comedy. His experience, and particularly his sense of timing, counted for a lot; there was much witty repartee, and the one-liners had to be delivered *just* right:

Diana: You need a sentimental reason for them to vote for you. A dying husband would have ensured everything—you wouldn't like to get something fatal for me would you, angel?
Sidney: You should have told me sooner. I could have come over on the *Hindenburg*.

After the Oscar ceremony, from which Diana Barrie returns unglorified and drunk ('Did you get your eggs Benedictined?' asks Sidney), the mood changes as she confronts Sidney on the subject of his (homo)sexuality. There follows a blazing row before the two agree that the quality of their relationship is more important than convention.

When the film was released it was the Caine/Smith sequence of the four playlets that won praise along with the Fonda/Alda piece. 'Baldly, two of these are rather good and two of the filler variety,' wrote Derek Malcolm in the *Guardian*.

And in the *Sunday Telegraph*, Tom Hutchinson added, 'The only story that is remotely successful is that concerning an Oscar nominated actress (Maggie Smith) coming to terms with her husband's bi-sexuality, touchingly conveyed by Michael Caine who's better than he has been for many films: a

233

wry, tender look at love's vagaries.'

Maggie Smith was nominated for, and won, an Oscar for her portrayal of the caustic Diana Barrie whose acerbic wit concealed a needy heart. Caine was pleased enough to have confounded the critics by popping out of a different box. 'It's the first time I've never researched a role thoroughly,' he told the *Daily Express*, 'but it was fun to play. A lot of actors might shy off playing a role like that, but it didn't worry me, for two reasons.

'First, there is my known reputation as being a straight guy, so there were no worries on that score.

'And, two, I don't mind what people think anyway.'

The role has become one of his own personal favourites. 'I'm very fond of the homosexual I played in *California Suite*,' he told *Time Out* magazine later. 'I tried to get away from the sort of whoops-dear-limp-wrist and show a man in some pain. I got a letter from the chairperson of some Gay Association in the States thanking me for portraying a gay without ridicule. I rather cherish that. Especially not being gay myself.'

★   ★   ★

Ashanti, on the other hand, is that rare thing; a film that Michael Caine has always admitted was a dreadful mistake. Says Caine of the experience, 'It was the only film I ever did for the money alone and I was never so unhappy in my whole career.'

Ashanti originally set out to explore the possibility of a modern-day slave trade, with Caine cast as a doctor whose wife is kidnapped by slave trader Peter Ustinov. But the plot never lived up to its serious intentions and soon degenerated into a farcical adventure yarn.

It's virtually impossible to take any film seriously when the plot involves the hero leaping from an exploding helicopter into a crocodile-infested river, only to reappear in the very next scene walking impeccably dressed down a city street, with no word of explanation as to how he got there. And the poor storyline isn't, unfortunately, salvaged by the kind of innocence that captivated the audiences for *The Swarm*.

Various stars had accepted cameo roles, but it was left to the two leads, Peter Ustinov and Michael Caine, to try to salvage some kind of order from the chaos. It proved impossible, as the *Spectator*'s critic, Ted Whitehead, remarked:

> My congratulations to Rex Harrison, Omar Sharif and William Holden who are prominently displayed in the advertisements for *Ashanti* but have had the good sense to limit their appearances to about five minutes each in the course of almost two hours' inexecrable dullness ... Poor old Peter Ustinov (or is it rich old him?) and Michael Caine actually STAR in the movie ...

Right from the start of shooting, in July 1978, *Ashanti* seems to have been doomed. 'I'd been working on it a week and they fired the leading lady, the director, the art director and the editor,' Caine said later. 'So I had a faint inkling we might be onto a spotty project there.'

Having survived his encounter with a camel in *The Man Who Would Be King*, Caine was horrified

235

to be confronted by another of the species. 'You know the advice they give actors? Don't ever work with children and animals,' he told the *Sunday Mirror*. 'Well, they're right. And the worst children to work with are those who've never acted before because they're so natural. And the worst animals are camels.

'So there I was in the middle of the Sinai desert—which the Egyptians can have back as far as I'm concerned—doing my big emotional scene in 130° heat with children who did everything and a camel that would do nothing.

'Then you know what? My camel fainted. I thought, Hello this is a bit much, the camels are fainting from the heat and they still expect me to act.

'I tell you it was the real depths.'

At least it gave the critics excellent raw material for some wittily scathing reviews ... 'only one tiny scene works,' declared the *Spectator*'s Ted Whitehead, 'as Caine tries to mount a camel which doesn't appear to understand English; the camel's acting leaves everybody else with sand on their face.'

Derek Malcolm in the *Guardian* added:

All I can say is that it is a toss-up as to whether Ustinov or the camels have the best lines. 'People have not gone up like petrol,' says Ustinov to a beautifully accented African trying to sell him a boy for the purposes of sodomy.

'Aaargh!' says the camel at the slightest provocation.

Caine had to draw on all his acting experience to

236

help him out, and there was the occasional opportunity to flex his acting muscle, such as when he was called on to show his anger. Harking back to his own experiences as a child during the war, Caine drew on his memories in order to arouse feelings of fury, and the result is powerful and effective. 'It felt good to be on the receiving end of that anger,' says Caine's co-star in the film, Peter Ustinov, 'but of course the person I was playing *fed* on that sort of cold anger ... I think [Michael] does it terribly well!'

Caine was impressed with the wit and erudition of Ustinov. 'Peter was funny,' he says. 'We were on the set and there was an Indian actor who was making curry that night. And we had an Italian crew.

'I was sitting with Peter and the actor came up and said, "Do you think the Italians would like curry?" And Peter said, "No—they didn't have Abyssinia for long enough."'

Despite the refusal of most critics to take it seriously, the film still managed to upset people. '*Ashanti* is one of the most virulent examples of Israel's supporters attempting to prejudice Western opinion against the Arabs,' announced a press release from the Council for the Advancement of Arab-British Understanding, in January 1980. But most distressed were those who were beginning to worry seriously about Michael Caine's career, like the *Sunday Telegraph*'s Tom Hutchinson, who ended his review: 'It is yet another thoroughly bad film for Michael Caine, who seems to have a sort of death wish about his career these days. For all our sakes he should do something about his choice—or his agent.'

'Beyond Poseidon, beyond logic, beyond me!' was the reaction of an unknown critic to Caine's next film, *Beyond the Poseidon Adventure*.

Using the same formula as the original, the second Poseidon picture placed Caine, Sally Field and Telly Savalas in the same upturned hull that Gene Hackman, Ernest Borgnine and Shelley Winters had inhabited in *The Poseidon Adventure*. This time the plot revolved around several attempts to steal the ship's booty, featuring Caine as a salvage tug skipper intent on looting the contents of the ship's safe, and Telly Savalas as an illicit arms dealer seeking the missiles he has heard were on board.

Beyond the Poseidon Adventure might have been better if the literary standard of the original author, Paul Gallico, had been reproduced on screen. Most of the reviewers pointed out that it wasn't so much a sequel to the original *Poseidon* as a poor remake. 'Lamentable is the only word for Irwin Allen's *Beyond the Poseidon Adventure*,' wrote Clive Hirschhorn in the *Sunday Express*, continuing 'The latest offering is more a movie disaster than a disaster movie, which does the reputations of its two stars, Michael Caine and Telly Savalas, no good whatsoever ... Neither, however, is able to salvage the film, which deserves to sink without trace.'

And Clyde Jeavons in the *Monthly Film Bulletin* called it 'A fairly dismal, cut-price [re-make] ... The real absurdity of the situation is that so many people would actually wander about in the bowels of an exploding, up-turned liner, whatever its mercenary attractions.'

Caine's co-star Sally Field was none too happy with the resulting picture either. During her acceptance speech for the Best Actress award for *Norma Rae* at the Cannes Film Festival she declared: 'I am apologetic if not apopleptic at my involvement with *Beyond the Poseidon Adventure*. My character survives but I don't. I'll never do that again—boy that certainly taught me something.'

According to Sally Field, director Irwin Allen indulged in some rather bizarre working practices. Apparently he was in the habit of addressing the cast from the top of a ladder and, to signal action, would fire a gun into the air three or four times.

Naturally enough, the plot involved much tossing and turning of the boat, and rather than get a moving set Allen would simply shout 'Flail' at the actors when he wanted to show the boat moving. As Sally Field put it, 'Most of his direction was "Flail" and, you know, Karl Malden's flail was very different from Michael Caine's, which was very different from Shirley Knight's, we could never get our flailing together. No matter how much you study, flailing is never really down to a science.'

Once again, though, the disparaging remarks of the critics were aimed at the movie and not at Caine himself, who was regularly attracting pleas from the British critics to give up all this Hollywood tosh. 'Come back to Britain, Michael; taxes have been cut and the punishment you're taking out in Hollywood now hurts far more,' pleaded Alexander Walker in August 1979.

Caine, as usual, was unrepentant: 'I made *Beyond the Poseidon Adventure* for a friend of mine, Irwin Allen. I liked the idea of it. I had never been in a
239

big Hollywood special-effects picture before, and I thought the experience would be interesting. Trying to make something of the rather cardboard characters in those movies is quite difficult...

'I wanted pictures in America. I was just moving here, I needed to start making a living here, and that was a very important consideration as well. I obviously didn't read the scripts for either *Beyond the Poseidon Adventure* or *The Swarm* and say, "This'll get me an Academy Award, I must do it at all costs," but I wanted to do American pictures. And frankly, I thought both of these movies would be much better than they were. I had tremendous thoughts about the special-effects possibilities in each—but the bees in *The Swarm* didn't work, and the effects in *Poseidon* were so much smaller than in the original *Poseidon*. Kind of chintzy really.'

★   ★   ★

If Caine was mildly disappointed though, it made no difference. His next picture, *The Island*, was of the same vintage as some of his other Hollywood films, and showed no signs of bringing relief to the hard-pressed film critics. It was based on Peter Benchley's novel of the same name. Two of Benchley's novels, *Jaws* and *The Deep* had already been made into successful films, spawning sequel after sequel (later Caine would take on *Jaws The Revenge*) and in autumn 1979 *The Island* was set to receive the same Hollywood treatment. The water-based terrors of *Jaws* and *The Deep* had been a huge box office success, and hopes were high that *The Island* would keep up the trend.

Apparently Anthony Hopkins had originally been

asked to play the central role of Blair Maynard, but had been unavailable. Caine accepted the part instead, to the evident satisfaction of Benchley himself who had always envisaged him in the role.

There may also have been another reason, as Michael Caine says, 'I heard that one of the reasons I got *The Island* was that an executive's wife had seen me in *The Swarm* and had told her husband, "This man has carried that picture all on his own. If he can carry *that* then he can carry *this*." So they gave me *The Island*.'

Caine, ever mindful of his creature comforts, was undoubtedly also swayed by the promise of Antigua as a location. However, the weather didn't quite fulfil expectations, as Caine's co-star Frank Middlemass remembers: 'In Antigua they found an idyllic location and re-created a native village. Then the heavens opened and washed the whole thing away. There was a great delay while we were all wading about in all this mud, waiting for the floods to subside.'

Blair Maynard is an investigative reporter who sets off to find out more about a series of Bermuda Triangle-style disappearances, taking his son along with him on the trip. The pair are captured by a gang of isolated and inbred pirates who intend to kill Maynard after he has improved their bloodline by impregnating the only sane woman left on the island. They brainwash his son and turn him against his father, leaving Maynard to save them both.

The Island never lived up to the success of its predecessors. Critics felt the opening hour of the film worked, but from then on it seemed to lose its way, and, as John Pym pointed out in the *Monthly*

Film Bulletin, 'the pirates included several honours graduates from the Bernard Miles School of Pirate Impersonation'.

'*The Island* is a lethargic venture by the *Jaws* production team into the dubious terrain of cannibalistic degeneracy, inhabited by those low-budget money-spinning shockers, *The Texas Chain Saw Massacre* and *Hills Have Eyes*,' wrote Philip French in the *Observer*, concluding, 'It's like an episode of *Biggles, Charter Pilot* rewritten for *Playboy*.'

Nigel Andrews in the *Financial Times* decided that: 'Michael Caine ... has been Hollywood's walking talisman of doom. From *The Swarm* to *Ashanti* to *Beyond the Poseidon Adventure*, if it starred Caine it was usually a disaster by name, disaster by nature. No disrespect to the actor himself, that deadpan, chipper East End charm has been a light to lighten the most stygian darkness, and sure-to-goodness Caine is at it again in *The Island*, a Caribbean-set clinker.'

'I've never seen it because I hate to watch myself,' says Frank Middlemass, 'but I think it's fair to say it was a flopperoo.

'I think Michael has defended it by saying it was ahead of its time. I think the problem was that it fell between two stools, they started to soft pedal in the middle and it ended up being neither one thing or another, part Disney, part thriller.'

In one respect, however, the film did resemble *Jaws*, as Caine vividly remembers: 'We were on a coastguard cutter—you know, those things that chase the druggies—and we were anchored in one spot for about four days, with all the rubbish going over the side in the same place.

242

'On the fourth day they said, "Right, Michael, over you go and swim round the boat."

'And I said, "Have you looked in the bleedin' water!"

'There were all these sharks. Richard Zanuck said wasn't it amazing—on the entire shooting of *Jaws* they never saw one real-life shark, and now they were doing *The Island*, which has no sharks in it, they'd seen nothing but sharks all the time.

'"Well," I said, "I'm terrified of sharks, and I'm not a great swimmer, either!"'

★   ★   ★

Since *Carrie* and *The Fury* Hollywood had been avidly debating the question of whether director Brian de Palma was a worthy successor to Alfred Hitchcock. His new film certainly paid homage to his mentor with its opening and closing shower sequences, reminiscent of *Psycho*.

Dressed to Kill featured Angie Dickinson as a sexually frustrated middle-aged wife who, after making a pass at her psychiatrist (Michael Caine), is murdered leaving the flat of a man she has picked up at the Metropolitan Museum of Modern Art. The murderer who carries out the frenzied attack appears to be a tall blonde woman. The only witness is a high-class call girl played by de Palma's wife, Nancy Allen, who is then stalked by the murderer as her next victim.

Meanwhile, the psychiatrist is receiving messages on his answering machine from a patient called Bobby who confesses to the crime, and declares that the psychiatrist's own missing cut-throat razor was the murder weapon.

Dressed to Kill was by turns praised as a brilliant and effective thriller and derided as a gratuitous piece of cinema with a gory murder scene. Either way it was an immediate and resounding success in America and Caine was highly praised for his successful underplaying of the character of the transvestite psychiatrist who is eventually exposed as the murderer. The film rocketed to number one in the ratings in its first week and took the (then) huge sum of £10 million in twenty-four days.

'Despite its plot faults, *Dressed to Kill* is a film that puts the long-absent crackling tension back into the auditorium,' wrote David Castell in the *Sunday Telegraph* adding, 'If you can watch this merciless, mordantly funny thriller without being seduced by its razzle-dazzle, then the loss is yours.'

In the *Daily Express* Ian Christie had praise for all concerned:

Angie Dickinson puts on a nice display of frustrated sexuality and Nancy Allen is beautifully confident as the high-class tart. Caine coasts through his part with his usual aplomb ... It doesn't matter that the plot has more flaws than a second-hand suit and that the ending is something of a cheat. This is a masterly piece of film-making with the grip of a hangman's noose.

In the *Standard* Alexander Walker analysed the connection with the master of suspense:

Hitchcock made great play in *Psycho* with the transvestite twist—Tony Perkins assuming his dead mum's persona and wardrobe to become the killer. De Palma knows this is old hat—why any

244

gay disco can show you as good (or as ghoulish).

He takes his film into the further regions of transexualism—the sex-change itself—with Michael Caine—there's style for you!—as a fashionable psychiatrist whose svelte patients are always threatening his professional standards or his life.

The film opened in Britain at the time of the Yorkshire Ripper killings when feelings were running high. In Bradford a group of women threw a bucket of pig's blood at the screen. Said Caine, 'They said he was doing it because he'd seen *Dressed to Kill*. Of course, when they arrested Peter Sutcliffe, it turned out he'd never seen it.'

Angie Dickinson appreciated her co-star. 'Michael is one of the best storytellers I know,' she says. 'No one does it better than the English actors. I had a great time filming with him; he was funny all the time on the set and when I wasn't laughing I was listening to him telling stories. It was very difficult to concentrate on the serious business of being murdered by him.'

'It's Michael's talent and humour that make him so sexy,' she told *Interview* magazine several years later. 'If a man walks into a room and he's a hunk you think to yourself "Wow". And that's it. Michael takes you way beyond that.'

But while it was easy for Caine to judge his interplay with Angie Dickinson, Brian de Palma was an altogether different proposition. 'De Palma is not a very emotional man,' says Caine. 'I did a scene at the end where I was the transvestite, and I had to cry on the floor. I always have a cigar somewhere around, and I stick it on the side of the scenery, while I do the scene.

'I finished the scene and De Palma came over and put his hand out and pulled me up off the floor and said, "Cut." He gave me my half-a-cigar back, and he got out a lighter and lit it.

'And the Assistant said, "Wow, he must really think that's great!"

'I said, "Why?"

'He said, "Brian De Palma would never do that unless you were absolutely fabulous!" That's how emotional he is.'

One thing worried Caine. 'I thought, Jesus, I'm putting on tights and a bra. Supposing I get to like this? Fortunately I hated it, I really hated it. A stunt girl played my double and you really couldn't tell the difference until one electrician said, "I know the difference between you two." I said, "What?" and he said, "You've got hairs coming through your tights."'

★　　★　　★

By 1980 Michael Caine had appeared in every conceivable kind of film, apart from Westerns and horror movies. He has still to make a Western, but his horror début came with *The Hand*, the first feature from a new director—Oliver Stone. The story, adapted by Stone from a book called *The Lizard's Tail* by Marc Brandel, featured a cartoonist who loses his hand in a horrific car accident and gradually becomes obsessed with the dismembered limb.

Although Stone was an unknown director in 1980, Caine decided to take a chance with him: 'I wanted to do a horror film, and they introduced me to this man who'd never directed a film; I thought he was very good and we got on immediately. All he ever talked about was this film he wanted to direct about Vietnam—it wasn't called *Platoon* then—so I kept saying there was nothing in it for me, because there were no British soldiers in Vietnam.

'But he desperately wanted to direct his first film.'

If the bees in *The Swarm* couldn't act, the Hand in *The Hand* certainly could. Created by Carlo Rambaldi, the special effects man from *ET* and *Alien*, the hand had a life of its own. Whether crawling through the undergrowth in hot pursuit of Caine, or trying to strangle him, the severed limb dominated the film but couldn't manage to save it. It simply wasn't well written enough for a psychological thriller, nor quite horrific enough for a straight schlock horror movie, *Variety* declared:

In reality, it is perversely funny to view this small hand scurrying around the floor or skulking in corners awaiting its next victim, and the visual image of its bringing a fully grown man to his knees is akin to sitting center ring for a wrestling match between Tweety Pie and Dumbo ... Although Caine evokes some sympathy after he loses his hand and particularly in scenes with his daughter Mara Hobel, he spends most of his time sweating and grimacing into the camera lens. It's not a pretty sight.

While David Denby in *New York* magazine commented, 'Stone takes a considerable risk in making his hero a bastard (Caine gives a creepy flaring-nostril-and-bared-fang performance). The movie is skilled, but it's all so damned *unpleasant*.'

The Hand never appeared in British cinemas. In 1983, two years after it came out in America, it received a low-key video release in the UK.

Oliver Stone was later to win Oscars as director of *Platoon* and *Born on the Fourth of July*; and Caine moved on to his next project, again having managed to survive unscathed. Critic Alexander Walker has observed Caine's ability to shake off bad movies through the years: 'Michael can walk away from a bad film, brush it off and it doesn't harm him. There are other stars who, if they have a run of two or three bad films, their popularity starts to slide, their agent gets worried.

'Oddly enough with Michael he can detach himself from a disaster. To some extent it's that he's played well in a bad film, but it's not always the case. There are some films that even he looks bad in, but he can still be unaffected professionally.

'The good ones are the ones that you remember and that's the test of a star.'

*　　　*　　　*

Escape to Victory reunited Caine with director John Huston, with whom he had enjoyed such a happy working relationship five years earlier on *The Man Who Would be King*. In the intervening years Caine and Connery had visited Huston on what they thought was his deathbed after he had undergone open heart surgery. Caine later recalled the moment: 'I'll tell you how sick he was: as visitors they gave us just two minutes. John was lying there, his eyes half open, and Sean and I stood there, two grown men, crying, and we said, "Hello John," and he looked up, he could hardly speak, and he said, "Peachy, Danny, you've come to see me." We knew he was dead.

'Six weeks later he was directing another film.'

Escape to Victory is a story of escaping prisoners of war, using the game of football instead of a wooden horse as the escape device. The plot revolved around a football match, set up for propaganda purposes between the Allied prisoners and the German national team, which becomes the cover for an elaborate escape plan.

Caine added a new rank to his acting military career, as Captain Colby, a former West Ham and England star who becomes involved in the German plans for a propaganda victory over the Allies. Caine describes him: 'Captain Colby is uncomfortable with himself, the sort of person who is always looking to see where others are uncomfortable with themselves, where there's an opening, somewhere for him to smack in. So I tried to play him with great watchfulness, tremendous stillness. Very, very quiet, so that the tiniest movement was a violent act.'

To add realism to the picture, professional footballing stars had been cast in the parts of the team. 'In the beginning all the footballers thought they were just there to be footballers, but we ended up having parts as well,' says one of those cast, Mike Summerbee. 'Michael and I had a scene where I had to keep diving and heading the ball into the net. Michael would then come up to me and say some dialogue and I had to reply.

'Michael said to me, "I'll tell you what to do; follow me around and I'll keep you in camera. They see enough of me, it'll be nice for them to see you for a change."'

As well as Summerbee, the list of genuine footballers trying their hand at acting was impressive. Pele not only took a role, he also choreographed the matches, or 'designed the soccer plays' in the words of the credits. He was joined by Bobby Moore, Osvaldo Ardiles, Mike Summerbee and John Wark as well as several other European internationals. It was certainly a new experience for the footballers. Says Mike Summerbee, 'All the actors wanted to be footballers and all the footballers wanted to be actors. The whole experience was like one long booze-up, one long football team tour.'

The location for the film was Hungary. 'They needed a stadium that looked pre-war and the only one left in Europe without any floodlights was the one in Budapest,' explains Bobby Moore.

One of the footballing actors was Tim Pigott-Smith. 'The combination of footballers and actors worked very well, socially,' he says. 'I think the footballers were under great stress when it came to acting, and the actors were under great stress when it came to football.'

Sylvester Stallone, who as Rocky had made his name with another sport, joined the cast as Hatch, an American who eventually joins the team as goalkeeper. 'Sylvester Stallone was a very different type of person to Michael. He kept himself to himself a lot more,' says Bobby Moore. 'But when he was with us he was fine, though not as easygoing and accessible as Michael.'

Stallone had more than football on his mind as Caine remembers: 'While we were doing *Escape to Victory*, Sly Stallone was writing *Rocky III* or *IV* or

V, I never know which one. He'd come in to dinner and then say, "No, I gotta go write this goddam movie", and he would go and write.

'Then he'd come out again and say, "Sod it, I'll come to dinner anyway."'

'Michael was very much one of the boys,' says Mike Summerbee. 'While we were out in Budapest they had an election, although there was only one candidate. It meant that there was no drinking allowed on the day of the voting. Michael had been away in Paris and when he came back he was wearing combat trousers with pockets all down the sides. The pockets were full of booze, everything you could think of, vodka, whisky, gin, everything.

'That night we sat down for dinner in the restaurant and the waiters couldn't understand what was happening. We weren't having anything to drink but we were getting absolutely legless. It was all being passed around under the table.'

By his own admission, Caine was not universally known for his sporting prowess, and the physical activity required proved something of a strain. 'I have never been so footsore, so bloody weary, with a bad back, swollen ankles, pulled tendons. I suddenly realized I was nearly fifty, on the field with people fifteen years younger than me and already retired.'

'I believe Michael Caine could have done a little bit more about getting himself into shape considering he was appearing with Pele and Bobby Moore,' says Tim Pigott-Smith, 'but he didn't seem to care and I doubt very much if anyone who saw the film did either!'

Caine got through by trading footballing tips for acting advice with the professionals. 'From our

251

point of view it was a great opportunity and a great experience to be involved in,' says Bobby Moore. 'Michael was a true pro. When it came to our lines, he told us just to be ourselves and be relaxed about it.

'He did pretty well as a footballer too. He was a great delegator, and he got the younger people doing a lot of the running. The whole thing was great fun to make.'

Just as the film was virtually completed the actors' strike of 1980 was called and Caine had to return home to Los Angeles. When the strike was over, he had to make a 'day trip' from LA to Budapest to complete the final scene!

Unfortunately, when the film was finally released in the UK in 1981, the combination of footballers playing actors, and actors playing footballers failed to work on the critics.

'*Escape to Victory*, the most egregiously silly sortie into Nazi Germany the cinema has yet given us, is *Match of the Day* meets *Stalag 17*,' declared Nigel Andrews in the *Financial Times*, and Alexander Walker commented in the *Standard*:

Michael Caine, playing a pre-war soccer star, gives the film what bite it has. But you feel he's fighting against the hopeless odds of Huston's slack direction as well as the fact that the POW camp, except for a token bunch of East European 'slave workers' introduced for plot purposes, looks like a fat farm where people go to lose flab, not regain freedom.

The chubbiness of the players did not go unnoticed by the *Daily Mirror*'s Arthur Thirkell either:

The match compensates for the flabby screenplay. The soccer skills of Bobby Moore, Osvaldo Ardiles, Mike Summerbee and Pele are skilfully blended to obscure the panting efforts of Michael Caine and other overweight actors. Sylvester Stallone plays a goalie who would be considered a joke even in Chelsea's colours.
Small boys will love it.

But Eric Shorter in the *Daily Telegraph* demurred, 'Mr Caine is Mr Caine wherever he goes and nobody would want him to be anybody else even if he tried.' Tim Pigott-Smith, describing his feelings on meeting an actor who had been a well-known film star for over fifteen years by now, agreed: 'It came as a complete shock to me that Michael Caine was so completely normal!'

*　　　*　　　*

Caine swapped his football boots for a pen in his next role as playwright Sidney Bruhl in *Deathtrap*. Ira Levin's thriller had been a huge hit in New York, becoming the longest running mystery in the history of the Broadway theatre. By 1981 the play was to be turned into a film, with Sidney Lumet directing.
Deathtrap is a complicated thriller with more twists and turns than a route map of Monaco. Caine had seen it on Broadway where John Wood had taken the lead role of Sidney Bruhl, and had made no secret of the fact that he was interested in the film version. The play had been adapted for the

screen by Jay Presson Allen who was also the executive producer. Initially she had doubts about Caine's suitability for the leading role of the fading dramatist; so Caine's Hollywood agent at the time, Sue Mengers, invited her and Caine to a dinner party. By the end of the evening Jay Presson Allen had been won over, and Caine was to play Sidney Bruhl. Says Caine, 'Jay had obviously seen a lot of my films. But I've done a lot of lightweight stuff and if these were the ones she had seen, they would have given her no idea whether I could do *Deathtrap*. That's such an emotional role. So being able to talk to her made all the difference.' Being on the spot in Hollywood was finally starting to pay dividends for Michael Caine.

Sidney Bruhl is a thriller writer whose last four plays have been flops. Returning to his idyllic East Hampton home and his wife Myra (Dyan Cannon) after his latest disastrous first night, he receives a script from a young would-be playwright he tutored in a seminar on the art of thriller writing. Bruhl recognizes a sure-fire hit and decides to murder the young dramatist and claim the work as his own.

Bruhl invites the young man, Clifford Anderson (Christopher Reeve) to his home where he kills him. Later that night Anderson reappears in the house. The shock is all too much for Myra, whose weak heart gives out. It then transpires that Bruhl and Anderson have conspired to kill Myra for her money, their homosexual love affair confirmed by a screen kiss (which caused much excitement in the tabloid press). From there on the plot spirals in complexity, binding its characters ever more tightly to itself until finally it disappears almost in a puff of smoke. We're left with—the première of a new thriller, *Deathtrap*! Which is where we came in—or is it?

'Sidney Lumet had been promising me a picture for twenty years and he finally gave it to me,' said Caine. 'Sidney is very good for actors because he understands us, has tremendous sympathy, and is more interested in the performance than the "Look, Ma, I'm directing" school. If you're having problems he'll figure it out in a sentence. Only the great directors can do that. The others bend your ear for hours; instead of listening to you they're listening to themselves.'

Lumet chose an unusual method of shooting, each sequence being filmed in long takes, more like scenes from a stage play than the quick set-ups of movie-making. 'Comedy, particularly a macabre comedy like this one, requires delicate timing,' says Caine. 'Since Sidney knew his actors were all stage veterans, he felt free to take a theatrical approach. Thus there was no way for an editor to throw off the timing by hacking into the performance.'

And says Lumet, 'The line between good mystery and good comedy is very thin, a knife edge. Both take delicate timing. And when an audience is scared, their natural reaction is to laugh.'

Caine won universal praise for his portrayal of Bruhl and many thought the part would win him an Oscar nomination. The *Financial Times*'s critic, Nigel Andrews, wrote:

More of the plot you could not extract from me, though you try with torture instruments: the story being landmined with highly classified surprises. But the chief surprise of all is Michael Caine. Cast Caine as an SS *Poseidon*

255

salvage-hunter or an asbestos-clad bee pursuer in *The Swarm* and you wonder how he ever passed a screen test. But plunge him into word-happy comedy (*vide California Suite* and this) and he sizzles like a new-forged sword. Here as beleaguered Bruhl, firing off incensed aphorisms at all passers, he's a joy.

And Derek Malcolm in the *Guardian* agreed:

Caine is now not your average beddable leading man but a character actor of some note, quite capable of turning a moderate line into something that seems funnier than it is. And his performance as Levin's blocked playwright, stooping to murder for the sake of a Broadway hit, is the main pleasure of a concoction that otherwise depends for its effect on a succession of ever more unlikely surprises.

'Michael was very nervous about kissing Christopher Reeve in *Deathtrap*,' says Caine's director on *Alfie* (and *Educating Rita*), Lewis Gilbert. 'Reeve said to him. "Don't be nervous"; and Michael said, "Well, I am a bit." "Why?" said Christopher. "Well," said Michael, "suppose we like it?"'
'The most difficult thing I ever did in the cinema was to kiss Christopher Reeve,' says Caine. 'I said to him, "If you open your mouth I'll kill you." Before we did the scene I drank about half a bottle of brandy and he drank the other half. And I said, "If you stick your tongue out I'm going to put my leg up backwards—you know, the way Doris Day used to do."

256

'It wasn't a happy day, I'll tell you. Christopher is taller than me so I was the fluffy one. I would've had to dance backwards if there'd been any music.

'Bombed as we were, we made sure we only had to do one take. We got that son-of-a-bitch right the first time.'

CHAPTER TEN

'TURN RIGHT AT WOODY ALLEN':
1983–1986

'My success has been gradual. At each stage I've had time to draw breath and get used to it. I wasn't some kid who suddenly got handed a million dollars and was ruined by it. Each decade for me has been better than the last.'

Michael Caine

Caine's comment in 1984, that each decade was for him better than the last, was certainly to hold true during his sixth. He reached his fiftieth birthday on 14 March 1983, just a few weeks before one of his most acclaimed films, *Educating Rita*, was released. *Rita* immediately won its place among his best work and earned him a BAFTA award and his third Oscar nomination. Two years later *Hannah and Her Sisters* finally won him the Oscar itself.

Caine was also becoming a pillar of the Hollywood establishment. At one time he toyed seriously with the idea of becoming a US citizen, which would have allowed him to visit Britain for six months every year instead of just three; but, as he got closer to the top in Hollywood society, the idea faded as he became more of an 'honorary British showbiz consul' instead.

Caine was asked to be joint chairman of the campaign to raise funds for the British team at the Los Angeles Olympics, and as part of the fund-raising effort hosted a glitzy Hollywood party for Prince Andrew. (He also defended the Prince over the notorious incident when photographers covering the trip were sprayed with paint). Three years later, on 23 July 1986, Michael and Shakira were among the guests in Westminster Abbey when Andrew married Sarah Ferguson.

At another dinner event Caine found himself placed very close to the Queen. 'There was another man sitting between us who obviously wasn't too scintillating,' remembers Caine, 'and finally she leaned across and said "Mr Caine—" and I said, "Yes, Ma'am?"—"Do you know any jokes?" So I said, "Yes, I do. Do you know any?" She said, "Yes" so we started to tell jokes.'

Another milestone in Caine's life was his decision to take his driving test at last: 'I learned in three lessons,' Caine told the *Sunday Express*. 'My instructor said he knew I'd learn very quickly because I was an actor. He said, "The minute you got in the car you took on the role of an expert driver—and of course you were."'

More bizarre, the unmistakable Caine tones were immortalized on vinyl by the pop group Madness with their record *Michael Caine*. Caine couldn't understand what all the fuss was about, but at the request of his daughter Natasha he sat patiently repeating the words 'My name is Michael Caine' numerous times for the benefit of a sound engineer.

Among Caine's closest friends in Hollywood were the director Billy Wilder; agent Irving 'Swifty' Lazar; Leonard Goldberg, the President of Twentieth Century-Fox; and Jackie Collins and her husband the nightclub owner Oscar Lerman. Caine and Shakira were definitely on the 'A' list at all Hollywood parties.

Another neighbour and friend was the artist David Hockney. One day, Caine dropped round for tea while Hockney's mother was staying with her son. Conversation progressed, and after a while Mrs Hockney asked Caine, 'And what is it you do, dear?'

*   *   *

In Caine's career to date his finest roles had all shared a common link—good writing. *Alfie*, *Sleuth*, *California Suite* and *Deathtrap* had all started life as stage or radio plays, and their translation to the big screen had provided Caine with well-written parts with which he had done his utmost.

Whilst on a visit home to England Caine went to see a new play that was at the time the hottest ticket in the West End. The play was called *Educating Rita*, by Liverpool playwright Willy Russell and its star was a young actress called Julie Walters. It was a two-hander about a young woman who wants more from her life and the college lecturer who helps her find it. Caine had heard the play was to become a film and he was checking it out.

As soon as he saw the character of Frank Bryant, Caine knew he wanted the role. In the play Frank's part was by far the smaller, but that didn't worry Caine in the slightest. What Frank did in abundance was *re-act* and Caine knew that this was his greatest talent. From the time in rep in Lowestoft when the producer had told him 'the thing about you is you know how to listen', Caine had made it his business to be a *re*-actor.

Rita is a hairdresser in search of something more fulfilling than shampoos and sets, or human reproduction—the role her husband envisages for her. After signing on for an Open University course she is allocated her tutor, Frank Bryant, a local lecturer.

While Rita has a unquenched thirst for education, Frank's problem is the opposite. He has drunk too much and for too long at the fount of knowledge. Literature has become stale for him and his own poetry has been locked away at the bottom of a drawer. Now he only gets through his lectures—and his life—with the aid of a bottle of whisky.

In time Rita, with her raw enthusiasm, injects some life and hope into Frank's disillusioned mind. In response to an exam question 'How would you overcome the staging problems inherent in Ibsen's *Peer Gynt*', Rita's response is logical and winning: 'Do it on the radio', she announces.

Finally their roles are reversed. Frank has taught her all he can and now it is time for her to teach him. Waiting for Rita to return from summer school, Frank has eagerly been looking forward to teaching her the poetry of William Blake. When she announces that she's already 'done' Blake, Frank is crestfallen. He tells Rita that she has become like all the other students; he feels he has taken away her individuality. But the root of his problem, as Rita points out to him, is that he is scared she doesn't need him any more. He is too frightened to take on the world on his own behalf. He won't accept that his poetry is good, and has come to enjoy his self-pity.

Frank's behaviour worsens, culminating in a wonderfully drunken performance from Caine at the lectern in the University Main Hall. Frank is reprimanded by the authorities and, realizing the situation cannot continue, decides to take the sabbatical offered to him in Australia. Rita's farewell present to him is a haircut, symbolic of the academic and personal re-birth she hopes he is going to undergo. She, of course, has passed her exam with distinction.

The director of the film version of *Educating Rita* was Lewis Gilbert, who had directed Caine's first major international success, *Alfie*. Gilbert had already had Caine in mind for the role of Frank Bryant, and he also insisted on retaining Julie Walters as Rita, giving her her first film role and the chance to repeat on celluloid the role she had played to such acclaim on stage.

It was very different from the film envisaged by the financial backers, as Lewis Gilbert remembers: 'Originally the Columbia bigwigs wanted Dolly Parton to play Rita, set the film in the USA and get Frank and Rita to go to bed together.'

Caine had some difficulty explaining his decision to America: 'There was a picture lined up for me with Sally Field who had just won the Oscar,' Caine recalls 'And they said "So you're going to do the picture with Sally Field" and I said "No". And they said "What are you going to do then" and I replied "I'm going to do something called *Educating Rita*" and everyone said "What the hell is that" so I said "Well it's a play that's on in London and it's going to be turned into a film." And then they said "Well who else is in it" and I said "A girl called Julie Walters". "Who the hell is Julie Walters" they said and I told them "She's very good, she's in the play and she's going to do the movie and I'm going to do it with her." And then they said

262

"*Educating Rita*, that must be about Rita, what do you play in it." I said "I play a guy called Frank" and they said "Well you should be doing a picture called *Educating Frank* if you want to be the star of this picture."'

The film was shot in the summer of 1982 at Trinity College, Dublin; a convenient location for Caine as he was prevented by tax regulations from spending more than 90 days in England in any year.

Caine put his all into the part, physically as well as mentally. He gained 37 pounds in weight and grew a beard. He wanted to look like a full-blown academic and he succeeded. Walking through the cloisters of Trinity College he was approached by an individual with a very similar appearance to himself. Caine didn't need to ask who it was—he knew already, and he was right ... the Professor of English!

Willy Russell adapted his own play for the screen and vividly remembers Caine's verdict on his efforts: 'Michael Caine said to me at Dublin airport, "And do you know, I haven't had to change one word of this script!"'

It was Julie Walters' first film role and she feels she learnt a great deal from her experienced co-star. 'The most important thing I learnt from Michael was to save myself. If there was a scene where I had to get upset then I would already be upset in the car on the way to the location and I'd have nothing left by the time we came to do the scene. From Michael I learnt how to save myself for the actual take.

'I was amazed when on the first day he was already there as the character. I remember thinking, "My God", because we'd had no rehearsal, no read-through, nothing, but he was already totally the character.'

Caine gave Julie Walters a camera so that she could record the experiences of her first film and she racked her brain for a suitable return gift: 'I didn't know what to give him, so I gave him a plastic razor with some lines from the play engraved on it.'

Educating Rita attracted universal acclaim. In the *New Yorker* Pauline Kael wrote:

Michael Caine is the least pyrotechnical, the least showoffy of actors. He has prodigious ease on the screen; it's only afterwards that you realize how difficult what he was doing is. His role here is a masochistic one, but Caine transcends that aspect of it ... This is a master film actor's performance. The goal of Caine's technique seems to be to dissolve all vestiges of 'technique'. He lets nothing get between you and the character he plays. You don't observe his acting; you just experience the character's emotions. He may be in acting terms something like what Jean Renoir was in directing terms.

Alexander Walker, writing in the *Standard*, said:

Caine's unselfish partnering of the newcomer doesn't conceal the finesse that now shades his every appearance on the screen—only in one scene where he gets drunk in front of the class do you feel the actor is ill at ease and thus maladroit. There is something very satisfying in being a critic long enough to watch a *Rita* join the *Alfie* we discovered when we were younger. The job seems better than work.

And in the *Financial Times* Nigel Andrews declared:

Michael Caine wears an ill-kempt beard that looks as if he's been attacked by a small flying sheep, and his seedy jackets are strained to rupture point by expanding girth. Caine has the best deadpan comic timing of any straight-ish actor on the screen today. And it takes nerve of a high order for a movie star to combine this much underplaying with looking like something the cat would have left outside.

'Everybody says that *Educating Rita* is like *Pygmalion*,' Caine told the *New York Times*, 'but I saw it, and played it, as *The Blue Angel*. He loves her vulgarity and the more vulgar she is the more he loves it. Not that I'm as good as Emil Jannings, but as I watched her, grew more involved with her, in the picture, my character descended.

'I based the Professor on two friends of mine, one of which you wouldn't know, but the other is the playwright Robert Bolt (*A Man For All Seasons*, *Lawrence of Arabia*) whose brilliance has put even arrogant men at his feet.'

The friend that New York audiences would not have recognized is generally thought to be Peter Langan, who, together with Richard Shepherd, was Caine's business partner in Langan's, the restaurant they set up in Stratton Street in Mayfair. Langan's, modelled on La Coupole in Paris, soon became one of *the* places to eat and be seen in London, and has retained its popularity amongst celebrities and star-spotters alike. Peter Langan, who died

265

tragically in 1988 after a fire at his Essex home, was an extravagant and notorious character who, once met, was never forgotten.

The character of Rita was equally important to Caine. 'Although I'm playing the Professor in this, in real life I was Rita,' he told the *Sunday Telegraph*. 'When you're working class everybody expects you to be stupid. If you're halfway bright, which I was, everyone falls about with surprise.'

Both Michael Caine and Julie Walters received BAFTA awards as Best Actor and Actress of 1983 for their portrayals of Frank and Rita, and the film was named as the Best Film of the Year.

Educating Rita was also a big hit in America, and meant that Julie Walters went on her first American publicity trip, again under the tutelage of Caine. 'Michael was such an easygoing bloke and so sweet to me. When we went to America to publicize the film he said, "I'll take you to a couple of restaurants in New York." We were sitting in Elaine's and Michael was pointing out stars to me—"There's so and so . . . and look, over there is so and so"—and he was taking an innocent delight in pointing out the stars to me, even though he was the most famous person there.

'In fact when we went to Elaine's there had been a huge storm and I was late. And I rushed in and said to Michael, "I'm so sorry I'm late, I must just go to the toilet." And Michael said, "It's over there, turn right at Woody Allen."'

Caine and Walters were both also awarded American Golden Globes as best actor and actress in a comedy. And of course Caine received his third Oscar nomination for Best Actor of 1983.

The Oscar ceremony routine was starting to

become familiar. He had been through it twice before, for *Alfie* and *Sleuth*. But this time Caine was a little more nervous. He was deeply proud of his performance as Frank Bryant and felt that if ever he deserved the accolade of an Oscar it was now. Also nominated were three other British actors, Albert Finney, Tom Courtenay and Tom Conti, along with the sole American Robert Duvall. When the announcement came it was Robert Duvall who took the award for *Tender Mercies*.

Caine was, as always, philosophical: 'I was a bit suspicious when I arrived at the ceremony and I was put about six people in, because usually if you're a nominee you're put on the edge so you don't waste time.

'Bob Duvall and Shirley Maclaine were sitting there so I thought this is a bit of a hint as to what's going to occur. That was an awkward year because there were four British actors and Bob Duvall, so I think there was no chance.

'You know something about not winning the Oscar? It's one of the most negative emotions you ever have. Up until that time you're thinking, "I'm not going to win, am I going to win?" And then they say, "Robert Duvall" and you say, "Right, let's go to Swifty's party" and you don't think about it. You don't say, "Oh my God I'm going to have a nervous breakdown" or anything. It is absolutely nothing not to win the Oscar; it's not disappointing, it's not anything, I assure you. I've *not* won it three times so I know what I'm talking about.'

*　　　*　　　*

Apart from shaving off his beard Caine did not need

to change his appearance greatly to take on his next role. The gone-to-seed look he had created for Frank Bryant would adapt easily to the character of Charley Fortnum, the honorary consul of Graham Greene's novel. Fortnum was also a disillusioned middle-aged man with a dependency on the bottle.

Businessman Fortnum is the honorary consul (or official British government representative) of a small town in northern Argentina, a town run on the typecast South American principles of corruption and coercion. The new doctor is the half-English half-Paraguayan Dr Plarr (Richard Gere), exiled from his own country because of the political activities of his father.

Dr Plarr is attracted to a beautiful young Indian prostitute who works in the local brothel. He is amazed when several months later he is told she has left the brothel and married Charley Fortnum. Nevertheless they begin an affair which culminates in Clara's pregnancy.

Plarr is told by two rebel friends that they can obtain his father's release from prison in return for information about the American Ambassador's forthcoming visit. Plarr pumps the unknowing Charley for information, but in the event the rebels accidentally kidnap Fortnum instead of the Ambassador. Plarr realizes the group's mistake when he is summoned to the hideout to deal with the 'Ambassador's' hangover. Plarr is then told by Colonel Perez, the local chief of police (Bob Hoskins), that his father was shot dead a year ago.

Plarr flies to Buenos Aires to try to persuade the British Ambassador to intervene but meets with a refusal. Charley is then wounded in an escape attempt and Plarr discovers that he knows about his affair with Clara. The hideout is surrounded by police, Plarr goes out to talk to Perez and is shot. Clara and Charley are reunited.

'What fascinates me about this part is that he's a much older and weaker man than I've played before,' Caine told *Woman's Own*. 'I've always spent my time playing strong young men.

'The difference and the depth of this character attract me. Apart from being a tragic figure, there's a lot of humour in there too. I really enjoy doing him. And he's a human being. In the end, when he's been kidnapped and threatened with death, he proves to have tremendous strength and courage.

'It's like a lot of people—they look weak and vacillating until they're under stress. Then they react in a totally different way from what people expect, and come out heroes.

'I've always been fascinated by losers who turn out to be winners in the end.'

The original plans to film in South America were overtaken by the political events of spring 1982. 'First of all I went to look at locations in Argentina,' says director John Mackenzie. 'I followed in Graham Greene's footsteps and went all over the north looking at possible locations. Finally I flew to Mexico City and the day I landed I picked up a paper and the Falklands war had started. I had missed it by twenty-four hours. Mexico then became the obvious choice.'

Having suffered so much trouble with his stomach on location over the years, Caine was taking no chances when it came to Mexico. 'In Mexico one's stomach was forever in a state of chaos,' remembers John Mackenzie. 'Amidst the riots going on in my stomach I was very pleased to have a companion like Michael around. He is a pleasure to be with, witty and pleasant.

'In fact, he was the only one of us who never got ill. He took precautions and while the rest of us started off by eating out and were saying how wonderful and ethnic the restaurants were, Michael stayed in the hotel.

'He was the only one who left Mexico the same as he arrived, all the rest were thinner and paler. Richard Gere was the worst of all; he became very wan. Michael was his usual cheerful and convivial self, holding forth in the hotel dining room.'

The director John Mackenzie had worked with Bob Hoskins before, on *The Long Good Friday*, but *The Honorary Consul* marked the first time that Caine and Bob Hoskins had worked together. It was the beginning of a firm friendship—reputedly, Caine's first words to Hoskins were 'Come here, my son. You're going to earn a lotta money and you've got to learn how to look after your money. Come to your Uncle Michael and I'll tell you.'

'Bob is raw and lovable and Michael is more urbane,' says John Mackenzie. 'They liked each other very much. Michael always said he wished he'd had the role in *The Long Good Friday*. They are very different types so they don't clash.'

'The first time that Michael and I worked together he got me a diabolical bollocking,' says Hoskins. 'It was in Mexico, where we were filming nights for *The Honorary Consul*. We were due to do a scene where Michael was on first and then I would come on and he was meant to be drunk. This is the first scene we'd had together and we were both terrified. We thought, don't touch a drop for goodness' sake or we'll ruin it. So we sat there for about four hours drinking coffee. I had the shakes, we'd drunk so much coffee!

'Finally they said, "Michael, you're on!" and he said to me, "Come over and watch it." So we walked across this square in Mexico, and as we were walking Michael was getting more and more "drunk", and by the time we got there he was "legless". And I got a bollocking for taking him on set legless! I said, "We've been on coffee all week!"'

Just as the film was about to begin shooting, *An Officer and a Gentleman*, starring Richard Gere and Debra Winger, opened in America, making Gere a sensation. Paramount were reputedly less than happy that he was stuck down in Mexico playing a disaffected Catholic doctor. It was Gere, who has never been happy with his sex symbol image, who had insisted on doing the film.

With the success of *An Officer and a Gentleman*, however, that image became even more difficult to shake off; in the *Sunday Times*, Iain Johnston wrote:

Unfortunately Richard Gere, as Doctor Parr [sic] is too much a film star—i.e. someone bigger than the parts he plays—and cannot convey the man within. Perhaps William Hurt could have achieved it better, for he has the capacity to subordinate his presence to his parts.

Michael Caine, on the other hand, as the Consul, has never been better. Bibulous, cuckolded, a joke figure of no diplomatic relevance, he revels in the humour of the part—'My wife was an intellectual; she didn't understand human nature'—and enriches a slight

271

plot with a sizeable performance that is more than worthy of the character Greene created.

In the *Guardian* Derek Malcolm remarked on how *The Honorary Consul* had the:

> requisite brooding atmosphere that Greene demands; his seedy South American country positively festers with extinguished hopes and newly lit fear—so that the splendid performance from Michael Caine as the drunken British Consul achieves a sometimes spectacular veracity.
>
> Caine goes from strength to strength as he ages, here curling at the edges like Trevor Howard in *The Heart of the Matter* or Alec Guinness in *Our Man in Havana*.

And David Castell in the *Sunday Telegraph* concluded 'Michael Caine is again exceptional as the drab, disappointed man afforded one late chance of happiness and dignity.'

After some research work, it was decided that Americans had very little idea what a consul was, let alone an honorary one, and so the film was given the rather bland title of *Beyond the Limit* for the US release. John Mackenzie was furious, but his faith in the performances of his cast, especially Caine, was undaunted: 'Michael is never too professional, never too blasé not to try. His performance in that role was terrific, really terrific, sincere, warm and touching.'

*   *   *

If spy Kim Philby, who had defected to the

Russians over twenty-five years before, suddenly decided to return home to London, what might happen? That was the idea behind Caine's next project, *The Jigsaw Man*, first announced as a film as far back as 1976. He was cast as the Philby character, apparently to shudders of horror from the real Philby in Moscow, as Victor Davies in the *Daily Express* reported in 1982.

> Philby, now thought to be a major-general in the KGB, was reported as looking like a man who had a bad smell under his nose when he heard the news. Could they really be proposing to have this lower-class mummer Caine, this 'jumped-up milkman' impersonate him?
>
> Philby's son John, who had been left behind in England, insisted that his father was only 'mildly amused' at the casting of Caine. John himself voiced the thought that Trevor Howard (educ. Clifton College) would be a better choice...
>
> Caine says, '... I received a telephone call from Philby's son. He told me, "I can assure you that my father never said those things because he hasn't the faintest idea who you are or that you intended making a movie about him."
>
> 'Young Philby said, "Ring him and you'll find out." He offered me his father's telephone number in Moscow. I was surprised. I said, "Can you really get through as easily as that?" He said, "Yes, I talk to him any time I like."'
>
> Caine added, 'I thought about it, but then I declined. I have made too many spy pictures to want to get involved too heavily in any intrigue. As it is, I live a fish-bowl life. I wasn't looking for an extra swim.'

Michael Caine was to play 'Sir Philip Kimberley', a former Head of the Secret Service who had defected to Moscow many years earlier. Increasingly drunk and belligerent in old age, Kimberley is becoming an embarrassment to the Russians who also want to get hold of a secret dossier which he hid just before his defection.

The Russians fake Kimberley's death and make him undergo radical plastic surgery to change his appearance. Then they give him a new identity as 'Sergei Kuzminsky' and send him back to England to retrieve the dossier, with the promise of a million Swiss francs and a new life in Switzerland once it is handed over.

Arriving in England, 'Kuzminsky' goes instead to see an old friend, Admiral Scaith (Laurence Olivier) and, unrecognized by Scaith, offers to sell him the dossier on Kimberley's behalf. But the police give chase and, realizing Kimberley has turned on them, so do the Russians, who shoot and wound him. Kimberley flees to a country cottage belonging to his daughter, Penny Black (Susan George), who only recognizes him when he calls her by her childhood pet name, 'Lovebird'.

She then takes him to a local hotel for safety, while she goes back to London to get money and her boyfriend Jamie Fraser (Robert Powell) a narcotics agent with the UN.

Meanwhile, fingerprints have proved to Scaith that 'Kuzminsky' is in fact Kimberley. He tracks Penny down, and she agrees to act as go-between at the handover of the cash for the dossier, on condition that Scaith keeps the secret of 'Kuzminsky's' true identity and takes him to

Switzerland, unharmed.

At the rendezvous at a country church, a shoot-out takes place and it transpires that another high-level MI5 man, Sir James Chorley, has been working for the Russians for years, and Jamie Fraser is not a narcotics investigator but a Secret Service man.

In hospital Kimberley is the subject of another assassination attempt, but survives and he and Fraser shoot the assassin instead. The film ends with Kimberley and Scaith plotting to auction the dossier to the highest bidder.

After considerable delays, *The Jigsaw Man* was up and running in May and June 1982, but the production soon ran into financial trouble. Only a month after shooting began, Caine's co-star Laurence Olivier walked off the set on the advice of his lawyers, reportedly because he hadn't been paid.

Caine kept on working for as long as possible to try and hold the picture together, but eventually the set closed down with only six days' shooting needed to finish the picture, and Caine returned to California, still owed an estimated $900,000. 'It was a bit of a shock when I looked at my air ticket just before I came back and discovered it was only one way,' Caine told the *Sunday Express*, 'which meant I had to pay my own fare back to Los Angeles. It had never occurred to me to look at the ticket before. If I had, I'd have guessed that if they couldn't afford to give a return ticket they couldn't afford to make the picture.'

Back home Caine began growing a beard for the role of Frank Bryant. Even if the money to complete *The Jigsaw Man* was raised, it was now too late as there wouldn't be time for Caine to shave off his beard and re-grow it for the start of *Educating Rita*. Caine was philosophical about the fate of *The Jigsaw Man*. 'It's not as if this film were a masterpiece that we should be rallying round,' he remarked at the time. 'It's just a good, straightforward thriller. I'm sorry about what's happened. But it has taught me a lesson, I promise you; it won't ever happen again.'

However, the next few months produced a dramatic change of fortune. Producer Benjamin Fisz, who had also co-produced *The Battle of Britain*, was suddenly offered four million pounds to complete the movie by a man called Mahmud Zipra. It emerged that Zipra had been Fisz's next-door neighbour for four years although they had never spoken.

By another stroke of luck, director Terence Young was able to negotiate six days' shooting to complete the movie at Shepperton Studios, where Caine was by now, at the end of 1982, just finishing *The Honorary Consul*. The break in production meant that editing was a Herculean task, involving piecing together a labyrinthine plot with not quite all the shots in the can, not to mention matching up the sound between shots where it didn't match at all! Seven months after filming had ceased, *The Jigsaw Man* was finally finished. To complete the hard-luck story, the film never received a cinema release in the UK, although it has appeared on video.

The problems in the film's making were fully reflected on the screen, as David Edelstein's review in the American magazine, *Voice*, seems to show.

The Jigsaw Man reunited Laurence Olivier and Michael Caine in a senile John Le Carré-style espionage thriller with damp, gray settings, and skulking KGB moles, and more flabby exposition than a month in the House of Lords...

[It's] probably the most garrulous and doddering spy movie ever made. Even the great cinematographer Freddie Francis (*The Elephant Man, The French Lieutenant's Woman*) seems to be drowsing in his wheelchair.

After having expanded his girth so successfully for *Educating Rita* Caine now faced the task of losing the 37 pounds he had gained. Worse still, he only had six weeks in which to do it. The opening scenes of his next film, *Blame It on Rio*, would involve him romping on a beach with a slim girl less than half his age who was supposed to find him irresistibly attractive.

Caine took to a diet of pineapple and water and everyone else took flight. By Caine's own admission he was an extremely difficult man to live with over those next six weeks.

The location which had tempted Caine was the luscious beaches of Rio de Janeiro. The film was also billed as a sophisticated comedy, very much the direction in which Caine wanted his career to go. His old ambition to be the 'Cockney Cary Grant' was still strong.

The director of *Blame It on Rio* was Stanley Donen whose previous hits had included *Singin' In the Rain* and *Seven Brides for Seven Brothers*, and the screenwriters were Charlie Peters and Larry Gelbart; the latter (who was also executive producer) being one half of the duo that had written

The Wrong Box, Caine's first major venture into comedy on film, seventeen years before.

Caine played Matthew Hollis, a middle-aged coffee trader who decides to take a holiday in Rio with his business partner Victor Lyons (Joseph Bologna). Both estranged from their wives, they take their teenage daughters Jennifer and Nicole (Michelle Johnson and Demi Moore) with them.

Matthew is seduced by Victor's daughter Jennifer and then after his moment of madness spends the rest of the week worrying about his friend finding out as Jennifer's feelings for him become more and more obvious. His own daughter realizes what has happened and sends for her mother. Meanwhile Jennifer has told her father she is in love with an older man and Victor is pursuing every Brazilian male who could possibly be the culprit, enlisting an ever more agitated Victor to assist him.

Eventually a distraught Jennifer botches a suicide attempt and returns from the hospital in the arms of a young Brazilian. Matthew's wife arrives and he discovers that she and Victor have been having an affair. However, they decide to give their marriage a second try, and the adults fly back to São Paulo, leaving the youngsters to enjoy the delights of Rio.

The film was based loosely on Claude Berri's 1977 film *Un Moment D'Egarement* but the remake lacked any of the charm or subtlety of the original, which had managed to convey the effect of careless youth on mature middle age and the inevitable destruction of the friendship between the two men. The critics felt that Caine had done what he could with a lacklustre script, but concluded that the film looked like a rather seedy sex romp. The *New Yorker*'s Pauline Kael wrote:

278

The forty-three-year-old father is played by Michael Caine—he was born in 1933, and this picture seems to have aged him another ten years. I think this is the first time I've seen Caine on screen and taken no pleasure in his performance. He manages to give his flashy, 'smart' lines a reading that makes them sound humanly plausible, but the result is counter-productive. His acting comes across as overemotional; the near-incest keeps him sweating and rushing about anxiously, and you just want him to get free of this picture—which is like a splurgy, risqué episode of *The Love Boat*—and back to sanity.

Writing in *The Times* David Robinson said:

What is objectionable is not the affair itself (that has even its touching moments) but the way that the film milks its every comic or sexual possibility, trading on the Humbert Humbert in all of us, before turning around in affected moral disapprobation, to impose retribution on the poor man by sending him back to his odious shrew wife. Michael Caine is the hapless hero; the carefree, topless natives of Rio de Janeiro provide local colour.

And Andrew Sarris in *Voice* declared:

Fortunately Caine is a talented enough and likeable enough performer to create the illusion of a mature irony at work on catchpenny material. Caine's insouciance, rueful stoicism, and even poignant yearning are much more than

279

the movie deserve. Indeed Caine builds up so much sympathetic identification with his point of view that a great deal of warm laughter is built up over his fear, guilt, and remorse in acquiring carnal knowledge of his best friend's teenage daughter.

Caine, true to form, defended himself: 'I got very good reviews for it in the United States from critics I respect. I neither produced, directed or wrote the picture—so I couldn't be blamed for the taste. I did it in order to prove that I could do comedy, and with the reviews I got for it I had proved that I could do comedy.'

However, the love scenes were one thing that disconcerted him. 'I'm prepared to go to any lengths to make acting "real",' says Caine, 'but with love scenes I'm not. I'd rather not do them at all.

'I don't like to be with bare-breasted women on screen because no one is looking at me for a start! I'm wasting my time. Even the women are looking at her tits to see how they compare to their own!'

But over the years he has devised his own way of dealing with love scenes: 'The thing to do is to be very professional,' he advises. 'This is a job, this is what we're doing and the fact that we're in bed and have never met before is part of it. What I do is joke about a lot so the female is never under the impression I'm getting off on a freebie.

'I always carry a mouthspray and just before a scene, just in case anyone has got any breath problems, I always squeeze it in my mouth, and when the actress says, "What's that?" I say, "Here, have a taste"; and that gets round that one!'

One by-product of the film was that, on its release in Britain, it gave the papers a chance to produce some 'Michael Caine still sexy at 50' articles—a fact which Caine himself was forced to acknowledge, but always in his own dry fashion. *The Sun* reported:

> Caine's magnetism for Michelle in the movie may be the work of scriptwriters, but in real life he still has the power to attract women. 'Women I don't know still put pieces of paper with their phone numbers in my pocket,' he says with an air of resignation. 'It gives me a bit of an uneasy feeling. If they can put something in without me knowing, they could take something out.'

Dick Clement and Ian La Frenais, two of Britain's top comedy writers (responsible for such eternally popular TV series as *The Likely Lads*, *Porridge* and *Auf Wiedersehen, Pet*), turned their attention to making feature films. By 1984 their film credits already included one film for ex-Beatle George Harrison's Handmade Films, *Bullshot*. *Water* was a new film they were devising for the same company.

The new script was written by the duo and Bill Persky, with Clement directing and La Frenais as producer. Set on the mythical colonial outpost of Cascara, its central character was Baxter Thwaites (Caine), the island's rather vague Governor, whose liking for the sleepy rhythm of life on Cascara is not shared by his exuberant Latin American wife, Dolores (Brenda Vaccaro), who wants a posting with more excitement. The only disturbances are provided by a local rebel leader, Delgado (Billy Connolly) who has declared, rather wildly, that he

281

will only communicate in song until Cascara is given its independence.

When Delgado attempts to win support for his cause from Cuba, the Whitehall mandarins wake up to the existence of Cascara, and despatch Sir Malcolm Leveridge (Leonard Rossiter in his last film role) to tell Thwaites that the island must be abandoned and the population settled elsewhere, much to the delight of Dolores.

Before he leaves Cascara, however, Sir Malcolm learns that an American company has discovered mineral water of a unique quality on the island, and he secretly encourages the rebels so that British intervention, Falklands style, can be arranged.

Baxter Thwaites ends up at the centre of a raging political storm as Cascara is invaded by tourists, the media, an idealistic environmental activist played by Valerie Perrine, and a German-led band of mercenaries hired by the French to destroy the potential competition to Perrier water. Playing the leader of the mercenaries was television presenter Paul Heiney, learning how to become an actor for one of the episodes in his television series *In At The Deep End*.

Amid the publicity, Delgado decides to take his message to the United Nations, where, with musical accompaniment by George Harrison, Eric Clapton and Ringo Starr, his 'Concert for Cascara' is a huge success, and the island wins its freedom. French bombs, however, have destroyed the water supply and the future looks bleak—until a gush of oil signals a new change in the islanders' fortunes.

'Michael's name came up for the part of Baxter Thwaites quite early on,' says Ian La Frenais. 'We had wanted to work with him ever since the
282

seventies.

'One Sunday morning I rang Michael at his house and said we had a script and wanted him to read it. I took it round to his house, or rather my brother in-law delivered it for me. That lunchtime I was due to go to a party at Leslie Bricusse's house, and like a lot of parties in Hollywood they had valet parking. By sheer coincidence Michael was there and when he saw me he put his thumb up. Then he came over and said, "It's great, we've got to do it."

'I was so excited I couldn't wait to tell Dick, I rushed back out again—the valet parking guy hadn't even had time to park my car—and drove round to Dick's and we opened a bottle of champagne.

'Then I suddenly realized it must have looked rather rude to the Bricusses. It was a very rare situation.'

'The script arrived on a Sunday morning,' recalls Caine. 'I wasn't doing anything at that moment so I sat down to read it. I'm not kidding. Four times I had to stop because the tears were streaming down my face! It took me two hours. At the end I said, "I'll do it." Just like that. It's completely nuts, but underneath it's saying something.'

The Caribbean island of St Lucia became Cascara, except in the scenes involving the oil rig where the less exotic north Devon coast was pressed into service. The casting combination of Caine and Connolly meant there was lots of laughter on set—and off. 'Michael and Billy found each other enormously funny,' says Ian La Frenais. 'It made for some of the best dinners of my life. They used to treat it like a jazz concert and each take a sixteen-bar solo. Michael is a fabulous raconteur

283

and terribly terribly funny; they would just take turns to make us laugh.'

'Michael and I got on like a house on fire,' Connolly told Michael Aspel on *Aspel and Company*. 'We drank and talked together all night, every night. All the American actors would get early nights and do their weight training, and Michael and I would prop up some bar and make each other fall off the bar stools with laughter. Michael smokes the same cigar for hours and hours.

'The hotel rooms we were staying in were extraordinary. They only had three walls; the fourth was open to the fantastic view over the valley and the sea, with just mosquito nets to protect you. There was a plunge pool at the bottom of the beds overlooking the view—desperately dangerous when you'd had a few!'

Despite the late nights the ever professional Caine was always ready and waiting when it was time for filming to start. 'No one ever needs to tell Michael that he is needed on set, he seems to have a sixth sense and is always there just a beat before,' says Dick Clement. 'One day there was a change in the schedule and Michael and Valerie Perrine ended up in the same car going back to the hotel. "Did you shoot today," said Valerie to Michael. "No," said Michael. "But when were you called?" "Ten o'clock." "Aren't you furious?" she asked him. "No," said Michael. "Waiting around is what we're paid for, the bit in front of the cameras is the fun." Valerie Perrine told me afterwards that it really changed her way of looking at filming.'

The film opened to a mixed reception from the critics. David Castell wrote in the *Sunday Telegraph*:

The new comedy by Dick Clement and Ian La Frenais, *Water*, is a throwback to such films as *The Mouse That Roared* and *Carlton Browne of the FO* ... The central idea is fresh, the playing enjoyable (Michael Caine as the slovenly governor and Fulton Mackay as a roguish parson are particularly good) but the scattershot of comic incidents has no real bite.

In the *Guardian* Tim Pulleine lamented:

Sad to see the names of Dick Clement and Ian La Frenais attached to this whimsy about political manoeuvrings in a Caribbean Ruritania, which might be called neo-Ealing in conception but comes out merely puerile in execution, with glossy production values only emphasizing the TV sketch thinness of the writing. At least, as the harassed Governor, Michael Caine displays his customary practised ease. Caine could do this sort of thing standing on his head, and on this occasion might have.

But Iain Johnstone in the *Sunday Times* came down in favour, on balance:

'*Water* is a gentle comedy with a faint period feel about it but it is sustainingly and warmly enjoyable.'

Clement and La Frenais would certainly like to work with Caine again: 'Something that frustrates us, something that we're determined to do before we die, is to write a script for Caine and Connery, to bring them together again after *The Man Who Would Be King*. It's something we'd love to do.'

*   *   *

Only three days after completing *Water* at the end of July 1984, Caine took up an offer to replace James Caan in a thriller based on a Robert Ludlum novel, *The Holcroft Covenant*. Caan had apparently left the production over a combination of exhaustion and a disagreement with the producers. 'Jimmy Caan was unable to do it at the last minute,' says Caine, 'and they were in terrible trouble. I really did it in twenty-four hours—I did it so quickly I wore my own clothes because they didn't have time to make any.

'And it was also British Film Year. I thought *someone* ought to make a British film!'

Another reason Caine agreed to take over was his long-standing desire to work with the director, John Frankenheimer, who had been responsible for *The Manchurian Candidate*. Frankenheimer, who had always felt that James Caan had been miscast, was delighted to have Caine as his replacement. For Caine, it also signalled his total acceptance as an international star—instead of James Caan being replaced by another American, Michael Caine was now regarded as equally acceptable to the American studios—and audiences.

The plot revolved around the covenant of the film's title, a document signed by three Nazi generals, Clausen, Kessler and von Tiebolt, just before they committed suicide in 1945. Forty years later Clausen's son, Noel Holcroft (Michael Caine), a New York architect, is contacted by a Geneva banker and told about the covenant. Apparently the three guilt-stricken Nazis had set it up in order that some of the damage caused by their war crimes might be alleviated by their male descendants. Noel Holcroft is amazed to learn that the covenant is now worth four billion dollars.

Holcroft returns to his apartment block in New York to find a stranger dead in the foyer. A message on his answerphone from the same man urges him to go to London and make contact with von Tiebolt's daughter, Helden Tennyson (Victoria Tennant). Once in London he is taken by Helden and an MI5 escort, Leighton, to the home of Oberst, a dedicated anti-Nazi who wants to establish that Holcroft will not use the money to try and create another Nazi regime. Once Holcroft proves that his intentions are good, he is sent to meet Johann, Helden's brother, a journalist working in London, and a third man, Jurgen Maas, a prominent musician. However, unknown to Holcroft, Maas has ordered the murder of Holcroft's anti-Nazi mother back in New York. The attempt fails and she leaves for London to persuade her son not to take any part in the covenant.

After an attempt is made to abduct Helden, she and Holcroft travel to Geneva, but are intercepted by Leighton who takes them to Oberst. On arrival they find Oberst and Holcroft's mother both dead. From the hidden video camera Leighton discovers that they have been killed by Johann who is the leader of a worldwide neo-Nazi organization aiming to use the covenant to finance terrorism.

Holcroft is initially concerned for Helden's safety, but after a chance remark he realizes that she too is implicated and that she and her brother are involved in an incestuous affair.

The signing of the covenant takes place but Holcroft has organized a press conference to follow, where he exposes Johann and then shoots him. Alone with Helden, Holcroft tells her he loves her, but that he knows the part she has played in the affair. Handing her a gun he turns away.

'Robert Ludlum's books may be confusing, but the films based upon them are well nigh indecipherable. *The Holcroft Covenant* is tackled by John Frankenheimer with the gaudy zeal of a sixties spy film, ablaze with meetings held in tourist locations and frenzied camera angles during the action sequences ...' wrote David Castell in the *Sunday Telegraph*, adding 'Caine gives far more than the role of the puzzled heir deserves; others among the cast are less generous.'

The *Daily Telegraph*'s Patrick Gibbs pointed out that

Since *The Holcroft Covenant* is from a novel by Robert Ludlum it must surely have been persuasive originally.

Alas it is no longer so in the hands of the once esteemed director John Frankenheimer. Its story of Nazis having left a sum in a Swiss bank to fund a revival 40 years later seems more and more ridiculous as it progresses between New York, London, Berlin and Geneva, with much double-crossing by those who are heirs to the fund.

Even Michael Caine as the principal of these can make nothing of it.

And the *Mail on Sunday* commented succinctly, 'Michael Caine is the only dignified element in this Nazi-revival hokum thriller, which makes even the original Robert Ludlum novel look like a masterpiece.'

'I must say that Michael Caine is the best movie actor I've *ever* worked with,' said John Frankenheimer. 'He has such an understanding of a part that he's able to do it so well without any fuss. I once heard a definition of talent, that talent is doing easily what other people find difficult. He does it so—on the surface—easily, yet he works his tail off. He brings so much to the part. He brings not only expert professionalism and total dedication, but he makes my job so much easier, he gives me exactly what I want, and you can't ask for anything more than that, can you? He's also terribly intelligent and he's terribly professional. That's all terrific, but on top of all that is the enormous talent and craftsmanship, and that doesn't come from doing one movie. That comes from doing fifty movies, which is what he's done.'

'Michael has the ability to balance his own ebullient personality with his incredible facility as a professional performer,' says his co-star in the film, Anthony Andrews. 'One day he had an impossible scene where he has to deliver an immensely long speech, several pages of dialogue, at a press conference in the film. If it had been me I would have been huddled in a corner until the final seconds, but Michael was completely undisturbed at having to do that much. He was cracking jokes at his usual rate of five a minute up until the last second and then he walked up, hit the mark and did the whole thing in two takes.

289

'Michael has an incredible understanding of film and cameras, such that he can appear to be doing not very much and then when you see the rushes you realize that in fact he was doing an awful lot more than you thought. He is very much like Laurence Olivier in that respect.'

Even in a Nazi thriller, though, Caine couldn't escape his old enemy—the horse. 'There was one scene which we had to do in a riding school,' says Anthony Andrews. 'The whole premise of the scene was ridiculous anyway and it looked even more ridiculous when it was acted out. Michael was all dressed up in a suit, and he had to get on this horse. He was terrified out of his wits as he hates horses anyway. No one could speak, me for laughing and him from fear. In the end we had to get off the horses and do the scene walking around in circles leading them.'

★ ★ ★

Naturally, it's not just the actors who have to jump through hoops for the sake of showbiz. *Sweet Liberty*, made during the summer of 1985, was almost certainly based on personal experience of the way in which writers are often treated by the film business. Alan Alda was the writer, director and star.

Alda played Michael Burgess, an academic whose serious novel on the American Revolution is being made into a film. He looks on with increasing horror as the script and plot take twists and turns which are both historically inaccurate and far removed from the original. The director of the film dismisses his objections and tells him that in order to appeal to a young movie audience it is essential to do three things: 'Defy authority. Destroy property. And take people's clothes off!'

The screenwriter who has adapted Burgess's novel, Stanley Gould (Bob Hoskins) has more experience of writing game show questions than movies, but is keen to improve his rather boorish script. He advises Burgess to bypass the director and go straight to the leading characters with his suggestions.

Burgess does so and is entranced by the leading lady Faith Healy who is playing his beloved patriot heroine Mary Slocumb. In turn she is impressed with him and insists that he be present on set for all her scenes.

The leading actor Elliott James (Michael Caine), an ageing but charming Lothario, presents more of a challenge; but he is won over to Burgess's way of thinking after a fencing match.

Eventually Burgess wearies of the fickleness of the film people and realizes that the real Faith Healy is not at all the same person as his beloved Mary Slocumb.

The film climaxes with a key battle scene where Burgess and the extras (all historical battle enthusiasts) confound the director's expectations by charging, rather than running from, the British cannon.

The film reunited Michael Caine and Bob Hoskins after *The Honorary Consul*. Alan Alda had, according to Caine, come straight to the point when offering him the part of Elliott James: 'Alan Alda said, "I've written this role especially for you." So I asked him what it was, "A conceited old film star," he said, "and you'll be perfect."

'I said to Alan, "Thanks very much. Where are you shooting?" and Alan says, "In the Hamptons, all summer. And we'll get you a house on the beach." So I said yes. Wouldn't you?'

The location was the exclusive American resort of Sag Harbour in the Hamptons and Caine was extremely pleased with his house on the beach, apparently telling Hoskins that in fifty-three films this was the best treatment he had ever received.

Putting Caine's long movie-making career slightly in the shade, though, was Lillian Gish, a film star from the early days (her first film was in 1912), now appearing in her hundred-and-fourth film. She played Michael Burgess's mother, pining for the old flames of her youth. There was also a new young actress cast in the part of Faith Healy who would later make big waves in Hollywood. Her name was Michelle Pfeiffer.

When the film opened in Britain in September 1986 it was to a generally favourable reception, and Caine and Hoskins were regarded as a fine double act, Ian Christie writing in the *Daily Express*:

Alan Alda, who wrote and directed the work, also stars in it as a sincere historian whose book is being trivialized by Hollywood. He gives a likeable impression of the disgruntled author. But he is completely outshone by Michael Caine as a delightfully flippant English film star with a lecherous disposition and Bob Hoskins as a dim extrovert scriptwriter who used to write questions for game shows ... Bob Hoskins' enthusiastic naivety and Caine's amorous dexterity just about save the day.

292

And Tom Hutchinson in the *Mail on Sunday* commented, 'Caine and Hoskins act up a treat. Bob Hoskins' film name here is Stanley. If they're going to continue as a twosome, perhaps Michael Caine should change his to Oliver.'

★   ★   ★

The summer of 1985 continued for Michael Caine with work on *Half Moon Street*. This film, based on a novel by Paul Theroux, told the story of an American economist, Dr Lauren Slaughter (Sigourney Weaver), who arrives in London to work at the Institute of Middle Eastern affairs.

After a few weeks she realizes that she is not going to be able to exist on her tiny salary and is intrigued when, after a drinks reception, she is sent a tape from the Jasmine Escort Agency, outlining how she could improve her financial situation.

After some consideration she signs on with the agency and finds herself spending evenings, albeit in a rather different role, with the same top level politicians and diplomats she is researching by day. Among her clients is Karim, a Palestinian diplomat who arranges for her to move from her seedy Notting Hill bedsit into a flat he is vacating in Half Moon Street, an area heavily populated with Arabs.

Gradually Lauren Slaughter becomes emotionally involved with another of her clients, a lonely widower and radical politician, Lord Bulbeck (Michael Caine) who is currently heading delicate negotiations for an Arab-Israeli peace settlement. However, against his wishes, she insists on keeping on her other clients, partly a device to protect herself emotionally as she feels Bulbeck is himself keeping her at arm's length. In fact, his vagueness is prompted by the security precautions he has been forced to take as his life has been threatened over the negotiations.

After Bulbeck fails to appear for a rendezvous they planned in Geneva, Lauren Slaughter sleeps with a stranger she meets in the hotel who calls himself Sonny.

Back in London Bulbeck contacts her and agrees to slip his guards to spend his birthday with her at the flat in Half Moon Street. As she gets ready Sonny—who is in fact a hired assassin—arrives, ready to kill Bulbeck. Lauren, although terrified, manages to smash the glass shower door over him.

Karim then arrives and reveals that he set her up in the flat to destroy Bulbeck and his reputation by killing him in a love nest. But Karim is killed by Bulbeck's guards who unknown to him had been keeping the flat under surveillance. Lauren Slaughter is caught in the crossfire but only slightly wounded, and is reunited with Bulbeck.

In general the critics felt that the film adaptation had failed to do justice to Paul Theroux's novel and instead of being a study of power and victims had become just a conventional love story.

In the *New York Times*, Janet Maslin wrote:

Mr Theroux's Lord Bulbeck is a poignant, lonely septuagenarian, whereas the film's Lord Bulbeck is Michael Caine. And this elderly man's tangential importance to an intrigue plot has been modified, in a vain attempt to expand this into a leading role. But Mr Caine, as successful as he is in affecting quiet desperation, can never seem sufficiently bereft and friendless to explain his dependence on Lauren. When Mr Caine appears holding flowers in the rain so that Miss Weaver can sniff, 'How totally out of character, Sam—I'm touched,' the moment is too awkward for even this unfailingly graceful actor.

And the *Daily Telegraph*'s Victoria Mather commented 'It is an honourable failure which boasts an interesting subject and an intelligent performance from Weaver. Caine could have done without his glue-on moustache.'

★　　　★　　　★

As a leading actor, Michael Caine rarely considered roles that weren't the pivot of a film. But, Caine being Caine, there were exceptions, and he accepted a cameo role in *Mona Lisa* as a favour to his mate Bob Hoskins and to *Company of Wolves* director Neil Jordan. Squeezing it into his already hectic schedule in the September of 1985, Caine was only on the set for a week; but the result was an electrifying on-screen relationship between his character and Bob Hoskins'.

Director Jordan had also written the screenplay, an uncompromising vision of low-life and corruption in London.

Bob Hoskins played George, a small-time crook who is released from prison after seven years. He goes back home to South London where his wife refuses to let him come back and doesn't want him to see their daughter. George also needs to find work, not necessarily above board, but preferably something that won't land him back behind bars.

He goes in search of his old boss Mortwell

(Michael Caine), who he feels owes him a favour, having landed him in prison. Eventually George is given a job ferrying porn videos to Soho shops and driving 'thin black tart' Simone (Cathy Tyson) to her sessions with wealthy clients. Initially the two are antagonistic, but gradually a friendship develops and George agrees to help the 'thin black tart' find her friend Cathy, a young prostitute with a heroin habit, with whom Simone has lost touch.

George is contacted by Mortwell who wants to know what Simone does with one of her clients, a wealthy Arab called Raschid. But all that Simone will reveal to George is that they drink tea.

Now infatuated with Simone, George is determined to save her from the world she moves in and to find Cathy for her. As he makes his inquiries he becomes increasingly horrified as he sees deeper into the world of pimps and drugs, sick videos and exploitation.

Eventually a dope-ridden Cathy is found and rescued from a client, and Simone takes her to Brighton to recuperate. There George discovers that Cathy and Simone are lovers and that his love for her is pointless.

When Mortwell arrives to try to reclaim Cathy, Simone shoots him, and George, realizing that she might have shot him too, leaves and decides to pursue a quieter life and concentrate on rebuilding his relationship with his daughter.

Although the subject matter was bleak the film didn't reject the chance for humour, with Robbie Coltrane taking on a role as George's eccentric friend Thomas, absorbed in the manufacture of plastic food ornaments.

Caine was only on set for about a week, being

paid, as Hoskins put it, 'Two bob and a lollipop', but he still managed to make Mortwell a central character in the film.

'It is quite a violent film and I find that certain levels of violence are endemic in everybody, in actors too,' says Neil Jordan. 'Michael got a particularly empty sleaziness into that role, someone who was dead in the centre. What gratified me was that aspects of the character were able to be suggested in brief, but very telling strokes.

'It's interesting because what I wanted was for him to return to characters in films like *Alfie* and *Get Carter*. Over the years he's begun to play very cosmopolitan roles. I wanted him to be as a man of his age would have been if he had chosen crime rather than acting.'

Caine thoroughly enjoyed playing the hard character of Mortwell: 'I love to lose my temper on film, I mean it's so easy, doing that and crying are the easiest thing, you can get an Oscar for that. The hardest thing to do is comedy—and you'll never get an Oscar for comedy—that's the most difficult thing to do. But shouting and balling and crying is easy.

'Fortunately I'm very much the kind of actor who, when asked "Are you the character in the evenings?" says "I'm not even the character between takes." I had a whale of a time with it, shouting and screaming at Bob, frightening the life out of everybody and effing and blinding—he swears all the time. I'm not a tough guy at all, but I really look it when I play it.'

And Caine was responsive to Neil Jordan's ideas about the part. 'Every director has wild ideas but not all actors respond to them,' says Jordan. 'It was very important to me that something should happen which was ridiculous or comedic just before Mortwell's death. So George shoots him in the foot and he says, "George, you bastard, you've shot me in the bloody foot" and then he's killed.

'For an actor to be able to combine comedy and violence in one scene is very difficult.'

Bob Hoskins was delighted to be working with Caine again, and deeply impressed with his approach. 'He has incredible screen knowledge,' Hoskins told *LA Weekly*. 'He knows where his light is, he knows where to stand and he doesn't want to think about it until everybody's ready. When he did *Mona Lisa*, he just came in, smarmed his hair down, and Bam! he was the seediest man I've ever met in my life.'

Mona Lisa was a huge success and the critics felt that the presence of Michael Caine was an added bonus. 'In an imaginative and surprising piece of casting Michael Caine, proving that though you are big in status you can be big in professional generosity too, makes a relatively brief appearance as George's smoothly manipulative and unprincipled puller of strings,' commented Ann Totterdell in the *Financial Times*.

'Michael was wonderful for the film,' says Neil Jordan. 'I have always thought that Michael is the perfect Graham Greene hero; he has the style and ability to suggest loss and repressed emotions in *Brighton Rock* and *The Heart of the Matter*. He is the perfect embodiment of those men.'

*   *   *

Caine was increasingly keen to build his reputation as a comic actor, but so far the comedy scripts he had been involved in had often failed him. So when, at the end of a very busy 1985, he was asked to appear in Woody Allen's next film, Caine was delighted. He realized that if he made a success of his part he would gain the comic credibility he had been looking for.

The film was to be called *Hannah and Her Sisters* and Caine played the character of Elliot, a New York financial adviser married to the Hannah of the title (Mia Farrow). Elliot finds himself developing a middle-age infatuation with Hannah's sister, Lee (Barbara Hershey), which eventually leads to an affair. Among the other characters are Hannah's first husband Mickey Sachs (Woody Allen), an obsessive hypochondriac convinced he is suffering from a brain tumour, her other sister, Holly, a neurotic would-be actress (Diane Wiest), and Holly's friend April (Carrie Fisher), with whom Holly finds herself in romantic competition for the affections of an architect.

Overwhelmed by his obsession with Lee, Elliot is also guilt-stricken at having betrayed Hannah. Carried along by the situation he becomes ever more agitated until Lee finally tells him that she has become involved with someone else, a literature professor at Columbia University.

The film ends two years on where it began, at the family's annual Thanksgiving dinner. Hannah and Elliot are once again secure in their marriage, and Holly has married Mickey Sachs and is pregnant.

Also in the cast was Mia Farrow's real-life mother, Maureen O'Sullivan, and Lloyd Nolan in his last film role. They played Hannah's ageing theatrical parents, Evan and Norma, who can never leave theatricality behind even in their retirement, and are prone to bouts of geriatric squabbling: 'Your mother gets drunker and drunker and finally she becomes Joan Collins,' declares Evan, and Norma retorts, 'Your father could be anyone in Actors' Equity.'

The film was very much a close-knit family affair for Allen, and Caine soon felt accepted into the mix, even if elements of it were rather unorthodox ... 'In *Hannah and Her Sisters* I was married to Mia Farrow and we had an apartment in New York,' says Caine. 'The apartment we used was literally Mia Farrow's apartment and we had a love scene in bed, Mia and I, which in fact was her real bed.

'Now, I'm being directed by Woody Allen, who is her lover, and I look up and there's André Previn, her ex-husband, who's come to see the kids. Woody said "Action", and I couldn't remember a single line because I thought, "These two guys are watching me in bed with this woman" and I didn't know what to do. I got very embarrassed which is unusual for me in a movie situation.'

Putting Caine into the mix did at first seem an unusual decision and critic Alexander Walker later asked the director about it: 'I asked Woody Allen if he hadn't been just that little bit nervous casting Michael as the Englishman in amongst the Jewish Americans in *Hannah and Her Sisters*. "If the acting is good enough," Woody told me, "nobody bothers to ask what he's doing there."'

According to Caine, another reason that Allen had for casting him was that: 'I appear vulnerable, as if I might cry in a relationship. That's the difference between me and actors like Robert Redford and Clint Eastwood. Can you imagine *them* crying over a relationship?' Caine recalls that

'Woody kept saying to me, "Not so funny, Michael! Not so funny." I said, "Why can't I be funny? I'm making a film with you so I could be funny!" He said, "I don't want you funny; I want you serious. *I'll* be funny—*you* be serious."

'I said, "*I* want to be funny, Woody." He said, "All right, we'll do your one and then we'll do my one."

'He'd say, "You want to do your funny one?" I'd say, "Yes, can I . . . ?" He'd say, "Go on." He used to let me do a funny one.

'Of course we only ever used *his* one.'

Allen's advice worked and earned Caine some excellent reviews. 'The acting in *Hannah* is uniformly excellent, and Michael Caine fits into the Allen repertory company with evident relish,' wrote Iain Johnstone in the *Sunday Times*. 'The director creates his characters on the set rather than in the cutting room and accordingly shoots in long takes, so that the timing of the players remains undisturbed.'

And in the *Mail on Sunday* Tom Hutchinson announced, 'Best of all, though, is Michael Caine as the wistful Elliot, amazed at the way his glands have betrayed him into adultery. His Oscar-deserving portrayal makes up for some recent rotten films.'

The Americans agreed. Vincent Canby in the *New York Times* declared:

Equally stunning are the performances by Michael Caine and Max von Sydow, whose familiar, public personalities effectively disappear into the world of Woody Allen's Manhattan.

It isn't that Mr Caine's performance is all that different from other roles he's had. He doesn't

301

play something wildly off-the-wall, like a Lower East Side junkie or an Afghan freedom fighter ... It's just that *Hannah and Her Sisters* makes better use of his wise, mellow, comically self-aware talents than any film he's been in since John Huston's *Man Who Would Be King*.

Early in 1987 the 1986 Oscar nominations were announced. In the category of Best Supporting Actor the contenders were: Tom Berenger for *Platoon*, Willem Dafoe, also for *Platoon*, Dennis Hopper for *Hoosiers*, Denholm Elliott for *A Room With a View* and Michael Caine for *Hannah and Her Sisters*.

That year, for the first time Caine did not have to attend the traditional 'also-rans' Oscars party, hosted by his old friend Irving 'Swifty' Lazar. He should instead have been at the Governor's party with the other winners. He had finally won his Oscar.

In the event, however, when his moment of victory came he wasn't there at all, being contractually obliged not to stray too far from Paradise Island in the Bahamas where he was shooting *Jaws—the Revenge*.

Caine was naturally delighted to be an Oscar winner at last, though he has always admitted that, given the choice, he would have preferred to win an Oscar as Best Actor for *Educating Rita*, the performance he has always felt was most deserving of the award. And it is rather ironic that Caine and his friend Sean Connery, both leading actors, would finally win Oscars in the Best Supporting category, Connery's in 1988 for *The Untouchables*. Nevertheless, at the fourth go Caine was happy to

302

be the proud possessor of one of the golden statuettes, and even more so for what it represented. 'I took the role to get comedy experience, so that people would think of me as being able to play comedy,' he says. 'Woody choosing me to do *Hannah* made me respectable as a comic actor. I was only on set for four weeks and I got the Oscar for it.'

He certainly earned his spurs in Allen's eyes: 'Michael Caine has got one of the best natural flairs for comedy I've seen. A number of times in *Hannah* I had to ask him to do takes a little less funny.

'It's a talent I'd love to exploit one day.'

CHAPTER ELEVEN

'NOW YOU BUGGERS CAN SEE WHAT I GET PAID FOR!': 1986–1989

'I regard the theatre as an operation with a scalpel. I think movie acting is an operation with a laser. Because it's so tiny and so small half the people say, "I don't know what you're doing." And you say, "Wait until you see the rushes".'

Michael Caine

In 1987 Michael Caine ended his Hollywood exile and returned to British shores. His desire to come back had finally surfaced a couple of years earlier when his wife Shakira caught him lovingly watching repeats of *Black Beauty* for the lush English countryside. She reportedly told him: 'If you're missing it that much, then we'd better get on a plane, fly to England and buy a house there because that is what you need.'

Another factor also prompted Caine's decision. His daughter Natasha had been in America since she was six years old, and naturally regarded the United States as home. He now wanted her to know about her English background and to attend an English school.

Caine set about looking for a house, but his criteria were demanding. He wanted it to be by the river, but not near any locks. It also had to be inaccessible except by its own driveway. He was looking for a home in which to spend a number of years and he was prepared to wait until the right place came along. Finally he found what he was looking for, in a small village in north Oxfordshire. Caine bought the house and set in motion a programme of improvements to be completed before his return.

Finally, in 1987, Caine was ready for the move and said goodbye to his Hollywood friends and neighbours. 'I'm pissed off that he left,' says his friend the director and writer Billy Wilder. 'He always had the best jokes and was a great person to have at a party.'

Moving into his new home Caine made a point of integrating himself into the life of the village. He attended the summer fête, and at Christmas read the lesson in church. 'The Vicar said it was the best box office he had ever had.'

One very important feature of the house for Caine was its garden. As well as his love for gardening he had also become a keen environmentalist, supporting the work of bodies like the British Trust for Conservation Volunteers. In his own garden he wanted to create a sanctuary for wildfowl and was already researching which varieties of plants would attract them.

Natasha was enrolled at a private school in London. Caine wanted her to be a day pupil and to come home to her family each evening, so he also bought a flat in Chelsea Harbour where the family could spend their weekdays—filming commitments permitting—returning to the country for weekends and school holidays.

Caine had always said that his happiest moments had been loading up the station wagon at Harrods on a Friday afternoon, and then setting off for the country. Now he could go back to that routine.

Michael Caine eagerly set about the business of becoming an Englishman again.

*　　　*　　　*

Back on British shores, Caine's first film was *The Whistle Blower*; it cast him in a familiar role—as a spy-catcher—though in this case a reluctant one. The background was Cheltenham and the setting GCHQ, or General Communications Headquarters, the British electronic listening and intelligence-gathering station.

Caine played Frank Jones, a veteran of the Korean war whose son Bob (Nigel Havers) is a linguist in the Russian service based at GCHQ. Increasingly at odds with the world of intelligence, its paranoia, deal-making and disregard of individuals, Bob Jones confesses his disillusionment to his father who advises him to suppress his fears rather than abandon a good career. Unknown to both, their conversation has been monitored by the Secret Service.

Meeting up with a wartime colleague, Charles Greig (Barry Foster), Frank reveals his worries about his son, who is by now convinced that British Intelligence has allowed the Americans to 'plug' recent security leaks at GCHQ, which also explains the mysterious deaths of two of his colleagues, one under the wheels of a train and the other apparently by gassing himself with a car exhaust.

Frank is then shocked to learn of his son's death, apparently after a fall. However, on visiting his flat Frank finds his son's normally chaotic room immaculately tidy and his diary missing. His two flatmates, also both employees at GCHQ, tell him

306

they are not allowed to discuss the matter.

While he is trying to find out the truth about his son's death Frank meets a left-wing journalist who had been contacted by Bob shortly before his death. The reporter is then killed while trying to discover the identity of a mysterious contact whom Bob had been told would help him.

Frank discovers that the mysterious contact was Charles Greig, who had then arranged Bob's murder. Frank gets Greig drunk and extracts a confession, discovering that Bob was killed because he had stumbled on the identity of a high-level mole in the Security Service, Sir Adrian Chapple (John Gielgud). The Security Service now threatens Frank not to take the matter any further; they are unwilling to unnerve the Americans any more, and want to wait until things have quietened down before 'neutralizing' Chapple.

But Frank goes to Chapple's home and forces him to write a confession before killing him. Frank then disappears into the crowds at the Remembrance Day service around the Cenotaph.

The director of *The Whistle Blower* was Simon Langton who had directed the television film series of John Le Carré's *Smiley's People* and was now making his feature film début. 'I took short money on it and invested my time which is how it got made,' Caine told *Woman's Own*. 'And I'm extremely proud of the result, especially as it's also a first film for the director Simon Langton. Every now and again I do a first film, and I must say I seem to pick winners. I did Ken Russell's first, *Billion Dollar Brain*, and I did Oliver Stone's first, *The Hand*. I think *The Whistle Blower* is another winner.'

However, there had been some initial confusion. 'They sent me the script and after I read it I sent it back and said the part is really too small,' says Caine. 'It was the guy with the girls and everything, the young lover. They sent it back and said, "You've read the wrong part. We want you for the father!"'

The film was shot in and around Cheltenham, and many of the citizens took part as extras; except for the employees of the GCHQ, who were banned from doing so!

Caine won praise from the critics for his portrayal of the war veteran whose belief in justice and the established order is shaken by the realization that expediency often wins over truth.

'Michael Caine, having meandered through several parts of late as if they were hardly worth the trouble, is excellent again in *The Whistle Blower* . . .' declared the *Guardian*, 'Caine apart—and he does manage to lift things off the ground—the rest of the film is muted and rather dull.'

Michael Pye in the London *Daily News* wrote:

It's only after an hour of tangled exposition—fretful spymasters, prison breaks, echoes of real scandal at GCHQ—that the film acquires any kind of mainspring to start it moving: a father's need to understand, and perhaps avenge, the death of his son.

It also acquires its one strong point: the unshowy performance of Michael Caine as the kind of ex-serviceman who shines his medals for Remembrance Day, who respects authority implicitly, but comes to think that his kind of patriotism is betrayed by what authority actually

308

does. Caine does everything right; the stolid
vowels, the pain in the eyes, the anger and the
contempt at the end, but he's stuck in a sluggish
script, full of undramatized research; a vast and
terrifying subject trapped in a small film.

And *Today* agreed:

> Michael Caine, almost single-handedly, brings
> salvation. The actor doesn't get older. He gets
> better. Vulnerability suits him. Here, he's
> paunchy round the jowl and girth. But he makes
> something wholly dignified and touching of
> Frank.
> Among his many recent movie roles he's
> seldom been better.

Playing father and son was amusing for both Caine
and Nigel Havers. In real life their backgrounds
were just slightly different—Caine the son of a
Billingsgate porter and Havers the offspring of the
Attorney-General. 'He was a very good father,' says
Havers, 'though it seemed a very odd idea for him
to play my father because we're from such different
backgrounds. I remember meeting Michael before
shooting began, at Langan's probably. He said,
"Are you going to come down accent-wise, or am I
going to posh up?" And I said, "You'd better posh
up," though of course he didn't. But when it came
out no one thought it strange at all...
'In the film I wore glasses and Michael didn't.
I've got bad eyesight, but I've worn contact lenses
for years. I found my old glasses in the back of a
cupboard; I don't think I'd worn them for fifteen or
twenty years. I probably bought them at the time to

try and look like Michael Caine, so it gave me a sense of déjà-vu.'

★   ★   ★

Michael Caine had been friends with Frederick Forsyth, author of *The Day of the Jackal* and *The Odessa File*, for many years. In fact, Caine had been keen to take the lead in the film of *The Day of the Jackal*, but director Fred Zinnemann had decided that he wanted an unknown in the part and had cast a then unfamiliar young actor called Edward Fox.

When Caine read a copy of Forsyth's new novel *The Fourth Protocol*, he was immediately attracted to the part of John Preston, the rebel spy-catcher. There were definite similarities between the character of Preston and Caine's old friend Harry Palmer, whom he had played to such acclaim in the sixties.

Caine and Forsyth agreed to set up their own production company to make the film. Forsyth would, for the first time, adapt his own novel into a screenplay, and between them they would raise the finance. They made a start by deciding to defer a sizeable proportion of their own fees and plough the money back into the production. But raising the rest of the cash wasn't easy. 'We went round cap in hand for ages,' says Caine. 'You go to meetings in Hollywood and people you know extremely well—you're godfather to their children, or something—look right through you. It's a dreadful feeling being a producer. I wouldn't . . . well I don't know . . . no, I really wouldn't want to be a producer again, I don't think.'

John Mackenzie who had directed Caine in *The*

Honorary Consul joined the project as director. 'The part of John Preston was not so demanding of Michael as his part in *The Honorary Consul*,' says John Mackenzie, 'so it was more a matter of keeping the character interesting.

'Michael is a director's actor; he says, "Tell me", and then he does it. He's the sort of actor you look forward to working with. It's not eternal fights and egos, there's none of that.'

A young actor called Pierce Brosnan, extremely popular in his television role as Remington Steele in *Sapphire and Steele*, and at that time a contender to become the new James Bond, was chosen for the other major role.

The story involved a KGB plot to breach the Fourth Protocol, an agreement between the superpowers to ban the smuggling of atomic weapons into each other's territories. Pierce Brosnan played the KGB man sent to infiltrate Britain and secretly assemble an atomic bomb, and Caine played the unorthodox spy-catcher, unpopular with his superiors, who tracks him down. The film was shot in Finland and in the UK.

'Michael was allowed to choose his own wardrobe for the film,' recalls Frederick Forsyth. 'We started filming in early April 1986 and he chose his usual powder-blue lambswool polo-neck sweater, a black zip-up jacket and a heavy anorak. By the time we got to filming the sequence in which Michael had to run down the length of a traffic jam it was late June or early July and about 84 degrees Fahrenheit.

'We were filming on the as yet unopened Chelmsford by-pass. Prince Michael of Kent had come along to observe a film being made, and he and I were sitting under huge parasols with cool

311

drinks watching Michael do this quarter-mile run. Michael, of course, had to continue wearing the outfit he'd chosen for the film. It took eight takes, and Make-Up were following ten seconds behind, out of shot, to cover up his beetroot face between takes. Between puffs, Caine said, "Now you buggers can see what I get paid for!"'

Once again, the film, in the critics' eyes, did not live up to Caine's acting. In the *Evening Standard*, Alexander Walker wrote:

Most of the characters talk 'officialese'—the Russians talk it more slowly to show they are Russians, or maybe their tongues are just frozen: it's always midwinter in Moscow, even while, curiously, it's midsummer in England . . . It's left to Caine to provide the humanity. He's very good as a sort of up-dated Ipcress Man for whom his snooty bosses' titles and hyphens hold no fear and from whom he expects no favour.

And in the *Sunday Times* Iain Johnstone commented:

Caine is a true master of the screen, communicating so much with so little material, but here he is given—or has given himself, since he is an executive producer—too little. We skate over his broken marriage, his relationship with his son, his relationship with his job, his personal moral code—sacrificial victims to the all-consuming plot. But if he were allowed these visual soliloquies our empathy with his dilemma would make us infinitely more involved in this high-speed international chess game.

312

'Someone asked me the other day what the difference was between John Preston, who I play in *The Fourth Protocol*, and Harry Palmer, who I played in *The Ipcress File*,' said Caine. 'I said Harry Palmer was Woody Allen and John Preston is Clint Eastwood—and I am one of the very few actors who can play both.'

When his next film, *Surrender*, was described to him as a classic screwball comedy, the kind his hero Cary Grant would have starred in, Caine was immediately attracted to the idea. His co-star would be Sally Field, who had suffered with him in the upturned hull of the SS *Poseidon* almost eight years before, and both had higher hopes of this new collaboration.

Caine played Sean Stein, a writer whose enthusiasm for the female form has been tempered by suits for alimony and palimony from his wife and lover, and by the final injustice of being robbed of his wallet by a prostitute who locked him in the bathroom. He now prefers to step into elevators containing fierce guard dogs rather than attractive blondes.

At a party Stein meets Daisy Morgan (Field), an artist who produces colour-coordinated pictures to which Hilton Hotel managers can match their sofas. She already has a rich lawyer boyfriend, Marty Caesar (Steve Guttenberg), but he won't commit himself to marriage.

Cautious after his track record, Stein tells her he is a penniless writer and they embark on a romance. From there the film travels the classic 'Will they, won't they?' course. The burning issue in this case, however, was marriage—this being the 1980s, the

313

question of sex had already been taken care of early on.

When the film came out in Britain in November 1987, the critics felt that it had missed its mark.

'Their stumbling romance is quite amusing for a bit and certainly fetchingly played,' wrote the *Guardian*'s Derek Malcolm. 'But Jerry Belson's direction is akin to a ghetto-blaster (loud and coarse) and some time before the conclusion what could have been a good example of a now neglected genre has blown so much steam that it has run out of it altogether. Pity.'

And in the *Mail on Sunday* Tom Hutchinson agreed:

To see Michael Caine and Sally Field at work is to watch the triumph of professionalism over very thin material ... There are just so many twists that writer-director Jerry Belson can't get out of a plot whose outcome is as foregone as any Rock Hudson-Doris Day movie. Michael Caine and Sally Field make it sharper and funnier than it deserves. I should have known. That, of course, is what makes them stars.

At least, Michael Caine—in spite of taking a Cary Grant-type role—was recognized as a star, which, apparently, his hero wasn't always ... 'I remember once I was standing outside the Beverly Wilshire hotel in Beverly Hills talking to Cary Grant,' says Caine. 'A woman saw me and she came up and said, "You're Michael Caine!" and she got my autograph. She went on, "You know, I've been here for three weeks and I haven't seen one movie star." And then she turned to Cary Grant and said,

"You *never* see movie stars any more, do you?" And he said, "No, my dear, you don't!"'

★　　★　　★

Michael Caine's next career decision, to accept a part in the fourth *Jaws* movie in February 1987, was largely due to the persuasive powers of his fourteen-year-old daughter Natasha, who told him she wanted him to do a film her friends would want to see.

It says a lot, too, about the changing tastes of teenagers. The last time Caine had done a film to please one of his offspring had been in 1971, when he accepted the lyrical *Kidnapped* so that his elder daughter Dominique, then also fourteen, could see one of his films. During the intervening years, man-eating giant white sharks had taken over where classic swashbuckling tales had left off.

With his usual candour Caine admitted that there were three other good reasons for accepting the film—'the location in the Bahamas, the script and the money.'

Caine particularly enjoyed the laid-back atmosphere of the Bahamas. 'One day we were shooting a scene in Paradise Casino,' he says, 'and a local lad came up to me and patted me on the back. He was about eighteen or nineteen and he smiled and said to me in all sincerity, "Next stop Hollywood—making movies!"

'Another sunny day, while filming I noticed a woman wearing a T-shirt with the wording "Insanity is hereditary—you get it from your kids". On asking her where she got it from, she took the T-shirt off and gave it to me as a gift—at the same

315

time revealing that she had nothing on underneath!'

Caine was paid £1.5 million for his role as Hoagie, the dissolute pilot and gambler who befriends Ellen Brody. To update on the *Jaws* saga so far—Martin Brody, Amity Island police chief and survivor of several shark attacks, has finally died of a heart attack. Shortly afterwards his son Sean is killed by a Great White shark while attempting to clear a piece of flotsam out of a marker buoy.

Ellen Brody is convinced that the shark has developed some kind of grudge against her family, and goes to the Bahamas to try to persuade her other son Michael to give up his job as a marine biologist. Michael has been working on a study of sea snails with another scientist, Jake; and Michael's wife, Carla, a sculptress, has been working on a commission to brighten up the seafront.

Michael and Jake come across a Great White shark, out of its territory in the warm waters of the Bahamas. They decide to study it in secret, but at the unveiling of Carla's sculpture the shark attacks, and almost catches Michael's daughter. Ellen takes Michael's boat out to sea, determined to face up to the shark as her dead husband did. Michael and Jake follow in Hoagie's seaplane and confront the shark. Jake risks his life to plant an electrical device in the shark's maw, which Michael uses to disorient the fish before Ellen finally impales it with the broken bow of the boat.

In fact the film had more than one ending. In America the character of Jake was eaten by the shark, but for the British version he survived, and an extra scene was shot, in which the shark is finally

316

blown up. Test marketing in Japan revealed that the character of Jake was also popular there, and he was allowed to survive in that version too!

The film received a critical battering, but Caine managed to escape the jaws of the critics as well as the shark. The *New York Times* decided that:

> What's missing from *Jaws—The Revenge* is the intensity of the first film, where the characters were truly quirky and the action was focused in the man versus shark battles ... Mr Sargent and the screenwriter, Michael de Guzman, make some sincere but lame attempts to create characters who are more than fish bait. The pilot has an eccentric name, Hoagie, but even Michael Caine can't turn him into more than a shaky subplot device.

Caine had already earmarked a use for his fee from *Jaws—The Revenge*: 'When I went to America I had this house picked out and it was $430,000, and by the time I actually got there it was in the middle of a property boom and it was a million five so then I made *The Swarm* and *Poseidon* and *Ashanti* to try and get all this money together.

'And then when I was coming home there was a property boom here, and I thought, Christ, they're going through the roof again here, so I went out and made *Jaws IV*, which I got criticized for.

'I was at a sort of seminar, a very serious seminar, and this man said to me, "Did you learn any lessons in your career from making films like *The Swarm* and *Jaws IV*?" So I said, "Yes, never move during a property boom."'

In the summer of 1987 Caine accepted a highly unusual role, as a real-life teacher. His brief was to give a TV masterclass, on *Acting in Film*, to five young actors and actresses. The programme was to form part of a BBC series of three; the others being *Acting in Opera*, taken by Jonathan Miller, and *Acting in Restoration Comedy*, with Simon Callow.

Caine was persuaded to undertake the challenge by actress Maria Aitken, the co-producer of the series, who had worked with him on *Half Moon Street* and had noticed how he had helped a young actor improve his performance with a mixture of anecdotes and suggestions.

Caine was initially wary, but took up the gauntlet. He used material from *Alfie, Educating Rita* and *Deathtrap* as the basis for the programme, and tutored his pupils on many aspects of his art, from how to deal with stunt arrangers to love scenes. All was peppered with a liberal sprinkling of stories and illustrations from his own career.

When the programme was transmitted on 27 August 1987, it fascinated audiences as Caine spoke lovingly of the camera and taught his pupils how to use the all-seeing eye of the lens. Even his fellow professionals were impressed. 'As I watched Michael teach his students I was thinking, I've spent my *entire* life trying to teach actors *exactly* that, and you've succeeded where I've failed. You've demonstrated it consummately with an economy I couldn't achieve,' says David Wickes, who would later direct Caine in *Jack the Ripper* and *Jekyll and Hyde*.

The critics were captivated too; in the *Daily*

Mail, Mary Kenny wrote:

The first thing to be said about Michael Caine's master-class *Acting* is that it shows you what a marvellous screen actor he really is. By instinct, he knows that you must love the camera if you are going to communicate across it. 'Once you are in front of that camera, nobody else exists.'

In communicating on screen, too, the eyes have it all. Michael Caine will not be insulted to hear that his eyes are not exactly the windows of the soul; they are not shimmering dark pools, but rather frog-like and protruding, with that slightly bland look of the myopic.

Yet the range of minute expressions that Caine can call up with those eyes is breathtaking.

And in the *Guardian* Nancy Banks-Smith added, 'Michael Caine's *Acting*, a movie workshop, was so intense, yet funny, that Jonathan Miller and Simon Callow who follow in the series will have trouble topping this one.'

For Caine's five pupils, his advice continues to prove invaluable: 'I remember when Maria Aitken asked me to do it a few of my friends said, "You don't want to do that, you don't want to look like a student,"' remembers Celia Imrie. 'But I said, "I'd like to be able to say *Hello* like Michael Caine." In every job I've done since it still comes back to me.

'When we were at drama school we weren't taught anything about acting for camera or film. Michael taught us about the third eye, about bringing your face round to camera.

'I wouldn't have missed it for the world.'

During the programme Caine paid tribute to the

goddess of his career: 'The camera is like someone who loves you deeply. It is the most incredible of mistresses or lovers because it will love you forever, in spite of the fact that for the rest of your career, except for given occasions, you ignore it. It does not exist. You never look into it, you never know it's there ... if you do it right for the camera it will catch you every time you fall back. It's watching you, it's your friend, it loves you and it is listening and watching everything you do.'

*   *   *

After his interlude as a teacher Caine's next role was as Sherlock Holmes. Over the years possibly more films have been made about Conan Doyle's hero than about any other fictional character. During the silent era alone some seventy comedy or burlesque Sherlock Holmes films were made, and through the years, everyone from Buster Keaton through Basil Rathbone to Gene Wilder has tackled the genre. The most recent had been the Steven Spielberg production, *The Young Sherlock Holmes*.

The latest offering in the genre (in 1987) revolved around the idea that it was really Dr Watson who was the brilliant detective. Co-writer Gary Murphy came up with the 'flip-flop' notion after watching *The Sign of Four*, in which Holmes humiliates Watson in front of detectives from Scotland Yard. The resulting script—*Without a Clue*—became a sort of Victorian *Odd Couple*, in which Watson, finding that the readers of *The Strand* magazine didn't take to his stories about 'The Crime Doctor', creates a more flamboyant alias in the fictional shape of Sherlock Holmes. He then makes the character flesh and blood by hiring an actor to take on the role, but is unfortunate enough to land up with one Reginald Kincaid (Michael Caine), a womanizer and drunk.

The two set about solving the theft of printing plates from the Bank of England, Watson having the dual task of tackling the clues while trying to keep Holmes sober and in order.

Dr Watson was played by Ben Kingsley, classical actor and star of *Gandhi*. 'The Holmes/Watson relationship is the key,' says Caine, 'and I was fortunate enough to have Ben cast as Watson. An expert in dramatic acting is just right for comedy, because it's only funny when it's real. You could say it's a case of straight man, funny man.'

For Ben Kingsley the attraction was to work in a comedy alongside Michael Caine. Their relationship was generally regarded as the best bit in an otherwise undistinguished film.

'The film gives Michael Caine and Ben Kingsley as H and W some fair-to-moderate chances to display the lighter side of their professional prowess and they take it like true troupers,' remarked the *Guardian*, while *What's On* magazine declared succinctly, 'Every now and then Michael Caine makes a decent movie. *Without a Clue* isn't one of them.'

Lysette Anthony, who later turned up as one of the prostitutes in *Jack the Ripper*, was cast as the voluptuous Lesley, providing quite a distraction for Reginald Kincaid. 'Michael was brilliant in *Without a Clue*,' she says. 'The script stinks but he transcends all that in the way he dealt with the comedy. The director gave him a free rein and I roar with laughter every time I see it.

'He goes out of his way to include people. He is aware of his fame and he knows that people can find it difficult to handle. He is one of the people I would most like to be like. He is such a professional, and he's very down to earth.

'Michael has a wicked sense of humour and I'm a terrible giggler. The make-up lady must have got through boxes of tissues and gallons of mascara, because he made me laugh so much.'

★   ★   ★

It was now nineteen years since Michael Caine made his last television drama appearance in Alun Owen's *Cornelius*, and it would take a very special offer to tempt him back.

The man who finally persuaded him was producer/director David Wickes. Wickes had been researching the story of Jack the Ripper for over a year, gaining exclusive access to case files held at the Home Office and Scotland Yard. Euston Films in Britain and CBS in America had commissioned a four-hour mini-series about Britain's most notorious murderer, to be shown on both sides of the Atlantic, coinciding with the 100th anniversary of the murders.

Wickes approached Caine with an offer of a million pounds to play the role of Inspector Frederick Abberline, the detective who would finally expose the real identity of Jack the Ripper. In reality of course the Ripper was never caught, and Abberline retired after the file on the killer was closed.

Caine was impressed by the script and the financial offer, and viewed the concept of a mini-series as really a film, only made for television instead of the cinema. He accepted.

Wickes met Caine to talk about how he would play Abberline, and their discussion made a lasting impression: '"Shall we do our rehearsal now?" I said.

'"I tell you what," said Caine, "the way I see Abberline, I want to play him fucking *relentless!*"

'I grinned and said, "I think we just finished the rehearsal."

'There was no need to carry on—here was a consummate actor who had grasped the essence of the part in a sentence.'

Jack the Ripper had a $6 million budget, and would involve sixty-two different sets and seventy-two major speaking roles. The whole thing was shot in less than three months during the spring of 1988, and Caine noted, 'We're making a film forty-five minutes longer than *Gone with the Wind* in eleven weeks.'

Caine reverted to the process of working in television with ease: 'What I found is that television is more interesting for an actor than movies because you concentrate on performance and face and movement and there is no point in having spectacular scenes or special effects. The actor is all-important on TV, which I had forgotten.'

A disused asylum in Virginia Water in Surrey formed the basic location and in its grounds Victorian Whitechapel, the scene of the Ripper's grisly activities, was re-created. Also in the cast were Lewis Collins, Susan George and Jane Seymour. 'I've worked with many experienced actors over the years and have never been intimidated,' says Seymour, 'but I really was frightened the first day on the set with him because he is just brilliant on camera, there's always something hidden about him.

'He has this extraordinary talent. In rehearsals it doesn't show, but when the camera's on him it's like he presses a button and turns on a waterfall in his eyes, and you're just drawn to them.'

When the time came to shoot the ending in which the true identity of the Ripper is finally revealed, David Wickes shot four different alternatives. Wickes didn't want the real secret of the Ripper to leak out before the series was aired. Even Caine asked not to be told which of the four was the correct one. That way if anything did happen, he certainly couldn't be held responsible.

Jack the Ripper was aired in the UK on two evenings, 11 and 18 October 1988, and went straight into the Top Ten programmes for both weeks. It broke new ground in the USA by being that extremely rare thing, a high-rating British import; it did well in Canada, and was one of the highest-rated programmes of the decade in Australia.

On the other hand, for the first time in years it gave the television critics the chance to get their teeth into Caine, and some of them bit hard.

In the *Daily Telegraph*, Richard Last castigated:

What *Jack the Ripper* also needs is not a star, but an actor. Mr Caine may have charisma, but his histrionic range as Inspector Fred Abberline, pride of the Metropolitan Force ('Abberline's on the case'; 'Hold the front page'), could be described as limited.

In the *Sunday Times* Patrick Stoddart wrote:

> There was a lot of heavy breathing in the final slice of *Jack the Ripper* and with half an hour to go, I thought I'd cracked it. Obviously, it was the inspector wot dunnit. Other characters might have looked a touch dodgy, but the one who was clearly going off his chuff was Michael Caine, who by the fourth hour was wild-eyed and screaming, knocking people around and generally behaving like an unreformed Millwall supporter.

But Thomas Sutcliffe in the *Independent* defended Caine: 'As Abberline, Michael Caine is the saving grace, butting his way through a positive scrum of suspects with an engaging deadpan which avoids ever quite endorsing the whole enterprise.'

Caine was undisturbed by the critics' reaction. For him the production fulfilled all the promises it had made, he was pleased with his performance, and the public had evidently enjoyed it. He was satisfied and so was David Wickes: 'Caine is one of the great actors,' he says. 'He's burnished his technique—he'll glance at the camera knowing *exactly* which lens is being used, and how high to hold the newspaper. He's like having a Stradivarius on the set.'

As Jane Seymour points out, there is a good reason behind Caine's desire to get it right first time: 'He always does it in one take. He's a One-Take Wonder because he's always got a lunch appointment.'

★   ★   ★

After freezing through the winter shoots of *Without a Clue* and *Jack the Ripper* in London and the Lake District, Caine felt he deserved a treat. So when the script of *Dirty Rotten Scoundrels*—set in the South of France—arrived, he readily accepted.

Caine had already met his co-star, Steve Martin, when Martin's wife, actress Victoria Tennant, appeared with him in *The Holcroft Covenant*. But at that time Caine couldn't envisage a suitable vehicle coming along to enable them to work together. As he says, 'If you think of Steve's history in movies and mine, you couldn't imagine where the two of us would ever get together.'

The film that did bring them together was in fact a re-make. *Bedtime Story* had been released in 1964, the year Caine first came to prominence with *Zulu*, and had starred the unlikely combination of Marlon Brando and David Niven. The film was the story of two con-men in the South of France, the suave and sophisticated Lawrence Jamieson, played by Niven and the streetwise bum, Freddy Benson, played by Marlon Brando. In a *Playboy* interview at the time Brando said that he and Niven 'giggled like schoolgirls' throughout the making of the picture.

When it was decided to update the film for the late 1980s, Steve Martin was originally approached to play the Niven role and Kevin Kline and Bill Murray were among those mooted to take on the Brando character. But the more Steve Martin worked with the director Frank Oz, who had worked with Jim Henson on The Muppets and had directed Martin as the maniacal dentist in *The Little Shop of Horrors*, the more comfortable he felt with the character of Freddy Benson. It was then that Michael Caine's name was first mentioned. 'I remember seeing *Bedtime Story*,' Caine told *Time Out*. 'I don't think at that time people were ready to see Brando in a comedy, and they didn't laugh. I know I didn't. I know that he and David liked making that movie, but whenever we laugh too much on the set I always say, "Remember what David told me; 'we laughed all the time making that picture, and when it came out no one else did'."'

One of the major considerations for Caine was that the film would actually be shot where it was set. 'When I saw the setting was the Riviera I thought, "What if they decide to shoot it in Yugoslavia or someplace with a comic gendarme in the back to make it look like France, and a guy with a moustache and a string of onions going by on a bicycle who's really a Yugoslavian peasant?" They do that a lot, you know, because it's very expensive to make a movie in the South of France.'

Caine's fears were allayed by the producer Bernard Williams, who many years earlier had been location manager on *Alfie*. Being in the South of France during the summer had another advantage: it meant Caine could see a great deal of his friend Roger Moore who was also spending the summer there. 'Michael rented a house a couple of spits up the road from me,' explains Moore. 'And he asked me where I got my wine from because he wanted to fill up his cellar for the summer. He doesn't drink much—he spills most of it.

'Michael happens to like the wine that I like which is a blanc de blanc of the domaine Ott. Michael said, "Where do you order it?" and I said, "Well, there's a *cave* down in Antibes. If you call them up, they'll come and deliver." So being, as you know, very modest, he ordered twenty-four cases of blanc de blanc and of rouge d'Ott.

'The next day Michael told me that the fella had been and delivered it in a battered old station wagon. When he had finished Michael said, "Here you are here's a *pourboire* (tip)—have a drink." And the fella said disdainfully, "Monsieur, I am the brother of Olivier Ott. We own many vineyards, and I do not need a *pourboire*." And I said to Michael, "That's strange, Olivier himself delivers to me."'

Caine also ran into another old friend, Donald Pleasence. 'Michael and I bumped into each other in the South of France,' says Pleasence. '"Where are you off to, Donald?" he asked me. "I'm off to play boules on the village brown," I told him.'

Caine's character, Lawrence Jamieson, is the resident con-man in the Riviera resort of Beaulieu-sur-Mer. The income he needs to keep up his beautiful cliff-side house comes from convincing elderly matrons that he is in fact a prince in exile. Then Freddy Benson arrives in Beaulieu, meeting Jamieson on the way, and begins operating his own smaller but just as effective con; getting money for his board and lodging by telling rich women he is saving to pay for an operation for his grandmother. Jamieson advises Benson to leave town but Benson threatens to expose him; so instead Jamieson agrees to teach Benson all he knows if he will then leave. Eventually the rivals make a wager. The first one to extract $50,000 from the next woman they meet wins, and the other must leave town . . . The shoot was lengthy, leading Caine to coin the phrase 'I'm Riviera'd out'.

When the film was released in the UK, in July 1989, the critics gave it high praise, considering it an improvement on the original version, and Caine was lauded for his careful underplaying opposite Martin's maniacal character. In the *Sunday Times*, Iain Johnston wrote:

> Michael Caine faces a gamut of gags from Steve Martin in *Dirty Rotten Scoundrels*. Given space to operate by the director, Frank Oz, Martin jerks his way through the film like a cross between a Muppet baby and an electric eel. In the face of such frenzied energy Caine reacts with the accumulated screen wisdom of a quarter of a century: he does as little as possible, as calmly and suavely and economically as possible.

Clive Hirschhorn in the *Sunday Express* agreed:

> Though Caine doesn't quite have the sophistication of Niven, his skill and technique convince you he does ... It's a subtle, beautifully controlled performance that contrasts well with Steve Martin's extrovert 'scoundrel'.

The *Daily Telegraph* held a similar view:

> Despite a plot that comes with a neon sign saying 'Twist', the pairing of Caine and Martin as the naughty boys is rumbustious. Martin is an acknowledged comic talent, but Caine too, is well up to the task, the ideal foil, and between them the film becomes a compulsively watchable exercise in refined vulgarity.

In the cinema trailer advertising the film, Caine and Martin stroll down a quay on the Riviera taking in the passing parade of children and vendors. They seem like two harmless men enjoying themselves, until Martin nonchalantly extends an arm and pushes an elderly woman into the water and, seconds later, Caine shoves candy floss into the face of a young boy. Don't watch out for the scene in the finished movie—it isn't there! The film was one of the first to adopt a new trend: making a separate trailer to publicize a film. Orion Pictures sent Steve Martin and Frank Oz five or six different scripts for a trailer which Steve Martin then rewrote and sent back. Ideas were exchanged and then one whole day on location was spent making the 'bespoke' trailer that was seen by cinema audiences all round the world.

* * *

Working on his next film, *A Shock to the System*, Michael Caine presented the scriptwriters with something of a problem. The 'lovable rogue' he was required to portray proved so charming and so charismatic that it soon became obvious the original ending—featuring his demise—would have to be dumped. It wasn't until five weeks into the actual shooting schedule that they came up with another, more satisfactory, dénouement.

Frank Perry, the film company boss, said he found changes like that at such a late stage frankly terrifying, but not surprising—films often took on a life of their own, and executives ignored that at their peril.

A Shock to the System is a comedy thriller set in New York's advertising world. Advertising executive Graham Marshall (Michael Caine)

330

discovers it's possible to remove, with extreme prejudice and without being found out, the human obstacles in the way of his promotion. Murder works!

It starts when a bum in the subway won't stop pestering him, and Marshall accidentally knocks him into the path of an oncoming train. When the police decide the crime is in fact suicide, Caine's relieved mind turns to other possibilities—a few other 'accidents'. His nagging wife is got rid of by means of an electrical 'accident', and he acquires a mistress. The yuppie who pipped him to the post he'd been waiting for for years is also disposed of—a boat explosion—and suddenly Caine's career is on the way up. Unfortunately, he can't stop using his 'magical little solution' in his continuing pursuit of success.

There is no strong social message intended in this somewhat dark comedy; but the director, Jan Egleson, sees the movie as demonstrating the intolerable pressures of the business world in a city like New York, telling the *New York Times*, '[It's a] cut-throat, unfeeling attitude about money and power. Here's a man who's worked hard all his life and he gets a raw deal. The Young Turks, the new young driven people, move in and discard people with experience and skill. It's a waste.'

Michael Caine was as intensely aware of the pressures of the business world, but typically described it differently.

'I was walking to my trailer when all of a sudden everybody came cheering out of the buildings.

"Is it a fire?" I asked, and was told, "No, it's lunch."

'Then the restaurants emptied out all at the same

time.

'This regulation—it's not a natural life for any human being.'

★   ★   ★

David Wickes, who persuaded Caine to take on *Jack the Ripper*, appears to be responsible for Michael Caine entering a 'Victorian period' in his work. After *The Ripper* and *Without a Clue* Caine was about to embark on his third film set in the nineteenth century in less than two years.

Fortunately Caine himself is drawn to the period: 'I like the Victorian era very much. The only thing I don't like is the stiff collars. And they always have fog in Victorian pictures, and you're always breathing in rotten smoke which I'm sure is dreadful for you . . . Someone once told me that I've got a Victorian face, once you see it in a Victorian costume. I'm not quite sure what to make of that!'

Caine's new project was *Dr Jekyll and Mr Hyde*, a £4 million, two-hour telefilm, adapted and directed by David Wickes from Robert Louis Stevenson's classic horror story, and shot for London Weekend Television during the summer of 1989.

Cheryl Ladd co-starred as Sara Crawford, the beautiful sister of Jekyll's dead wife, who is prepared to flout the strict moral code of Victorian society to become his lover.

While *Jack the Ripper* was based on fact and so bound by conditions of accuracy, the fictional *Dr Jekyll and Mr Hyde* allowed Wickes to keep the essence of the story and widen it.

Caine has said that *Dr Jekyll and Mr Hyde* is 'the epitome of everything I have ever done'. And there's no doubt it was physically very demanding. Presenting in one role the story of one man's experiments on his own body, releasing the uncontrollably evil creature within himself in a schizophrenic frenzy, is a challenge for any actor. And not just to his acting ability, but also his stamina. Very early calls, four hours of make-up, and an hour at the end of the day to remove the hideous Hyde make-up was gruelling.

The mask was made up of twenty disposable pieces of foam latex, which had to be stuck meticulously on to a base on his face with a special glue, leaving holes for ears, eyes and mouth. Caine had to restrain himself from smoking his famous star-sized cigars, as any smoke would have discoloured the artificial skin. The problem was finally overcome by the invention of an extra-long cigar holder.

Eating was another hazard. Anything greasy would have damaged the mask, which meant Caine was limited to a diet of lettuce leaves, radishes and dry bread. By the end of filming, he had lost almost half a stone.

'I see a point every other day where I want to retire,' says Caine. 'When I sat in the chair for the first day of *Hyde* and they started on the make-up, I looked at the clock and it was 6 o'clock in the morning. They said we'd be called at 10 for the first shot, "when we've finished this"!

'Then I wished I was anywhere else...'

Weeks of this left the actor feeling the pinch. However, 'He's a very even-tempered man, except on a cold morning at 4 am!' says David Wickes, adding, 'He's meticulous, very careful about preparation—he'll mutter his lines obsessively from his motor-home to the set . . . At the end of a shot, as soon as I yell "Cut!" he'll find me with his eyes. I'll give him a look and he knows with just an expression whether it was OK.'

'I didn't want to do *Dr Jekyll and Mr Hyde* on film as it had been done so well before by Spencer Tracy, Frederic March and John Barrymore. The only medium left is television . . .' says Caine. 'The great thing about TV filming is they concentrate on the actor. It's your performance they're shooting, and you don't have to wait for the cavalry to come over the hill for an hour before they shoot your close-up. I like that because I'm lazy . . .'

Even for a workaholic like Michael Caine there comes a time when his home is preferable to his work. Despite his dedication to his craft, he still puts his family life above all else. When the factory hooter goes at the end of the day, he's the first to make for the gate: 'I'm a guy who likes to go home a lot. I'm a joke in the movie industry. They say, "Keep out of his way when they say 'Cut'; otherwise you'll get struck down when he rushes out."

'I wind up at the end of the day doing close-ups with just a collar on and all my own clothes and then I just rip the collar off and run.'

CHAPTER TWELVE

'BEEN THERE, DONE THAT'

'I once asked Michael Caine if he still went down the Elephant and Castle to see all his old mates. Standing there in his double breasted blazer and polo neck shirt, he said, "Nah. For one fing they fink I'm toffee-nosed 'cos of the way I dress. And the other fing is, they don't like the fact I don't talk like wot they do any more—I talk nice like this".'

Harry Landis

It could be said that Michael Caine has changed a lot since the early fifties—and equally that he hasn't altered at all. His life has changed around him but he still wears his 'cockney heritage' with pride, as if he's been working *towards* his roots all his life, instead of away from them.

But Michael Caine knows better than most that the world doesn't stop at the White Cliffs of Dover. His is a global view now. An actor of international stature, he moves easily about the world stage and yet, in apparent paradox, he prefers his Oxfordshire home to anything the jet set can offer. He's elected to return to what he left years ago—British family life.

Caine's finances have certainly improved since the early days. Thirty years ago Michael Caine had difficulty scraping together enough cash even for a cheese roll and a cup of tea at the National Film Theatre. He'd go to auditions on foot to save the bus fare of just a few pence, and he shared his clothes with his mates. 'For years Michael, Terry Stamp and I only had one dinner suit between us,' says Caine's tailor, Doug Hayward. 'We could never go to the same place at the same time, and the suit used to go backwards and forwards between the three of us.'

Michael Caine's interest in matters sartorial has always been relatively negligible. If Doug Hayward didn't stop him, Caine would probably still wear a blazer and a polo neck shirt whatever kind of trousers he was wearing—even pinstripes.

On the other hand, although his taste in clothes hasn't changed a great deal, his taste in food has become increasingly sophisticated. In the old days simplicity was all, and the traditional British working-class menu was what he craved, usually in quantity—as Gerald Campion, owner of the actors' haunt Gerry's, remembers: 'Stanley Baker and Michael Caine often came into Gerry's for lunch during pre-production for *Zulu*. Michael was obviously keen on my cooking as it was later reported that, when asked what he missed most in England, while he was filming in Africa, he replied, "Meat and two veg at Gerry's!"' 'I remember standing behind him in the dinner queue at the BBC canteen in 1957,' recalls Ronald Eyre, who directed Caine in one of his early roles, 'and hearing him say to the canteen lady, "I'll have a steak . . . No, hang on a minute", he said, "I'll have two."'

At that stage foreign food was anathema to Caine. When filming *A Hill in Korea* in Portugal he firmly rejected the local cuisine, according to fellow actor Harry Landis. 'He'd say; "Take this away—it stinks of garlic! I'll have an omelette." Then he'd say: "Pfwaugh! This stinks of garlic too!"'

'If it wasn't egg and chips à la Elephant and Castle, he didn't want to know. Now I hear he's a gourmet.'

Nowadays, of course, Michael Caine has a far more sophisticated palate and has even become a restaurateur. He is also a connoisseur of fine wines (and Havana cigars!). Such sophistication still surprises people who think of him as a pie-and-mash and a bottle-of-brown-ale man. 'People always think, "He's a cockney; he can't possibly speak French", but I do,' says Caine. 'A while back I was made a Chevalier de Méduse in Antibes, and I had to give an acceptance speech . . .

'I thought, "How am I going to get a laugh in French?" And suddenly I thought, "I know how I'll do it. My real name is Maurice, and so now I am Maurice the Chevalier." So I tried it in the speech in French and they laughed.

'And then I collapsed because before you get the award you have to try all the wines, and I never spat them out . . .'

Friends, particularly old friends who came from the same background and went through the same trials on the way up, are particularly important to Caine. His two closest male friends are Sean Connery and Roger Moore, both, like Caine, self-made men who started their careers with absolutely no advantages and—from a class point of view—several handicaps.

Michael will frequently tease Roger about his acquired upper-class accent, while Roger points out that, in his opinion, Michael has become even more cockney with success.

Richard Shepherd, Michael's business partner in Langan's Restaurant in London, recalls seeing the

337

three of them enjoying dinner together during Roger's reign as Bond. 'They were discussing the day's events,' he recalls, 'and Moore was describing his day's filming. The morning had apparently consisted of his having to say, "Hello, my name is Bond."

'"And what did you have to do in the afternoon?" queried Caine.

'"Had to say, 'Hello, my name is Bond' again," replied Roger.'

Caine certainly doesn't forget those he worked with in the early days either—like Victor Maddern, who appeared with Caine in his very first film. *A Hill in Korea*. 'My daughter, Sarah, had a bit part in *Educating Rita* in Dublin,' says Maddern, 'and the director, Lewis Gilbert, took the opportunity to introduce her to Michael.

'"Oh, Victor Maddern's daughter!" he said. "I did my first film with Victor Maddern. Hang on a minute, *everyone* did their first film with Victor Maddern!"'

Caine may be safe now from the financial hardship he once went through, but he is still deeply aware of the fickleness of his trade. 'If you're hot then they'll alter the part from a black midget for you,' he declares, 'and they say, "We'll work on it, we'll get round it!" If you're cold, then it's a case of, "We're making *The Michael Caine Story*, but unfortunately you're too tall for it."'

It is this awareness that has kept Caine working so hard through the years, never quite losing the fear that it might all suddenly disappear.

Caine's advice is now almost as sought after as his acting ability. For someone who's done quite well in the business sense, he's remarkably free with it.

Not that those on the receiving end will always be delighted by his directness: 'I get scripts that I send back to producers and say, "Not only will I not do it, but I suggest that you don't either! You're going to lose your shirt on this one."'

Over the years a large number of young actors and actresses, from Lawrence Douglas in *Kidnapped* to Julie Walters in *Educating Rita*, have benefited from Caine's advice. 'I remember Michael took Vivien Heilbron and me to lunch at Pinewood studios and introduced us to Roger Moore and Tony Curtis,' says Lawrence Douglas, 'and then we went back to his flat in Grosvenor Square, whisked round in his blue Rolls-Royce...

'He was full of fun and repartee, and very encouraging. I remember I once asked him, "What advice would you give to a young actor?" And he said, "Follow your own instincts."

'I've tried to stick to that.'

As a master of technique, any pearls of wisdom from Caine are gratefully received. 'One thing I learned from Michael was to go over your lines loudly between takes,' says Saeed Jaffrey whose first film role was in *The Wilby Conspiracy* with Caine. '"Air it a bit," he'd say.

'I learned a tremendous amount from him.'

Caine is also admired for his unselfish partnering of other actors. 'Michael is extraordinarily generous as an actor,' says Frank Middlemass who starred with him in *The Island*. 'I remember once we were doing a close-up and he said, "Frank, don't look into both my eyes. Look into my right eye, and that will bring your profile round more into the camera."

'He is extremely relaxed, which must come from

being tremendously experienced. He's ready for it all; he knows his lines, the angles, where he ought to be. He's uncomplaining and unflappable—a splendid fellow.'

Caine sees himself above all as a *movie* actor: 'I'm a professional movie actor, and within that framework I'm not a picture that I hold up and say, "Look at me." If I'm doing my job right I hold up a mirror and I say, "Look at you!"'

He feels that his enthusiasm for film is partly a result of the age he was brought up in, as a conversation with Laurence Olivier, his co-star in *Sleuth* illustrates: 'We were talking one day about our generations, Olivier and I, and I said, "When did you first see an actor?"—talking about the differences between him and me. He said, "Well, my nanny took me to the local something or other and I sat there and the curtains went up and the lights were bright. Oh," he said, "it was enthralling, that's when I decided to go into the theatre."

'He said, "What about you?" I said, "Well, I went to what used to be called the threepenny rush, which was a children's cinema, on a Saturday morning, and the first actor I ever saw was the Lone Ranger. And," I said, "all my youthful life I lived a quarter of a mile from the Old Vic but I never had enough money to go to it, but I had enough money to go to the pictures twice a week." He said, "That's why you're in cinema." I said, "That's right. I've been a cinema person from the day I was born."'

And Caine has always rejected any form of acting snobbery: 'People say to me, "Who did you watch in the theatre, or films, as an actor?"

340

'I say, I didn't. I say I sat on the Tube to learn it—you learn more about acting in ten minutes on the Tube than you can watching a three-hour drama at the Old Vic.'

Caine never really felt particularly comfortable in the theatre and he hates the school of thought that maintains that theatre is in some way more valid than films. There's very little that is likely to tempt him back: 'I went to see a serious play and I couldn't take it seriously. It was three hours long. I laughed; I had to go to the gents, I had to go to the ladies, I had to go everywhere. I thought I was going to get a hernia. I can't take it when it gets too pompous.

'The thing about being a movie star is that when I go to the theatre I always get the giggles for about the first five minutes in a dramatic play because I can't get used to the idea of what they are doing.

'If it's a comedy I'm fine. If it's a musical, it's great. But when the lead comes on and says the baby is dying of appendicitis and the wife says she's having an affair—I still to this day can't keep a straight face in a straight play.'

Michael Caine has carefully analysed his own appeal, and is sensitive to those who have accused him of always playing the same character. He has a suitable riposte for such allegations: 'Actually, I've never played a millionaire.'

He has a firm vision of how he wants to be regarded as an actor: 'I don't think people go to see "a Michael Caine film"—there isn't any such thing. I think I really am a sort of new species of actor. I mean, I'm not the first of it, but I'm a product of it—the Leading Character Actor.

'It started with the Lee Marvins and the George

C Scotts, and people like that, who starred in films playing definite characters. If you went and saw a Cary Grant movie, you knew what you were going to see. If you go and see a Clint Eastwood movie the same applies. But really, you can't vizualise what you're going to see if you go and see a film starring me. You may have read about it, but you can't say, "Oh, Michael is going to be doing this with his glasses on; or, he'll have a lovely old cockney accent and we'll have a wonderful time and sing 'Knees Up, Mother Brown' and then eat sausage and mash."'

Directors universally regard him as a pleasure to work with. Provided that the production is well organized, and that he feels everyone else is putting as much into it as he is, Caine is a very straightforward man to work with. 'Michael is completely devoid of bullshit,' says Sir Richard Attenborough, who directed him in *A Bridge Too Far*. 'Someone once asked Noël Coward what catchphrase he would use to sum up his approach to characterization and he said, "All you have to do is get on, say your lines, and get off without bumping into the furniture."

'Michael is like that, there is no nonsense, no pretentions. He is like Olivier; he is always prepared, always word perfect, but that doesn't mean to say that Michael is not malleable too, if he accepts your point of view. He is a superb craftsman.'

'*Get Carter* was the first time I had worked with a film star,' says Mike Hodges, who made his directing début with Caine. 'The first scenes we shot were on the train going up to Newcastle, and then in the bar just outside the station. In the scene,

Michael had to walk all the way up this bar which is the longest in Europe. He came in, walked up, and stepped up to the camera . . . and completely filled the screen.

'Then I knew the film would be completely different from the way I had envisaged it. A star was a kind of species I had never really encountered before. There is a total difference between acting for TV and acting for film.'

Not everyone feels he has fulfilled his potential, though. 'I think there is a well of unused talent in Michael,' says one of his *Alfie* co-stars Shelley Winters. 'I know that many British actors pooh-pooh the Method style of acting, but there's a lot of truth in finding a parallel experience and using that to create a character. Michael showed that in *Alfie* and used his past for the cameo in *Mona Lisa*. But if Michael used his own life experience he could be the greatest.'

Despite his star status, Michael Caine is still seen by his public as very much 'one of us'. He is consistently popular on set with every member of the crew, and off-set, casually attired in his favourite leather jacket, with an open neck shirt or roll neck jumper, his fans usually feel that he'll have time to say a few words: 'When I walk along the street, people just say, "Hallo, Mike! Hallo, Mike!" No one is ever surprised to see me anywhere.

'Except, I remember, I was once walking along the street and a guy stopped me and said, "You're here!" I said, "Yes."

'"But you're here," he said. "You're right here!"

'So I said, "Well, I have to be somewhere, don't I?"

'And he said, "I never thought of that, yeah."

And he just walked on.'

'I like to think that there are a few of us who have stayed ordinary,' says another of Caine's *Alfie* co-stars, Millicent Martin. 'Sean Connery and Michael are both like that; you can meet them again after fifteen years and there are no walls between you.'

And another *Alfie* star, Julia Foster, agrees: 'One of the most remarkable things about Michael is that he has remained the same. I once worked with Deborah Kerr who was also very much down-to-earth, and I asked her, "How have you managed to stay the same?" She said, "When you're brought up properly everything will be all right."

'I think Michael's personality is a great credit to his mother.'

What of the future? Michael Caine's home life is very important to him, and he's completely at home in the English countryside. His days as an evacuee in Norfolk have left their mark: 'I'm big in green. I'm the merry green person. I always have been. I've even got my own green place in my garden. I've got two acres fenced off for four kingfishers. They're always there, they live there all the time. I've never seen so many kingfishers so close together; they're usually on their own. I've put little guppies in everywhere so they get something to eat—it's not very kind to the guppies, but...'

Would Caine like to diversify a little in his career? He once expressed a desire to become a director, and to 'grow old disgracefully' behind the camera, as he put it. But recent years seem to have brought about a change of heart, although many believe he would make a very fine director. 'I've always thought it would be nice to direct,' says Caine, 'but the first thing I do as an actor, after I've accepted a script and gone through all the serious bits, is to count the number of days I have off. Whereas as a director you don't get any days off. You're there three months before the picture starts, and you have to interview actors and turn them down. I was turned down for so many parts in my life I would find that extremely difficult to do. And then the most dreadful thing, which people don't know about, is a thing called "post-synching"— putting the words in afterwards—which is agony. You just sit there in the dark [editing], for week after week.

'No, I wouldn't like to be a director.'

Caine wasn't enamoured of the difficulties a producer faces either when he came up against them as Executive Producer on *The Fourth Protocol*. Basically he's still Michael Caine the actor, looking for new parts to play: 'What I'd love to do now is a drug-busting character to push, propaganda-wise, against drugs. There was a wonderful cartoon in the *Evening Standard*—the US troops are marching into Colombia, and the boss of the drug cartel is saying, "Oh, wonderful! The customers are coming to us!"'

Or, indeed: 'I'd love to play the Orson Welles role in *The Third Man*. It's my idea of a great role. You get all the kudos and you don't have to be there for very long. That's the kind of role I'm looking for.'

And others are willing to offer suggestions as well. Neil Jordan, who directed Caine in *Mona Lisa*, would like to see him tackle another Graham Greene character, and Dick Clement and Ian La

Frenais would love to write a script for Caine and Sean Connery. Shelley Winters has an idea too: 'I'd like to see him do a modern film and use his life story as its basis. On stage I'd love to direct him in a Eugene O'Neill play like *Long Day's Journey Into Night*.'

Whereas another former co-star, Glenda Jackson, comments succinctly, 'I think it's about time he got back to acting!'

Michael Caine is a survivor, not by being over-protective about his image, or by being careful about selecting his roles. He's just gone hell-for-leather for it: 'People say, well you know Dustin Hoffman has made about three or four failures, and Michael Caine has made about twenty!

'But Dustin Hoffman has only made ten or twelve films; I've made more than sixty. It's the same ratio. It's just that I like to work, and I've liked it all my life.'

For Caine work is play. He's still as keen on acting as he was forty years ago: 'I take it very seriously. I try to be as good as I can at it, but remember, it goes right back to Clubland and the Amateur Dramatic Society that I was in.

'I'm getting paid for something I would do for nothing. You can't beat that!'

Michael Caine was once asked if he had a motto: 'Yeah—Been There, Done That. It'll certainly be on my tombstone. It'll just say, "Been There, Done That".'

Photoset, printed and bound in Great Britain by
REDWOOD PRESS LIMITED, Melksham, Wiltshire